English through drama

A way of teaching

From the same author

For teachers

The Mummery. Teaching English in a specialist room
  (Chatto & Windus 1967)
'Drama' in *Directions in the Teaching of English,* edited by Denys Thompson
  (Cambridge University Press 1969)

For use in schools

Transatlantic. Twentieth-century stories by American writers
  (Chatto & Windus 1968)
The Playbook Series. Drama for schools and colleges
  (Cambridge University Press 1969)
Leopards (with Denys Thompson). Short stories in packs
  (Cambridge University Press 1972)
The Open Boat. Stories by Stephen Crane
  (Chatto & Windus 1972)

English through drama

A way of teaching

Christopher Parry

Cambridge

At the University Press 1972

Published by the Syndics of the Cambridge University Press

Bentley House, 200 Euston Road, London NW1 2DB

American Branch: 32 East 57th Street, New York, N.Y.10022

© Cambridge University Press 1972

Library of Congress Catalogue Card Number: 72-184902

ISBNS

0 521 08483 0 hard covers

0 521 09741 x paperback

Printed in Great Britain

at the University Printing House, Cambridge

(Brooke Crutchley, University Printer)

Contents

Illustrations

Acknowledgements

I owe warm thanks to many people: to Raymond O'Malley for the kind suggestion out of which this book arose; to David Holbrook for introducing me to the publishers with such expeditious grace; to Michael Black for giving such a prompt and provident go-ahead; to the Cambridge Institute of Education for a generous grant from the research fund at a critical time, and to F. F. C. Edmonds for showing me how to apply for it; to Ian Brown for his services as an amanuensis; and to 'X' for letting me use the letter that makes the last chapter.

Thanks are also due to the following for permission to quote copyright material: Heinemann Educational Books Ltd for an extract from *Teaching English* by J. H. Walsh; J. M. Dent & Sons Ltd and the Trustees of the Joseph Conrad Estate for an extract from *The Nigger of the 'Narcissus'* by Joseph Conrad; J. M. Dent & Sons Ltd for an extract from Shakespeare's *Julius Caesar* in their King's Treasuries edition, and an extract from Malory's *Le Morte D'Arthur* in their Everyman's Library edition; Chatto & Windus Ltd for an extract from *The Disappearing Dais* by Frank Whitehead; The Hogarth Press and Harvard University Press for an extract from *Essays on Literature and Society* by Edwin Muir; Mr O. Gaggs for an extract from an article by him in *The Use of English*, Vol. 21, No. 2 (Winter 1969); Mr B. Hankins for an extract from an article by him in *The Use of English*, Vol. 19, No. 4 (Summer 1968); Faber & Faber Ltd and New Directions for 'Lament of the Frontier Guard' from *Collected Shorter Poems* by Ezra Pound; Penguin Books Ltd for an extract from their edition of Shakespeare's *Julius Caesar*; University of London Press Ltd for an extract from *Free Writing* by Dora Pym; Curtis Brown Ltd for an extract from *The Play Way* by Caldwell Cook, first published by Wm. Heinemann Ltd; Longman Group Ltd for an extract from *Our Living Language* by A. P. Rossiter; Constable & Co Ltd and Alfred A. Knopf Inc. for 'The Herd Boy' translated by Arthur Waley and included in *170 Chinese Poems*; Frederick Muller Ltd for an extract from T. C. Worsley's 'Teacher and Taught' in *The Quality of Education* edited by Denys Thompson and James Reeves. 'Snake',

viii   Acknowledgements

'Baby Tortoise' and 'Fish' from *The Complete Poems of D. H. Lawrence* edited by Vivian de Sola Pinto and F. Warren Roberts, Copyright 1964, 1971 by Angelo Ravagli and C. M. Weekley, All Rights Reserved, are reprinted by permission of The Viking Press Inc. and Laurence Pollinger Ltd and the Estate of the late Mrs Frieda Lawrence.

The diagram of the Mummery on page 10 and the photograph taken by Edward Leigh on page 11 first appeared in *Use of English Pamphlet* **4** published by Chatto & Windus Ltd. The plan of the original Mummery on page 8 first appeared in *Play Way English for Today* by D. A. Beacock, published by Thomas Nelson & Sons Ltd. The photograph on page 12 is by Peter Dunne. Other photographs are by Photo-Reportage Ltd, London.

The author and the publishers thank those concerned for their co-operation in allowing material to be used.

For
JOSIANE

Introduction

I began this book while I was teaching at the Perse School, Cambridge. It seemed sensible to continue writing in the present tense when I left the staff.

I have tried to describe an educational situation truthfully; and to write simply. I hope the result will not strike the reader as merely simple minded or narcissistic. The first-person-singular style of narration is adopted because I believe that a teacher must 'watch himself' to have a chance of working to some real purpose. Most of the places where I repeat myself occur intentionally; as do some of the places where issues are suggested rather than dissected. I have tried to enlist the active support of the reader's imagination, in the hope that something near the truth of the matter may be achieved collaboratively.

To avoid causing embarrassment to the people whose work is quoted I have disguised their names by the use of a simple code. I am sorry that from time to time (particularly in the chapter on Writing) the reader has to endure the minor inconvenience of keeping the book open in two places at once. I am even sorrier that I have not been able to avoid altogether the pitfalls indicated in the last paragraph of the first chapter.

My debt to the late Douglas Brown is deep and lasting. It goes far beyond those passages where I have quoted his wisdom directly. If he had lived, he would have written a different, and far better, book. His teaching is the source of any virtue this one may have: the faults are entirely my own.

1. Beginnings

My first clear memories of English in school are that it wasn't a class-room subject; that you acted and talked, recited and chanted and perpetually did things.

The name of Henry Caldwell Cook first came to my ears when I was an eleven-year-old 'new boy' at the Perse School in Cambridge in the autumn of 1948. I gathered that he was remembered as 'a Good Thing'. He had done something special about English when he began to teach at the school just before the First World War. He had founded the little classroom-theatre in which we were having many of our English lessons. We were told that some of our stage-furniture 'went right back to his day', which seemed, impressively, to be ages in the past. He had started the school dramatic society. And he had written a book called *The Play Way* which, to judge from its dusty and secluded position on the library shelf, was more often mentioned than read. I learned that he had died in 1937; and eventually I discovered that *our* English teacher, Douglas Brown, had been one of his pupils as a boy of our age. I sensed a tradition and did not discover much more about the past until I was much older. The present was interesting enough.

Our little theatre was an intriguing part of Pendene House, an old private residence which the school had bought long ago and converted into classrooms (in 1914, in fact, shortly after Caldwell Cook joined the staff). On the ground floor a front living-room and a back dining-room had had the wall between them removed, leaving a kind of proscenium arch. The rear room became the main acting area and its floor had been raised about a foot and a half and extended forward a couple of yards into the front room. There was thus a fore-stage as well as a main stage. Heavy orange curtains were fitted to draw across the proscenium opening, and round the three sides of the main acting area dark blue drapes hung down to the floor. It was just possible, I remember, for a thin boy to creep round in the space between these drapes and the outer walls without giving sign of his presence. In the middle of the back wall a bay window had been boarded up, and the enclosed space could be made to serve as a tiny inner stage. It was illuminated from above by three bare electric light bulbs. Light for the main stage came from a row of bulbs set in the ceiling just behind the orange curtains; and there were two or three more serving the fore-stage and the auditorium. All these lights were controlled from a small panel of noisy switches located just off-stage at one side of the proscenium.

Rows of folding wooden chairs filled the auditorium, which was warmed in winter by an enormous, unreliable gas-fire, a primitive monster. There was just enough room for thirty boys to sit down. Behind the last row of chairs some thick dark-green curtains covered the large windows, and round the edges the heavy material was stuck to the woodwork with drawing-pins to seal out all trace of daylight. And down the sides of the room – perhaps to relieve the somewhat austere impression – four big pictures of scenes from Shakespeare had been stencilled on the cream-painted walls.

Outside, on our left as we faced the stage, ran a narrow corridor, and three doors opened into the room from it: the first was at the back of the auditorium, the second at the side of the fore-stage, and the third beside the switchboard. Opposite this last, across the corridor, was a cubby-hole – a spot bigger than a cupboard but too small to be called a room. It had been, perhaps, a waiter's retreat in the days when our stage had been a dining-room. Now it housed an electric gramophone and a collection of records (the old-fashioned sort made to play at 78 revolutions per minute). Music on the turntable emerged behind the stage from an extension loudspeaker rigged up in a corner. Near the cubby-hole a staircase descended from the corridor to a vast, dim and musty cellar where umpteen bits and bobs of costume and properties were stored – tunics, cloaks, hats, sashes, caskets, swords, shields, goblets, and so on.

It was, I suppose, very cramped and inadequate accommodation for drama. The whole room measured just eleven yards from end to end. Our stage was barely fifteen feet across. A cumbersome oak settle and two carved wooden thrones stood on the fore-stage, and for many an acting project they had to be cleared into the corridor, where they effectively obstructed all movement. Boys operating the gramophone could not see the stage directly. Boys in the cellar would often lose touch with upper regions, by accident or by design, and time would be wasted. The list of shortcomings was infinite and the place was a far cry indeed from the miniature Elizabethan playhouse that had been Caldwell Cook's ideal; but, with its limited scenic resources and its intimacy of relationship between actors and audience during performance, it did revive some of the beneficial conditions in which English lived at times for the Elizabethans. And the thought that our facilities were inadequate or makeshift never crossed our eleven-year-old minds. We were too busy – perpetually doing things.

We live in a world created by applied science, and our present is unlike the present of any other age. The difference between our world and the world of imagination is growing greater, and may become so great that the one can hardly understand any longer the other. Applied science shows us a world of consistent, mechanical progress. There machines give birth to ever new generations of machines, and the new machines are always better and more efficient than the old, and begin where the old left off. If we could attribute sentience to a new machine, we should find that it simply did not understand the old, being too far ahead, in another world. But in the world of human beings all is different; there we find no mechanical progress, no starting where a previous generation left off; instead there is a continuity ruled by repetition. Every human being has to begin at the beginning, as his forebears did, with the same difficulties and pleasures, the same temptations, the same problem of good and evil, the same inward conflict, the same need to learn how to live, the same inclination to ask what life means. Conspicuous virtue, when this creature encounters it, may move him, or a new and saving faith, since the desire for goodness and truth is also in his nature. Nevertheless he will pass through the same ancestral pattern and have the same feelings, the same difficulties as generations long before he was born. All this may seem dull to the thinker, but it enchants the imagination, for it is an image of human life. But when outward change becomes too rapid, and the world .

around us alters from year to year, the ancestral image grows indistinct and the imagination cannot pierce to it as easily as it once could.

Yet at the same time we are bound, even when we do not know it, to the past generations by the same bond that unites us with our neighbours, and if only for the sake of preserving the identity of mankind we must cherish that connection. Fortunately, in spite of our machines, the habits of the human heart remain what they have always been, and imagination deals with them as no other faculty can. It is more urgently needed in our time than ever before.

From 'The Poetic Imagination' in
Essays on Literature and Society by Edwin Muir

For us the room was spick-and-span and special. During the summer of 1948, Douglas Brown and a small group of volunteers from the Sixth Form had restored it. There was much to restore; for as a teaching room it had died with Caldwell Cook and become the school junk-store. (Today it has disappeared altogether and new offices for a Schools Examination Board stand on the site.)

The renovated room was known to us, as to earlier generations of Perse boys, as the Mummery – a name that strikes the imagination strangely at first hearing. Under its impact an adult friend recently retorted, bluntly – 'It seems to me to carry overtones of "Mummerset" and wholemeal-bread-and-honey types dancing round a maypole in hairy tweeds and flat shoes.' But as children we did not find it distasteful. Indeed the very oddness of the word gave it a kind of appeal that ensured its currency. It seemed right and proper to us that a special place in the school should have a special name, and it rolled off our tongues smoothly enough, as Caldwell Cook no doubt intended it to do. Perhaps he meant also, when he chose the name, to imply that activity and a sense of the past belong to English as a subject; and some of us may have felt this, dimly.

A child's mind is inclined to take lucky circumstances as simply the way of the world; so in my first term, and for some time after, I took it for granted that every school had a Mummery. Most schools, after all, had an Art Room, a Science Laboratory, a Music Room, so why not a specialist room for English? I supposed that English was everywhere the most important school subject since it occurred more frequently in our week than any other – on seven occasions, in fact, and four of these were regularly in the Mummery. I imagined that an emphasis on dramatic activity was a general rule in schools and that what one did for most of the time in English lessons everywhere was to work with the other people in one's class at the interesting business of 'putting on' plays and 'doing' stories and poems and talks.

For us English meant, chiefly, a happening in which we were all involved. In the Mummery we worked in two groups and each of us had a special responsibility in one of them. Some of us acted, some stage-managed; some looked after the lighting, some provided music; some coped with costumes, and one boy in each group was elected leader. The groups were performers and audience by turns. And I assumed that all this imaginative collaboration was a vital part of English in most other schools. Since it filled four of our English lessons out of every seven, it seemed obvious to us that it was quite *as* important as all the reading and writing that we did in a conventional classroom in the remaining three periods of English every week and in our homework time.

4   Beginnings

We did English, then, in a prevailing atmosphere of *social* effort. We were strongly aware of our little communities and of our individual purposes within them. Everyone contributed something. A boy whose talent or inclination did not draw him towards acting found outlets for other kinds of practical skill; skill that his whole group depended on. Every 'specialist' found that his work involved him directly in concern with other people's efforts. In the preparations for staging a short play, a boy in charge of the lights, for instance, could only plan effectively if he knew what plans the stage-manager, actors and musicians were making. Underlying all that we did was a sense of our small society's need for each individual's effort; and it was this that put the worth in the work for us. Almost always we came away from lessons in the Mummery with some sense of achievement. It was not always very mighty achievement, but it was something we had done together; something we shared.

We experienced in the Mummery, I realise, some of the qualities of human relationship and personal expression which inform all creative and responsible social living. And in a real sense this made English the heart of our curriculum.

Teachers of English are, necessarily, concerned with the use their pupils make of their native tongue to live more humanly. Some teachers are more concerned with certain uses than with others; but all try to some degree to stir 'the use of imagination'. The essential task is to reach, and to exploit positively, resources of sensibility. As a task it is not solely important, but it is *more* important than the surface-work of polishing the formal skills of literacy, because the ability to read and write well depends basically on the capacity to feel, and to feel deeply. So teachers of English share the purpose of the artist as Conrad described it in his preface to *The Nigger of the 'Narcissus'* (though few, perhaps, would speak of it with the same ardent eloquence). Like the artist, the English teacher strives in his work to speak

to our capacity for delight and wonder, to the sense of mystery surrounding our lives; to our sense of pity, and beauty, and pain; to the latent feeling of fellowship with all creation – and to the subtle but invincible conviction of solidarity that knits together the loneliness of innumerable hearts, to the solidarity in dreams, in joy, in sorrow, in aspirations, in illusions, in hope, in fear, which binds men to each other, which binds together all humanity – the dead to the living and the living to the unborn.

If, as teachers, we do not help English in school to nourish that conviction of solidarity which binds men to each other, in a generative union of young imagination and the resources of our language, then we do next to nothing.

Of course, speaking to children's various capacities for delight, wonder and so on is not just a matter of talking or reading to the class. It is, rather, a matter of setting the word *in action*, encouraging children to give it active expression in many modes. As Frank Whitehead puts it in his excellent book on the principles and practice of English teaching, *The Disappearing Dais* –

> The main business of the English teacher is not instruction in any direct sense, nor even teaching in the sense which may be applicable in some other subjects. It is the provision of abundant opportunity for the child to use English under the conditions which will most conduce to improvement; opportunity, that is, to use his mother tongue in each of its four modes (listening, speaking, reading and writing) and for all the varied purposes (practical, social, imaginative, creative) which make up its totality; opportunity moreover to use it under expert guidance and in situations which will develop ultimately his power to be self-critical about his own efforts.

As children in the Mummery we enjoyed both abundant opportunity and expert guidance. Douglas Brown provided both.

The words at the head of this chapter are his words, but they describe my own memories exactly. He remembers the main business of English taught by Caldwell Cook as warmly as I remember it taught by him. But the English I remember was no mere repetition of the English of Douglas Brown's schooldays.

Caldwell Cook taught with the pioneer's intense devotion to his cause. Through one form of dramatic activity or another he roused in most of his pupils a vigorous, imaginative power of expression and frank enjoyment of literature in an age when English teaching concentrated almost exclusively on the conventional drills. As *The Play Way* shows on every page, he believed passionately that 'a natural education is by practice, by doing things, and not by instruction'. If the book also shows that some details in his methods arose more from personal idiosyncrasy than from insight into the ultimate ends of education, these were perhaps a consequence of his singleness in the field. The heart of his work, his grasp of the main business of English, was strong and sound. As a practising teacher his gifts were remarkable, and his methods inspired many. Some of his followers simply imitated what he did, without the original flair. Others, with more wisdom, adapted his ideas carefully and selectively, fitting them to their own circumstances and personalities. But Douglas Brown saw straight to what was best in his work; and he refined it, developed it, and applied it in his own teaching with the distinctive brilliance of a rare, regenerative spirit.

So, when I had the good fortune to be appointed as Douglas Brown's successor a month or two before he left the staff, the greatness of my predecessors daunted me. What I hoped to do was to keep alive the *spirit* of a tradition that stretched back through two generations of pupil-taking-on-from-teacher. I was no pioneer or reformer. Indeed, fresh from a university course, the disciplines of which I found difficult to relate in any direct or comforting way to the practical problems of teaching boys aged eleven and twelve, I was a complete, and rather frightened, novice. In his last summer term at the school Douglas Brown let me observe many of his lessons. He made for me a very full set of notes on his teaching programme and procedure. During the holidays we had several long discussions about Education in general and English at the Perse in particular. Then in September 1961 he left me to it.

My situation seemed to teem with pitfalls. Into some of them I fell, hard – as into the assumption that 'my' children would have the patience and poise of reasonable adults – and I quickly found the folly of my ways. Into others I probably fell without realising it. A few dangers I foresaw and avoided. And others – such as that from the surface impact of his own personality – Douglas Brown warned me of in advance. This was a typical instance of his far-reaching concern for all his pupils as individuals. For many of us he became the most profoundly influential figure in the whole course of our secondary education; and he accepted this position as the simple fact that it was, without alarm or conceit, fulfilling meticulously the responsibilities that it entailed. He told me candidly how easy it was for the appearance of good teaching to be copied in isolation from the substance. Like his predecessor, he found a number of self-styled disciples adopting, in more or less conscious admiration, many of his habits, mannerisms, gestures, even his style of dress – and he knew well what debilitated affectation that kind of admiration could be.

In the circumstances it was good to be left to it. But I worried a lot at first about my lack of professional training. Without a Diploma of Education, or anything like it, I felt I must have missed a lot of crucial instruction. Then gradually, during the first year, the worry departed. What I needed most to know, I learned, albeit painfully on occasion, through the effort to do the job. Caldwell Cook's first principle – 'Proficiency and learning come not from reading and listening, but from action, from *doing* and from experience' – applies as strongly to the student-teacher as to the child.

The notes that Douglas Brown left me were particularly useful for two reasons. They focused always on actual issues arising from the conduct of lessons: and they took the form of descriptions 'for information only'. They offered possible tactics, not a set of commands. Once the first term had begun, one of my earliest mistakes was to refrain from consulting these notes when I was in difficulties. The reluctance was a misplaced form of pride, combined with too acute a fear of becoming a slavish

THE 'OLD' MUMMERY

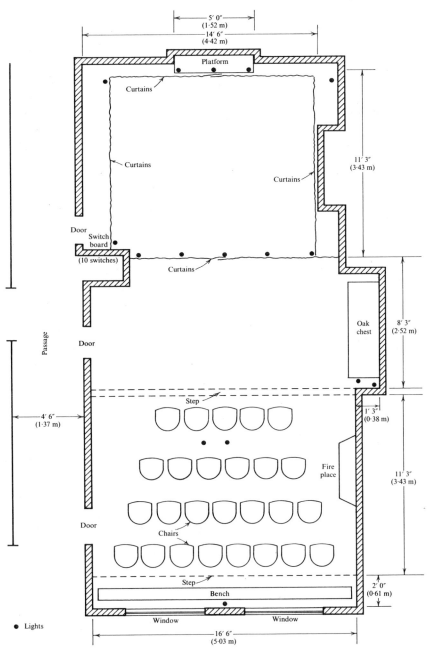

Labels within the figure:

5′ 0″ (1·52 m)

14′ 6″ (4·42 m)

Platform

Curtains

Curtains

Curtains

11′ 3″ (3·43 m)

Door

Switch board
(10 switches)

Curtains

Oak chest

8′ 3″ (2·52 m)

Passage

Door

Step

4′ 6″ (1·37 m)

1′ 3″ (0·38 m)

Fire place

11′ 3″ (3·43 m)

Door

Chairs

Step

Bench

2′ 0″ (0·61 m)

• Lights

Window

Window

16′ 6″ (5·03 m)

imitator. I felt I should prove my power of independence. Such foolishness did not last long. Before the term was out I had learned that a teacher of English needs all the humane, informed support that he can get – and I consulted the notes frequently.

Recollections of my own childhood in the Mummery proved useful too. I could remember clearly much of the work we had done in our English lessons at the age of eleven and twelve, how we had done it and – in some ways most important of all – what we had thought and felt about it at the time. I learned a lot about how to behave as a teacher from such memories. Perhaps they gave me some kind of training after all.

This book, then, is about teaching English in particularly fortunate and helpful circumstances. It aims to give an account of experience, not to lay down a set of precepts. Conditions in secondary schools differ enormously, *and where the reader's situation is vastly different from mine I hope not to breed mere envy or mere impatience.* 'That may be all very well with the kind of children you teach, but it would never do with mine' is a common enough reaction among teachers listening to another talk about his work. Yet the more we give that thought its way, the less we are likely to be able to help each other, for it magnifies our sense of division, when we should be looking for the spots of common ground.

So what follows is largely a personal narrative. On the subject of English in school there are many general dissertations about the way others ought to do things. I have come to prefer greatly the detailed accounts of the things others do. They seem to me to be much more useful. The reader can take as much or as little as he wishes, and act on it as he thinks best. Whatever he takes, he takes it in a practical aspect, not just as theory. There is a great need for a wider sharing of knowledge about principles and methods in English teaching – of knowledge about methods especially. For lack of it too much English in school is still done drill-fashion.

Any account of teaching experience is also an act of exposure. In steeling himself for it a teacher may unconsciously adopt a tone that becomes hectoring, preachy or too sternly didactic. Therefore it is perhaps best, as well as fitting, to close this chapter with some words of Douglas Brown's which, like those that began it, express my own feelings precisely.

How very difficult it is for a teacher to talk to others about his convictions, his methods, his findings or his disappointments, *without* slipping unaware into the wrong stridency, or into the appearance of knowing more of the answers than really he does. If I remind you and myself of this, I hope to have your sympathy when and if I fall.

THE 'NEW' MUMMERY

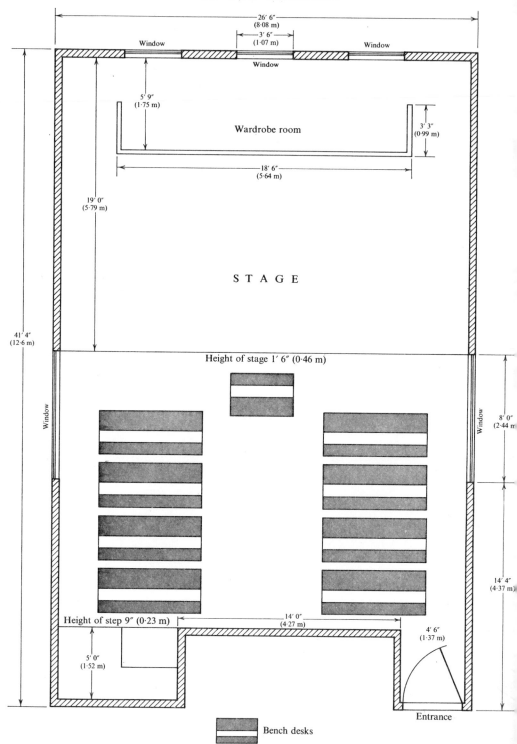

- 26' 6" (8·08 m)
- 3' 6" (1·07 m)
- Window
- Window
- Window
- 5' 9" (1·75 m)
- Wardrobe room
- 3' 3" (0·99 m)
- 18' 6" (5·64 m)
- 19' 0" (5·79 m)
- STAGE
- 41' 4" (12·6 m)
- Height of stage 1' 6" (0·46 m)
- Window
- Window
- 8' 0" (2·44 m)
- 14' 4" (4·37 m)
- Height of step 9" (0·23 m)
- 14' 0" (4·27 m)
- 4' 6" (1·37 m)
- 5' 0" (1·52 m)
- Entrance
- Bench desks

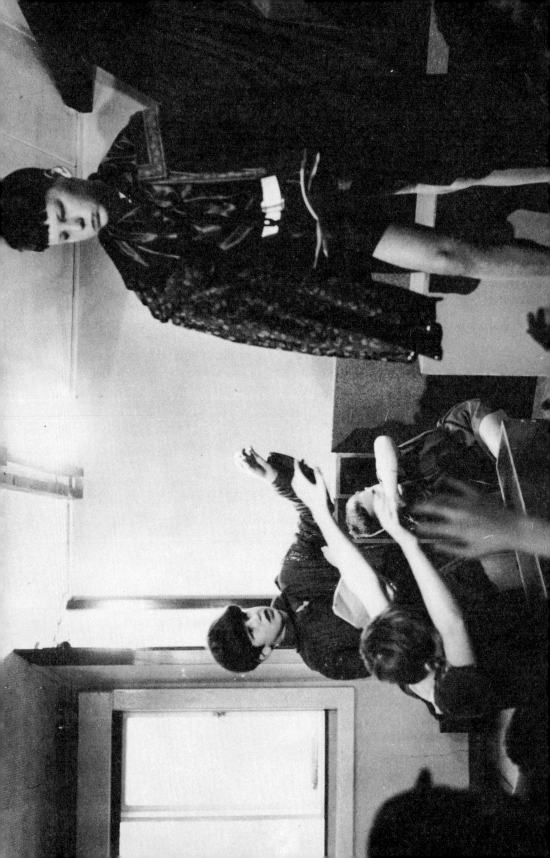

2. Taking possession

A welcome provision in larger schools would be rooms for English large enough to take a few low rostra and some classroom furniture. It is surprising that the simple but purposeful 'Mummery' at the Perse School, Cambridge, has not been imitated.

From *Drama. Education Survey 2. Department of Education and Science*

The Perse is a direct-grant grammar school. Most of the pupils attend as day-boys. In September every year, with their entrance-examination ordeals behind them, sixty boys enter the First Form; thirty of them go into 1 A and thirty into 1 Alpha. The division is purely arbitrary as the content of the timetable is the same for both classes at this stage. Later, at the start of the third year, the letters indicate the Arts/Science division as the processes of specialisation begin, all too soon.

As a boy I went into 1 A. In those days, as now, most of the teachers taught in the same room all day and the boys moved round from one to another – Room 1 for History, Room 10 for Latin, Art Room for Art, and so on. Four times a week we trooped over to Pendene House for English in the Mummery, where Douglas Brown taught A and Alpha classes for the first two years. He also took us once a week for Business Period (a name to be explained later) and this lesson was held in an ordinary classroom because we needed desks for it. Two other lessons each week were taken in ordinary classrooms by other members of the English staff – a Reading Period and a Grammar Period. (Both of these disappeared from our programme for the second year, though we continued to do much reading and some grammar.)

Organising the school timetable is usually a tricky undertaking – a sort of juggling act in which teachers' wishes have somehow to be reconciled with inadequate amenities and administrative necessities. The result is a network of more or less feasible arrangements in which some staff almost certainly will have had to make more compromises than others. When Douglas Brown came to teach most of the English for the first two years (with the rest of his schedule filled with Sixth Form work) he was fortunate in having almost no compromise to make with his convictions. There was only one Mummery in the school and he was the only teacher eager to use it. He was convinced that the opening years of secondary school are a crucial time – and dramatic activity a crucial medium – for the cultivation of young people's sensibility in English. He was a man who stood firmly by his convictions; and so it was agreed that the Mummery's resources should be used intensively with Forms 1 and 2 instead of being spread lightly throughout the school and being diluted by other, and to some extent alien, methods of teaching the subject.

So English for most of us in the first two years was absorbing, exciting work. It made plenty of demands and it gave plenty of delight. *After* the second year it turned into a bleaker business, no less demanding but a good deal less delightful. For the third, fourth and fifth years the demands were chiefly demands for written answers to exercises in one text-book or another: and it slowly dawned on us that preparations for the O Level exams had started in earnest in the Third Form.

When I began to teach at the Perse the two senior members of the three-man English Department accepted their former pupil as a colleague with an amiability and tolerance that I deeply appreciated. They did not fuss or harry: they simply and tactfully left me to get on with things. The timetable arrangements for English had remained fairly constant since my childhood. I slid into a vacated slot. In effect this meant that I took full responsibility for English for the first two forms, and a rough third of the Sixth Form work.

Many of the faces in the staff room were familiar from the old days; but the school buildings were not. In 1960 the Perse had sold its old site and moved to a less congested area on the edge of the town. There it had re-built. When the plans for the new buildings were being drawn up, Douglas Brown seized the kind of opportunity that Caldwell Cook must have longed for. He devised a new Mummery which gave his English classes really adequate living conditions. Although financial considerations imposed some economy of space and affected some details of the design, all the major facilities for teaching English through Drama materialised in a more practical form than in the old Mummery.

The new room was empty when I saw it for the first time, and my first impressions were of space, light and airiness. It was one of four specialist rooms that had been built as a suite for Arts subjects at one end of the school, projecting as a limb from the main teaching block. Daylight came in from both sides through large windows halfway along each wall. There was no proscenium arch and no ceiling to hide the structural rafters that supported the roof, whose high peak ran the length of the room about fourteen feet above the floor. Later I learned that the place was just over forty-one feet long and twenty-six feet wide. Ten feet added to the length and breadth of Caldwell Cook's room had made the new Mummery twice as large.

I stood at the sole entrance, at the back of the auditorium, and found my eye drawn straight to the stage. It was eighteen inches high and filled the full width of the room and half its length. At the back was a plain white wall, ending at left and right in high square arches that led behind. On the stage a number of rostra, rectangular and various in size, were arranged tidily together in formal order. There were two blocks of steps in front of the largest rostra.

I went up to the middle of the stage. With the tips of my fingers I could just reach the rafter over my head. Fixed to its side were four light-sockets holding ordinary household bulbs, with swivelling metal shades around them. There were three more of these on the rafter that came immediately in front of the back wall. And on another rafter that crossed the room about a foot ahead of the front edge of the stage two baby spotlights were fixed, one near each end, on simple hinged brackets. The absence of ceiling boards made all these fixtures unobtrusive yet quickly accessible. At each side of the stage, close to the front, a vertical bank of four light-sockets emerged from the wall. These were angled towards the acting area and masked from the audience by narrow wooden screens. In the middle of the stage-floor, at the back, I found a tiny trapdoor covering two more sockets.

From the stage I looked at the auditorium. Facing me were two groups of wooden lecture-desks; strong, rigid things. Each of them had its bench-seat joined at the bottom to the feet of the flat writing-top, making one integral unit. Each unit was long enough for four boys to sit in with elbow-room between them; and four units, one behind the other, made each group. The teacher's desk was of the same kind but half-length. It faced the class from the middle on the same level as the others, *not* from the stage. These bench-desks struck me at first as grim, cumbrous things, but they were more comfortable to sit in than they looked, and they had advantages that became apparent as time went on.

I noticed that the windows were fitted with spring-loaded roller blinds. When these were pulled down they ran in a wooden frame that enclosed the edges all round. Gone was the need for drawing-pins to seal out all sign of common day.

Beside each window was a large mural painting of a scene from Shakespeare – Macbeth meeting the witches, and Hamlet duelling with Laertes; scenes which the Sixth Form artist had first encountered during second-year dance-drama sessions in the old Mummery. In the middle of the back wall of the auditorium was a display board, and this was flanked by two recesses. The one on the left framed the doorway where

I had just been standing: the one on the right was wider and its floor was raised about nine inches. A gramophone stood on a table here, with a cabinet of records nearby. I could see a panel of light-switches; and a rack of coloured light-bulbs; and some shelf-space.

I turned and went through one of the arches into the area behind the stage, a narrow, inner room where the sun streamed in from three, small, roller-blinded windows. This was the equivalent of the wardrobe-and-props cellar of my childhood, and it still kept its old name: the Tiring House. The attire was all ready to hand. Two clothes racks lined the partition wall. They were the kind of thing one sees in dress shops; free-standing affairs, on castors. From one of them hung an array of cloaks, ranging from the sumptuous to the ragged: on the other were many tunics and a few long robes, in all sorts of material, colour and style. Midway between the racks I saw, with a twinge of nostalgia, two useful relics from the old cellar – a sort of ancient umbrella stand sprouting assorted sticks and flags and spears and swords, and a tall brown cupboard with numerous deep shelves for hats and belts and a thousand and one small props. Tucked snugly away behind the line of cloaks was the oak settle. The other juggernauts of my childhood, the two wooden thrones, now stood on the landing outside the Mummery door.

I came out of the Tiring House, crossed the stage, stepped down into the auditorium and walked round the ample gangways that surrounded and separated the two groups of seats. A springy, buff-coloured linoleum absorbed most of the sound of my steps. I sat down in the back row, a little breathless with pleasure. This room in which I was to teach for most of each day was bright and spacious, with its walls and roof painted white, the rostra a light grey, and the clean brown woodwork of the rafters and bench-desks giving it a thoroughly purposeful air. Empty of people it seemed a little bare – later I adorned it with long orange curtains hanging from the rearmost rafter across the back of the stage – but not at all depressing. It was clearly a room in which people were meant to be getting on and doing things: and it would clearly be as convenient and practical for doing drama or mime in, for holding poetry-sessions or listening to talks, as it would be for doing free writing or formal composition, for taking notes or for discussing or reading. Everything about it seemed planned to make it easy to use English 'in each of its four modes (listening, speaking, reading and writing) and for all the varied purposes (practical, social, imaginative, creative) which make up its totality'. It amounted to fully furnished accommodation for the learning and teaching of English, while the auditorium alone, with the addition of a blackboard and easel, could serve general classroom purposes, if need arose, perfectly – or almost perfectly.

One year I discovered one purpose which the Mummery did *not* serve as well as an ordinary classroom.

The O Level exams and the school exams usually occurred at the same time in the summer, and in this particular year a feasible timetable could only be produced for them, it seemed, if the Mummery was used as a G.C.E. examination room. So the bench-desks were removed. They were no good for examinations: people sitting in them would be too close together, it seemed, and exam candidates had to be kept apart. So thirty standard, individual desks and thirty single chairs were moved in and set down in straight, wide-spaced lines that ran the full length of the room, from the back of the auditorium to the very back of the stage, ignoring the change of level. All the rostra were stacked in the Tiring House, except for the two biggest ones which were made into a towering eminence for the invigilator. The O Level candidates did most of the laborious furniture-removing, without much relish, on the eve of Exam Fortnight.

The incident seemed to epitomise the anti-educational effect that exams produce. There was so much energy devoted so assiduously to setting people apart from each other. The Mummery was not designed to split a class into thirty separate 'candidates' in order to test the ability of each one to write answers to questions against the clock. It was designed to hold a class together in two small communities in order to use each individual's ability most effectively in developing powers of creative imagination.

3. Instruments

But if the teacher goes the right way about it, children using the stage will be as orderly as children using the classroom.

From *Teaching English* by J. H. Walsh

I find it takes about six consecutive lessons to introduce a new First Form to all the Mummery's equipment.

We usually start with the rostra on the stage. All of these are stoutly constructed, with tough composition-board tops and ply sides; and they can be arranged in countless ways. The two largest are four feet square and two feet high; two more have the same surface area and half the height; and there is a long dais, six feet by three feet and half a foot high. All but the dais have convenient hand-holes and these make it easy for four boys, working together, to carry them. To reduce the risk of accident, I tell the class with some emphasis that four is *always* the number of carriers required. The other items are smaller and more easily manageable. There is a seat block, four feet long and eighteen inches high and wide; and two step-blocks, each with three six-inch steps. The whole array stretches across the back of the stage in a roughly symmetrical pattern which I ask the boys to remember. It forms the standard order to which the rostra are returned at the end of each lesson, for the sake of neatness and for the convenience of the next class to use the Mummery.

After pointing out that the best stage-managers work quietly and carefully, moving one thing at a time without rushing, I divide the class into teams of six or eight, each with two 'foremen'. Then I give each team a scene to set – such as a rocky landscape or a court-room or a ship's deck – under their foremen's direction. The boys are inclined at first to treat the rostra rather as a giant construction kit than as a means of making functional acting areas and levels. So I point out, just before dispensing two minutes planning-time, that a good setting gives the actors room to move about unhindered; and this means that the foremen should decide just where the main entry and exit points for the scene are to be, and leave them unobstructed. (There are five main points to choose from, two from behind the stage and three from the back of the auditorium, down the gangways.) When planning-time is over, each team in turn comes out to arrange its setting while the rest of us watch and assess. It is considered disastrous to bang the rostra into each other or to drag them any distance (causing a great din, despite the springy linoleum): and it becomes apparent to everyone that success depends on clear instructions from the foremen and on alert co-operation among members of the team. When a team has finished, the boys in it sit down in their places again, I make a few brief comments on their procedure – laying on the praise for well-conducted and well-spaced efforts rather thickly – and then for a minute or two we all discuss how convenient the setting would be for actors to use. With luck all four or five teams have had their turn and restored the stage to standard order by the end of the forty-minute period.

When the class comes for its next lesson we attend to the Tiring House. Just as the stage has its standard order for rostra, so here everything has its appointed place: if it didn't, with four classes constantly using the same supply of costumes and props, the room would quickly be para-lysed in chaos. Cloaks belong on the cloak rack, each hanging by its chain-fastening from a separate hook. Tunics and robes belong on coat-hangers on the other rack, short ones on the left, long ones on the right. I open the props cupboard and indicate which shelf is for hats, which for masks, which for cups, bottles and dishes, and so on all the way down. The contents of the ancient umbrella stand arouse much interest. I show the boys how to wheel the cloak rack aside when they want to take out the oak settle from behind it.

The whole of this guided tour has to be done twice over because the Tiring House is so very narrow that only half the class at a time can squash inside. Once the inspection is complete everyone returns to his seat to hear how to make use of the costumes. Being so small the Tiring House cannot be treated as a self-service store or as a dressing room. In fact only two people, the Tiring Men, work in there before a performance, and it is their job, not the actors', to choose what each character shall wear. The actors make ready by taking off their jackets (all costumes go on over shirt and trousers) and leaving them on the bench-seats: then they go to wait at one of the entrances to the Tiring House. There the Tiring Men give them their items of costume and they come back to the auditorium to dress up. Actors only go into the Tiring House if they have to make their entry on to the stage from there. At the end of a performance the Tiring Men collect the bare hangers from the racks, give them out to the actors, and go back to the Tiring House to await the return of costumes. The fact that each actor brings back his costume ready for hanging up makes it possible to restore the Tiring House to order quite quickly.

Tunics make good basic items of costume. They give a quick all-over change of appearance, and they are simple to pull on over one's head; but boys, being boys, need fairly constant reminders to open the neck-fastenings fully before they begin to pull. Most of the Mummery's tunics and cloaks were begged from the school dramatic society years ago. Kind parents have made and donated others. Altogether they constitute an invaluable, if well-worn, basic wardrobe: and the boys often extend it with pieces of finery of their own, brought from home for particular performances; curtains, fur capes, leather jerkins, gaudy waistcoats, even bed-jackets have been pressed into service like this on occasion.

To try out the whole process of fetching, donning and returning costumes, we make new teams of six. Two boys in each are appointed as temporary Tiring Men, the remainder imagining themselves to be actors. We invent a group of characters for each of the settings used in the previous lesson – for the rocky landscape, say, a gipsy robber chief with two of his gang and a captured nobleman – and while one team dresses up another sets the stage; and the rest of us watch what goes on. When the characters are ready, they make a tableau on the stage for us to consider their costumes. From the start I try to encourage Tiring Men to aim for simple, bold effects and contrasts. They tend at first to swamp the actors with too many bits and pieces, treating costume as if it were thoroughly realistic period dress instead of seeing it as a stimulus for the imagination. All that is *really* needed to distinguish the captured nobleman from the gipsy gang, for instance, is a wise choice of cloak. From the start too I try to encourage actors to take pride in their appearance, so I show much concern that costumes should be worn trimly – belts not twisted, tunics hanging straight and level, cloaks descending comfortably from the shoulder-line and not tight about their wearers' throats. And I try to make this a less sergeant-majorly concern than it sounds.

In the activity of these lessons the boys begin to build the customs of carefulness and practical co-operation that are vital to their work later on. As they discover that all the equipment in the room really *is* for their own use, they see too that using it entails respect for Order. This Order is very different from Teacher's Orders. It is an orderliness in their relationships with each other, and it is aimed at making the most of resources. Everyone is called to contribute to it: and it is clear to everyone that the degree of self-discipline required is useful, in a direct way, to the common cause. From the beginning, in fact, the emphasis is upon social solidarity and shared achievement, not upon individual differences.

After the rostra and the costumes, we spend a whole period round the gramophone. First I show the boys how to turn the machine on and off, how to set the turntable going, how to handle the pick-up, how to use the volume and tone controls. Then we turn to the records. They are mainly recordings of classical orchestral music on standard-play 78 r.p.m. discs. They are stored in the open-ended compartments of a wooden cabinet and the stiff cardboard covers have a label stuck on each side giving the title of the music and the composer's name, as shown on the labels on the records. Each disc also has a short strip of coloured tape stuck to the centre of each side; and there is a strip of the same colour down the edge of its cover. In the cabinet the covers have these strips facing outwards, and the records are grouped together there according to colour. Beside the gramophone lies a card with the following information typed on it to guide the boys who take charge of music:

The Colour Code
Green: serenity, joy, happiness, high spirits, dance.
White: fanfares, heroism, ceremony, procession, dignity, power.
Blue: storm, the sea, violence, excitement, restlessness, danger.
Yellow: peace, quietness, sleep, gentleness, softly mysterious.
Black: serious, melancholy, funereal, sorrowful, elegiac.
Red: mysterious, uncanny, nervous, apprehensive, disturbing.

And underneath a note advises:

Don't regard the colour key as *too* sure a guide. Some records have more than one colour anyway; others have a colour that suggests only the *general* character – music may be very changeable. When experimenting, try the middle as well as the beginning of a record.

After drawing attention to all this, I show the boys how records should be handled – not with fingertips over the grooves, but with two hands round the edge – and how the volume should be turned right down before the pick-up is lifted on or off a record. Then, with a relay of volunteers taking over operations, we hear a short passage from a record in each of the colour-categories in turn.

We use the old-fashioned kind of records for the sake of their manageability and relative durability in young hands. For most purposes they are easier to cope with than tape-recordings – they are easier to 'match' to circumstances on the stage, for instance – and they are much more resistant to accidents or clumsiness with the pick-up than high-fidelity, microgroove, long-playing records.

Finally, we explore the lighting arrangements. In two shifts, as in the Tiring House, the whole class crams itself into the recess to look at the switchboard and the bulb rack (which is actually a set of padded pigeonholes containing red, white, green, blue and orange bulbs – about six of each). As the boys in the second shift return to their places, five of them pull down the window-blinds while I stay at the switchboard.

A single switch controls all six of the 'house' lights that are set in the roof over the auditorium. When I switch these out the darkness is sudden and total, and a clamour of surprise goes up. So I switch on again to say that the Mummery has no dimmers, that darkness is a way of moving into the world of imagination, and that actors and audience make that move best if silence reigns in the darkness. We try blacking out again, maybe three or four times, until silence really does reign. It is not unduly difficult for thirty boys to sit absolutely quiet and still for a few seconds in total darkness, but some of them find it difficult to believe that they are really expected to do it at the flick of a switch. I bother to insist because it is a useful piece of etiquette that is needed often in later lessons.

The demonstration of the stage lighting is usually punctuated with gasps of 'ooh' and 'ah' from the boys. Coloured light can stir the imagination and create mood and atmosphere most effectively, and instantly. For that reason it is much more useful in English lessons than conventional scenery.

The switches on the double-rowed panel are numbered 1 to 12 and at first I go through them in order to show that some control paired sockets and others control single ones. Then I spend a little time showing what can be done by using only one or two switches and different colours of bulb. The boys quickly appreciate the sheer variety of lighting that seventeen sockets and two spotlights make possible: but it takes them a little longer to realise the importance of mastering the switchboard. So, after quickly showing how the swivel shades can restrict or widen the spread of light, and how the spotlights can be reached and adjusted from a pair of folding steps kept for the purpose, I ask two or three boys at a time to carry out some simple, straightforward lighting opera-tions. There is never any lack of volunteers. One boy stays at the switches while the others change bulbs or adjust shades or spotlights. There is a key to the switchboard typed on a card in the bulb rack, and I urge the boys to commit it to memory if they can. The importance of knowing *precisely* which switch does what is vividly illustrated if the whole class, quite breathless with anticipation, watches a pair of boys carefully change a couple of bulbs at one spot on the stage only to find, when the signal to the switchboard operator is given, that lights snap on somewhere entirely different.

By design the Mummery's equipment is *simple without being primitive*. This is a point of basic importance. Machines like the gramophone and the switchboard, and facilities like the costumes and the rostra, are there to be instruments of young imagination. As such, they must not be so easy to use that they quickly become uninteresting nor so complicated that they breed frustration as often as satisfaction. They amount, after all, to more than child's play.

This preliminary series of lessons spent in careful attention to technical matters is valuable in many ways – not least in the way it begins to establish a particular relationship between teacher and class. In effect, the teacher is introducing discipline by sharing concern. He gives his pupils instruments for doing English on the assumption that they will want to use them as well as they can. And while he demonstrates their use he is also 'teaching' respect for materials, consideration for other people, and a commitment to English that is earnest without being solemn or pretentious. In taking the line 'Look and listen carefully... Now have a try for yourselves', he is sharing an imaginative *concern* with his children, as well as know-how: and he shows this concern most clearly through his pleasure on their account when they do well.

Order in English lessons stems from the teacher's sense of poise. If he sets himself up as a boss, his discipline may be a wonder to behold, but the possibility of truly creative collaboration in and with his class will be stifled. If he sets out to be 'one of the boys', he is likely to find himself quickly losing the means of all effective control. He needs to be accepted as a part of the class-community, yet as a part distinct – child-like, perhaps, in his enthusiasm for instruments and tactics, and in his basic regard for standards, but not child*ish*. When the boys explore the technical facilities of the Mummery and put into practice what they see and hear, they are not so much seeking to please Sir as creating their discipline for themselves and, in discovering that recommended procedures do work, discovering its value. The whole class, teacher and all, shares the discovery; and the discipline is seen by all to be more constructive than repressive.

4. Forming groups

And the ordinary clamant needs and drives of their age (the need to be liked and accepted, the drive to experiment and master) will be seeking a suitable satisfaction. Children welcome, it is worth remembering, any legitimate mode of expression you can provide which really does give their needs and drives the chance to be expressed. Drives and energies will, of course, go into what we call bad channels if we don't provide adequate good ones. But if children can find satisfactory constructive outlets, they will. They will be on your side in this. Normally people prefer being social to anti-social.

From 'Teacher and Taught' by T. C. Worsley in
The Quality of Education, edited by
Denys Thompson and James Reeves

'Now that you have all had a good look at the Mummery and learned a little about its equipment, I'd like each of you to choose, by next time, which kind of work you would most like to do in future lessons. There are really five kinds to choose from – stage-managing; lighting; being in charge of costumes and props; being in charge of music; and, of course, acting. I know I haven't said much about the business of acting so far, but I hope that some of you will want to be actors all the same, or there'll be no work for the others to do. It may happen that you find *two* kinds of work attractive, in which case you should make the one which you honestly think you could do best your first choice and keep the other as a reserve. In fact, it will help matters if you *all* make a definite second choice, because it's not always possible to give everybody the job they most want to do. Suppose, for instance, that half of you were to make lighting your first choice and only one or two wanted to act: the class would be hopelessly lop-sided. But with second choices we can usually keep a reasonable balance. When we meet again tomorrow I'm going to divide the class in two, and each half will need some actors, some stage-managers, somebody to look after the music, and so on. When we have arranged all that, I'll tell you a little more about what we are going to do in English this term. Now there's a minute or two before the bell goes: has anybody any questions?'

There is a pause. Then the first anxieties begin to emerge.

'Please sir, do actors have to *learn* their parts?'

'Oh no; I should have made that clear. When we do a play from *The Curtain Rises* the actors act with the books in their hands. It would be too much to expect them to know their lines by heart every time we do a play. Besides, there wouldn't really be time for the learning because we do a lot of other things each term as well as plays.'

A shorter pause.

'Sir, when we've got a job, can we change it?'

'There's a chance to change at the end of this term, if you find that you're really not suited to your post: and we have a general change-round at the end of the year – or rather, at the very beginning of the Second Form.'

The next question comes from a doleful-looking lad.

'What happens if you can't even have your second choice, sir?'

'Well, that happens very rarely, but when it does it means – for a very few people – being content with a third choice until the first job-swapping session comes round. Then things are usually sorted out to everyone's satisfaction.'

He looks as if he plainly doubts it, and seems about to launch into one of those long, long questions that begin 'Yes, but if . . .' when somebody else pipes up urgently.

'Sir, if we choose to be *not* one of the actors, do we *never* do any acting?'

'No. In practice-lessons everyone may be asked to take part. And in some plays, later on, there are more characters than the number of official actors. So then the big parts go to the regular actors and the "back-stage boys" do the smaller bits. I usually ask Stage-managers and Tiring Men to do this because their regular work comes before and after a performance, so they are available to help.'

'Please sir, do we have a producer?'

'Not exactly. Each group has a leader, though. He is in general charge of the group, but he doesn't make all the technical decisions himself. He decides which actors shall play which parts; he gives the word for a performance to start when he sees that everything is ready; he settles disputes if members of the group can't agree among themselves. It's a good thing if he gives himself an acting part from time to time, but he leaves staging, music, lights and costumes to those who have special responsibility for them. If a crisis arises – say, for instance, that one of the actors is absent on the day of his group's performance – then the leader decides what emergency measures to take. As the leaders' jobs are specially important ones, you vote for them instead of leaving them to choose themselves; and I'll show you how to do that tomorrow.'

The bell has just stopped ringing.

'Don't forget, then – acting, stage-managing, lighting, music, Tiring

House. Come to English tomorrow with a first choice *and* a second choice. All right, off you go.'

The room empties with animated discussion to be heard on the lines of 'I want to do such-and-such. What do you want to do?'

The next day I begin the lesson by talking for a while about the Whitsun cycles of miracle plays and the medieval guilds of tradesmen and craftsmen who presented them. Though I digress a little about pageant-wagons, property lists, mechanical devices and such-like, my main purpose is not to give a history lesson but to make it clear that these early 'trade unions' were both the very first independent theatrical companies and (for all their amateur and occasional nature) very competent concerns. Then it is a simple step to draw an analogy between the guildsmen's situation as beginners in the theatre and the boys' situation as beginners in the Mummery. I exploit the analogy to set up a group structure that gives the boys 'constructive outlets' for their drives and energies with a large measure of responsibility for the way their English lessons are conducted.

In re-shaping the class in two halves I call the groups Guilds and give them distinctive names – The Haberdashers and The Costermongers in 1A, The Ironmongers and The Merchant Taylors in 1 Alpha: and, with more regard for traditional spirit than historical accuracy, I give each officer in each group a formal Guild title: Master Player, Master of Music, Master of Lights, Master of the Stage, and Master of the Tiring House (the latter two generally being shortened, in practice, to Stage Manager and Tiring Man). This nomenclature is not merely quaint. Because it catches their imagination the boys take to it readily, and it gives us all a set of terms by which to keep life in the group organisation. The titles sharpen the boys' sense of their particular rôles while imparting a faintly glamorous aura to them: and there are occasions when the very formality is a help; occasions, for instance, when it is more tactful for me to refer to 'one of the Master Players' or 'the Master of Lights' than bluntly to Smith or Robinson.

The Guild-idea encourages in the boys the notion that English as a subject has something to do with the experience of past generations coming alive in the present; and as this notion seems to me to be of fundamental importance, I foster it in this way. In some schools, however, children would certainly *not* take readily to Guilds and Guild-titles. It is not very difficult to find other bases for group-organisation, and other names. The important thing is to have a clear structure and a definite terminology to work through.

After introducing Guilds and emphasising the 'team' idea, I briefly recapitulate the scope of each office and turn to the business of electing group-leaders, who have the glowing title of Masters of Revels. The boys propose candidates, and if the number of those agreeing to stand exceeds two – as it usually does – we go on to a ballot. (It is important to ask for 'agreement to stand' since it sometimes happens that boys are nominated who are popular with their peers but very timid; and they may regard the leader's post with such awe and axiety that they would much rather forego the honour altogether. A teacher's poise ought to respect such feelings.) The ballot is held either orally, with candidates asked to wait outside the room, or by writing votes on slips of paper which are folded up tightly and collected in a hat. In both cases we display great care for secrecy, in order that justice may well and truly be seen to be done.

There are about thirty boys in the class, and in each Guild I hope there will be six or eight Master Players (though a Guild once managed very well with only four), two or three Stage Managers, two or three Tiring Men, two or three Masters of Lights, and one or two Masters of Music. Once the Masters of Revels are elected, I ask them to stand at each side of the auditorium while we fill the other posts. First I call for Master Players. All the boys who have made acting their first choice put their hands up, and the Masters of Revels pick alternately. As each actor is selected he comes out of his place to stand with his leader. When the last volunteer has been picked, I call for Masters of Music, and so on. In this way, job by job, the Guilds gradually assemble.

I tell the Masters of Revels the minimum and maximum number of boys that it is practicable to have sharing each Guild office, and if some of the minimum numbers are not attained I don't worry too much. Things can usually be levelled up through second choices. Almost invariably there are more than six boys who want first and foremost to be Masters of Lights, and when three for each Guild have been chosen I try to ensure that all the unlucky ones secure their second choice, even if it means asking for a little swapping of personnel between the Guilds. It usually transpires that most of the boys get their first choice of job and the rest make content with second best. But sometimes, swap and shuffle as we may, it is simply impossible to reach such a satisfactory arrangement. Then perhaps three or four of the thirty have the mild disappointment of a third choice to put up with for a time. They rarely languish when the Guilds start work in earnest.

There are many other practical ways of forming a class into two self-governing groups, of course. The particular value of *this* way lies in the evidently democratic method – which does not in fact leave the boys free to do entirely as they please (the option of making *no* choice of job is not open to them, for instance) but they accept the small measure of constraint without demur, if indeed they notice it at all. Since each boy takes on his work in this voluntary way, his teachers and his fellows may legitimately expect him to try to do it as well as he can for the sake of his group. Standards of work are thus sanctioned more emphatically by a social ideal than by Sir's decrees: and in the daily relationship of teacher and taught this is a distinct advantage. So is the fact that this way of forming groups makes it clear to the boys that those who do *not* want, primarily, to act in English lessons are just as important, and needed, as those who do.

It seems to me hardly sensible for a teacher to *expect* more than half a class of thirty boys to enjoy acting or to have the ability to be good at it – though it is always pleasant to find a higher proportion. I see no great educational benefit to be gained from forcing shy, unwilling or even frightened children to act, when they have other skills to offer. The Guild-idea is a way of accepting different kinds of ability; a way of developing them in a common direction; a way of spreading the sense of shared purpose and achievement.

With the elections over, the boys go back to sit in the auditorium. Each newly formed Guild fills one set of bench-desks – The Haberdashers, say, on the left, The Costermongers on the right – and this simple arrangement is adhered to in all the ensuing lessons. It helps the Guild-idea along by giving each group an evident, external identity, a local habitation as well as a name.

Both Masters of Revels then appoint a volunteer as their Guild Scribe for the term. This post can supplement any of the others, the chosen Scribe being responsible for putting a clear, neat notice on the Mummery display-board before any main performance by his Guild, giving the programme-details.

Then this lesson usually ends with my saying something like this:

'Our arrangements for English are nearly complete now, but there are three more important things to remember; and they are – Business Period, Entry Music, and The Golden Rules. I'll go through these in order, so listen very carefully.

As I expect most of you have noticed already from the school time-table, you have five periods of English in the Mummery every week and two others – Reading Period with Mr Hulton in Room 3 on Wednesdays, and Grammar Period with Mr Caley in Room 7 on Saturday mornings. And I'm sure you have all noticed too that you have a half-hour piece of English *homework* on a Tuesday evening, and another on Thursday evening. It is my job to set you those homeworks, and if that seems to you a grim prospect remember that Mr Hulton and Mr Caley won't be setting you any at all. I have set aside *one* of our five Mummery periods to deal with the whole business of homework; hence the name, Business Period. It will always be the same lesson in the week, first period on Friday afternoons, and I should make a note of it in your timetables now if you think you are likely to forget it. At Business Period I shall always give you your homework for the whole week ahead, so you can start it before Tuesday or Thursday if you want to. As well as explaining the work ahead, I shall also use Business Period to collect in pieces of work that are due, to give you back homework that has been marked and go over points arising from it, and – occasionally – to give you a short test of one kind or another. By putting all these matters into Business Period I hope to keep all the other four Mummery periods free to do other kinds of work in Guilds – acting, miming, speeches, poetry and so on.

Now Entry Music, as you may have guessed, is music played while you enter the Mummery. Its purpose is to make the beginning of the period fairly pleasant and to help you settle down and turn your minds to English from whatever it was you were doing previously. Masters of Music take it in turns, for a week at a time, to supply Entry Music. When it is *your* turn, Masters of Music, try to be here among the first arrivals so that you can get your record on in good time. You can choose from any of the colours except Red or Blue; and this is a good way of getting to know some of the music you can use for other purposes too. Play Entry Music good and strong until the last person to come in has got to his place and then, when I give you a nod, fade it out fairly quickly. While the music is being played I shan't speak to anybody about anything (so it's no use bringing problems to me then, however urgent they seem to be) and I'd like you to be just as silent. For the rest of this week, then, let's have the Master of Music from The Haberdashers supplying the Entry Music; and let's see if you can all remember to be quite quiet and listen to the record as you cross the Mummery threshold for English after break tomorrow.

This brings me to the Golden Rules, which apply to all members of a Guild in the minutes they spend getting ready just before a performance. The rules are very simple, and the whole reason for *having* them is to reduce fuss and bother as far as possible. You will see the need for them if you think for a moment of the number of people who have to use the stage all at once at such a time: the Master of Revels will be keeping an eye on things; the Stage Managers will be moving the rostra about; the Masters of Lights will be arranging bulbs and shades; and the Master Players will be going to and from the Tiring House. All this Guild work can happen very smoothly so long as everybody remembers the three Golden Rules and carries them out. Here they are. First, whatever your post in the Guild may be, do your *own* job, and don't interfere with other people's. Second, *walk*, don't run – however much of a hurry you are in. Third, *whisper*, don't shout. These are called *Golden* Rules because they are precious; they make all the difference between order and chaos –

as you will be able to see for yourselves quite soon because the first thing the Guilds are going to work on is a play. We'll make a start on it next time: so please make sure that you have your copies of *The Curtain Rises* with you tomorrow.'

A hand shoots up.

'Sir, does that mean we're going to start doing English properly?'

'Well...er...yes, I suppose it does.'

5. Drama

What we want is that our lessons should resemble more than anything else an early rehearsal for a co-operative form of dramatic production – a production which would be, in the result, not the interpretation of a single mind (the teacher-producer) but the collective interpretation of the group.

From 'Drama Lessons' in *The Disappearing Dais*
by Frank Whitehead

Although it first appeared over forty years ago, *The Curtain Rises*, compiled by J. Compton and published by Methuen, is still one of the best anthologies of dramatic pieces for use in the early years of secondary school. Unlike many more recent collections, it contains far more living matter than dead wood. David Holbrook's *Thieves and Angels* (C.U.P.) offers an even better selection; but its greater size and weight make it less practical for young players to use for book-in-hand acting. There are six short plays in *The Curtain Rises*: two lively farces (one traditional, one modern); two simple and engaging pieces from the Irish Revival; and two plays written especially for children. One of the latter – *Piers Plowman's Pilgrimage* by Frances Chesterton – strikes me as decidedly dead wood. It is described as a morality play; and it has been drawn from 'Will Langland's great epic of a May morning on the Malvern Hills'. The quality of dramatic life seems to have been drawn from the language in the process. With most of the morality made into overt moralising, and most of the speech made starchy-stiff, the script invites more posturing than acting. So, when we embark on Drama in the first term, I choose one of the five other plays.

And I ask *both* Guilds to perform it.

By doing this I hope to bring the boys' attention to bear as effectively as possible on the quality of dramatic life – the meaning carried by English in action – as they work on the play. They will do this for the next ten or a dozen lessons, interrupted only by the weekly Business Period, and if all goes well their interest and enjoyment will grow sharper as time goes on.

Getting all to go well can be very hard work for the teacher, much harder than merely running the show. To be truly 'a co-operative form of dramatic production' the play must be guided, not directed; and so must the class. Guiding children into achieving their own improvement requires considerable concentration, patience, tact, imagination and nervous energy – often simultaneously. The teacher has to know the play quite as thoroughly as any competent producer would know it; but if he makes the mistake of becoming a teacher-producer in class, he will seriously devalue the whole undertaking and he is more than likely to drive the children's enthusiasm into rapid decline too.

The new Guilds usually cut their teeth on the farce *Two Blind Men and a Donkey* by Mathurin Dondo. It's a brisk piece, with six strong rôles for the actors and no acute problems for the backstage boys. We spend a period – and never more than a period – on talk and preparation for the first Guild-performances. At the outset I say a little about the story in very general terms: it is set in medieval times; it involves several people, including the donkey, in practical jokes; and one of the jokers, who thinks it clever to be unkind, is shown up as the biggest fool in the play. A few more details of the plot emerge inevitably as I go on to talk about some dominant traits of the characters, concentrating on a few brief moments of dialogue, like this:

The blind men are two of a kind. Two professional beggars with a 'public' voice and a 'private' one. The public voice is a sort of miserable whimpering which they use when they hear 'clients' approaching; but their private voice is bold and quarrelsome. Early in the play they meet a strolling player, a Comedian as he was called in the old days, and when it turns out that he has no money to offer them we hear both sorts of voice in quick succession. You'll find this moment on page 58: look it up now . . . I'll start reading almost at the top of the page, as the Comedian approaches. Follow the script, please, in your books:

SECOND BLIND MAN   Have pity on a poor man born blind who will pray for your soul and for your happiness. Ave Maria . . .
(He mumbles a prayer)
COMEDIAN   My good folks, if you ask me for pity, I give it to you with all my heart. If you ask for money, all I can give you is the blessing of the Lord. I myself am a poor beggar.
FIRST BLIND MAN   You filthy beggar, get away from here.
SECOND BLIND MAN   Away with you. No beggar has a right to stand here.

Now as a matter of fact the blind men are being deliberately teased by the Comedian here. He is very fond of a joke; and very quick-witted; and very smooth-tongued. And although he has nothing of his own to give away for charity's sake, he cheerfully gives away other people's belongings. Later on, for instance, to do a bit of a good turn to the blind men (and himself at the same time) he gives the Donkey Driver's donkey to the Innkeeper. He pretends that he owns the donkey, and then he persuades the Innkeeper that the wretched animal has wonderful magic powers. Then, with a bit more tall story and some heavy flattery, he gets the Innkeeper to take it as a present. You will find this going on at page 70 . . . about halfway down:

COMEDIAN   Yes, sir, this donkey is almost human. I would not sell him for any amount of money, not even for his weight in gold. For that would be a sin. I have made the vow of poverty. I have renounced all worldly possessions as I am on my way to enter the monastery. What shall I do with my beloved donkey? I cannot give him away to the first stranger for fear the precious animal might be ill-treated. But here I find you, you with a noble, gentle and generous soul. You are the man who can understand my donkey, treat him with kindness and value his services. Take him, sir, he is yours. I give him away for charity's sake.

To call the man 'a noble, gentle and generous soul' is flattery indeed! Look back a couple of pages and you'll find that this same Innkeeper can become very rough and menacing when he finds the blind men can't pay his bill . . .

In this way I move on from one character to another, glancing at an outstanding quality in each. Such a brief guided tour does not take long to prepare before the lesson, and the effort of preparation is well worthwhile; for the play is then broached largely through the dramatist's own words, and the boys' careful attention is guided there from the start. I found it tempting at first to make this introduction to the play too long and too detailed, not realising that a full description of each character is as unhelpful to the drama lesson as a comprehensive account of the plot; both those tactics tend to weaken the very appetites that ought to be whetted. So now I allow myself to refer to only one short extract per character – and I try to render each one with plenty of relish and feeling, since lukewarm reading from a teacher does little good to anybody.

The Donkey is the character I keep for last; and I make him the means of turning to matters of costume. Years ago, after a school production of *A Midsummer Night's Dream*, the Mummery inherited a large, hollow, papier-mâché ass's head. This is fetched out now from the Tiring House and I demonstrate the way it should be worn so as to be most comfortable for the actor and most impressive for the audience. (There is really no harm in a teacher making an ass of himself in class occasionally, if he teaches the children something useful in the process.) Everyone is quick to realise the plain and simple effectiveness of the donkey's head; and I urge the Tiring Men to make such simplicity the aim of all their work, to select costumes that convey each character's occupation or 'type' as directly as possible. Then, after suggesting that 'the simpler the better' is also a very good policy for the lighting and the music in the performance, I turn to the question of staging. The play's opening stage-direction is more specific about the scene than the Mummery itself can be:

The scene is the public square of a quaint town of medieval France. To the left is shown an inn with the sign of the Green Dragon, and to the right one perceives the shadowy arch of a monumental gate. There is a stone bench by the gate, under a little shrine. In the background, we get a glimpse of tortuous streets and protruding gables. As the curtain rises, the Two Blind Men may be seen standing in their professional attitude, motionless, silent and expectant. Within a short time, the Comedian enters, and at once the Two Blind Men practise their art on him.

Once the whole class has read this through, I try to guide attention to the things that matter most –

A public square is, of course, an open, spacious place: and *a clear space* is the most important thing for the Stage Managers to provide. Then, the features to left and right are important. It shouldn't be difficult to make a simple inn-sign that you can fix quickly on the rafter to indicate the entrance to The Green Dragon: and on the other side we shall need some of the rostra arranged to suggest the stone bench and the little shrine. Who can explain what a shrine is? . . . Yes, that's right, a saint's tomb – a good spot for the blind men to carry on their 'profession', of course. So, with a sense of the inn on one side and the town gate on the other, we should all be able to imagine for ourselves the background view of twisted streets and jumbled buildings.

And there I stop, hoping to have encouraged everyone into some personal concern with the play by having mentioned the work of each Guild-department in turn.

It is very easy to start producing instead of guiding in an introductory talk of this kind. Yet one has to say *something* about the play – something more than 'Now let me see you get on and do *Two Blind Men and a Donkey*' – or the class will be unlikely to use the lesson-time to best advantage. After a point, however, the more one says by way of explanation the more one damages the very process of discovery-through-performance that drama lessons are intended to achieve. I have found it best to conclude my introductory remarks while I am still wondering if I have said enough to give the boys a useful start. If I wait till I am quite sure, it is usually too late and the damage has been done.

The next thing I do is to propose a full book-in-hand performance of the play by each Guild in turn in the next two English periods. The boys are invariably staggered; there is a loud gasp of alarm. Some of them think I must be joking; but it's quickly apparent from my (feigned) surprise at their surprise that I'm in earnest. They are suddenly face to face with the fact that they hold *real* responsibility in their lessons: and it is at this moment, usually, that the breath of life comes blowing into the Guild organisation. For the remaining fifteen or twenty minutes of the lesson a lot of planning goes on.

The Guilds go into council. This means that the bench-desks are shifted around to make two hollow squares, and the boys then sit round the sides looking inwards. This rearrangement takes less than a minute to carry out – because the units of furniture are large – and each group's planning is greatly facilitated. While the Masters of Music and the

Tiring Men go off to look through records and costumes, the Masters of Revels decide which actors shall play which parts, and the Masters of Lights and Stage Managers work out their plans together. My contribution is strictly limited to suggesting the order in which the acting rôles should be cast, to encouraging the boys to talk quietly ('so as not to give away all your ideas to the other Guild') and to giving advice *when it is requested* ('Sir, we haven't got enough actors, what shall we do?'). In each square the buzz of discussion rises and falls; and as an aid to efficiency we adopt the convention of 'man-in-the-middle' by which any boy who steps into the centre of the square must be listened to by the rest of his Guild in complete silence. This practice is particularly useful at the times when Masters of Revels want to make some general pronouncement and when Stage Managers want to describe in detail the setting they have planned for the actors.

I try to interfere as little as possible. But I do step in with reproof if boys start to quarrel with the decisions of their Master of Revels – 'I'm not going to be the Innkeeper. I want to be the Donkey. I shan't act at all if I can't be the Donkey!' – or if they waste time with chat that has nothing to do with the play at all. It is very important for future progress that the spirit of positive co-operation should catch on firmly at this stage.

If I have not said quite enough about tackling the play, the boys' questions, like 'How can we be blind men when we have to read our parts out of the book?' or 'Does the Donkey go on all fours or standing up?' usually remind me of what is missing.

At the end of the lesson the bench-desks are put back in place and we toss a coin to decide which Guild will give the performance in the English period next day. By the time that period arrives most of the boys, and fairly certainly all the actors, will have read the whole play once through carefully – out of interest and out of a sense of responsibility to the Guild. There is a world of difference in spirit between such work, done voluntarily, and a read-through imposed by the teacher as a homework task.

When I meet the class again, we get straight down to work. I remind the performing Guild of the Golden Rules, and then I hand the lesson over to the Master of the Revels. I move my desk to the back of the auditorium and settle down there quietly to watch proceedings.

In these early days the boys in the audience-Guild find the spectacle of their opposite numbers preparing for drama almost as absorbing as the performance itself. If the acting-Guild is careful and remembers the Golden Rules, the play is ready to begin after about five minutes' brisk activity. When all is ready a hush descends more or less spontaneously;

the Master of Revels makes a clear signal towards the lighting corner; and darkness and music introduce the performance.

Since the play lasts between twenty and twenty-five minutes, there will probably be about ten minutes of the lesson left after it – ample time for the boys to restore the Mummery to standard order and for me to make some comment on the Guild's work. No matter how well or ill the actual performance has fared, I include in my remarks some strong praise for the way the Guild used its initial five minutes. The *other* Guild is then almost certain to try to be ready to start in four minutes at the next lesson. In this way the boys are encouraged to regard preparations for acting as important and at the same time subordinate to the main enterprise. The play, after all, *is* the thing.

It may happen, however, that the stress of excitement, or nervousness, or simple carelessness, may lead the first acting-Guild to abandon the Golden Rules while it makes ready: in which case the muddle and fuss will probably go on for a good deal longer than five minutes. Sometimes more than a third of the lesson-time has passed before the acting has started, with the result that the performance has had to be broken off well before the end of the play. At such times a teacher may be strongly tempted to step in and put matters roughly to rights; but it is a temptation to become wholeheartedly a teacher-producer, and it must be strongly resisted. I sit quietly. But I look ostentatiously at my wristwatch as the minutes tick away; and I sometimes indulge in some pointed remarks to nearby spectators, rather heavily *sotto voce* – 'I wonder how many *more* actors will try to tell the poor Stage Manager what he ought to do?' or 'What a strange notion some people have of what *walking* means!' The boys in the audience sometimes grow rather smug, I am afraid; and some of them actually enjoy the sight of their fellows meshed in difficulties: but they learn from what they see. Usually the watchers make a more efficient job of preparing to act when their turn comes round at the next lesson: and the boys in the other Guild then learn from watching them.

That is one kind of learning-by-experience. Another kind, more important, comes to the boys through the imaginative extension of being that arises in the performance itself: and in cultivating *this* learning there is much direct, positive work for a teacher to do. One does not take a rest by sitting at the back of the room to watch the children's efforts without (if all goes well) interrupting them. Nor should one work with such an energetic attention (as in the over-zealous making of notes while watching) that one's presence distracts the children although one does not formally interrupt them. Rather, one needs to maintain a state of sympathetic watchfulness and critical awareness. This is a demanding occupation. It requires one to be feeling things from the boys' angle while assessing the art in what one sees them do: and simultaneously it requires one to be deciding how best to formulate one's comments for the end of the lesson.

The *whole* point of making comments at the end of the lesson ought to be to give encouragement. The teacher's remarks should lead the class to take a keener interest in the play and its performance: and children are most likely to do this if they find that what they have managed to do well *already* is frankly and openly admired. Praise should always come first and foremost – and not only praise for the actors. The back-stage boys will quickly feel relegated to second-class citizenship if they find their work being taken for granted: and relegated people feel resentful, naturally. So I always try to mention some good points about the staging, costume, lights or music in a performance, before I speak of the acting – though, for the sake of Guild solidarity, the core of the praise for good 'backstage' work is the fact that it helped the actors to do well.

I have found it best to limit the spectators' commentary in class to admiration by selecting particular aspects of a performance and inviting appreciation of them. In an unlimited discussion the boys usually pick up all the surface blemishes first – 'Willis kept losing his place, Sir; and the lights went out too fast at the end' – and if and when they do notice the positive achievements they tend to touch on them too loosely – 'Parker was good as the Donkey Driver', 'They kept it going very well' – though here the teacher's questions such as 'What did you like most about the way he did it?' or 'Why was that a good thing?' can lead to more substantial and incisive engagement.

But time may not allow this eliciting tactic. Fairly frequently only a minute or so of the lesson remains by the time the room is restored to order and all the boys are back sitting in their places. Then, I do not try to admire everything, but just pick out a couple of the best points, appraise them without hurrying, and let the rest go. Boys take more note of what they hear stated clearly and calmly than of what they hear uttered in a breathless verbal scamper.

By giving praise where praise is due a teacher-guide serves his class far better than by apportioning blame – so long as the praise is genuinely due. Nobody, adult or child, likes being jollied along with that kind of wholesale admiration that is manifestly overdone and under-considered. A gushing teacher is a menace: however, he is probably a little less of a menace than a teacher who habitually points out first and foremost the faults in his children's work. Such a teacher believes, no doubt, that he is doing the pupils some good, when he is simply wearing down their capacity for enthusiasm.

One cannot do entirely without criticism in drama lessons: but when it has to come it is best if it can be conveyed in some form of expression that implies 'here was a positive achievement just missed'.

In the lessons following the Guilds' first performances I hope to put watchfulness to work constructively. For several consecutive periods – perhaps as many as five – the class 'rehearses' collectively, working at my suggestion. It is essential, of course, that the work should really be by suggestion, and not by order. The aim is a sharper engagement by the boys in those parts of the play that were realised only superficially in the first attempt at acting: and the *engagement* is what matters, not the 'professional' kind of polish that an adult can give to the work. As a teacher one needs great restraint and patience here – with oneself as well as the children. When one is tired, or when the class seems sluggish, one is often tempted to step out to the front to act out for them a passage that is proving awkward to deal with, saying in effect – 'Can't you see that this is the way to do it?' But such personal demonstration is generally a short-circuit rather than a short-cut. To be properly helpful, one must let the children feel their own way into the life of the dramatist's words, and it is often a struggle to do this.

The ideal in these rehearsal lessons is plenty of action from the boys themselves. They demonstrate to each other their notions of the best ways to act the particular moments that I pick out from the play. There is a lot of coming and going between stage and auditorium as we work impromptu-fashion, without using full costume or 'proper' lighting. For the time being Guild distinctions are laid aside and the whole class works as one big group. I try to keep to a questioning approach which first invites attention to the text and then calls for practical demonstration. Anyone can volunteer to act, whether Master Player or not, and I try to pick the non-actor volunteers as frequently as may be. This is sometimes the way that shy boys make a first brief attempt at acting, and sometimes they discover that the ordeal is not as bad as they expected. After such a beginning, many a backstage boy has chosen, later in his Mummery career, to become a Master Player.

There seems no great advantage in going through the play strictly page by page. I hop backwards and forwards among the passages where earlier engagement was thin, sometimes starting by asking the actors of one Guild to re-do a scene for general consideration, sometimes simply referring briefly to the way a moment went in performance. Wherever possible I try to make strong moments into springboards for concern with weaker ones. For instance, most Guild actors render very well at their first shot the Blind Men's sudden change from whimpering to anger on meeting the Comedian (even if I have said nothing about 'public' and 'private' voices when launching the play). Their success here is a useful taking-off point for work on this later sequence, which is rarely managed smoothly at first attempt:

(The Donkey has just trotted off-stage after appearing on the scene for the first time. He has licked the outstretched hand of each beggar in turn. The Blind Men have both believed, for a moment, that a kind passer-by has been giving them alms; and each in turn has voiced loud and fulsome thanks to the supposed benefactor before realising his mistake. The text goes on as follows.)

FIRST BLIND MAN   Pierre!

SECOND BLIND MAN   Well?

FIRST BLIND MAN   You have been caught.

SECOND BLIND MAN   So have you.

FIRST BLIND MAN   You couldn't see through it.

SECOND BLIND MAN   Neither could you.

FIRST BLIND MAN   What was it?

SECOND BLIND MAN   'Twas a cow.

FIRST BLIND MAN   You idiot, 'twas a dog.

SECOND BLIND MAN   It's a cow, I tell you.

FIRST BLIND MAN   Cow yourself, I tell you it's a dog.

SECOND BLIND MAN   Dog yourself. You are more stupid than you are blind. You couldn't distinguish your nose from your thigh.

FIRST BLIND MAN   You threefold idiot, tell me if you can distinguish my stick from my boot!

(Both sticks strike the air, right and left, and the following can be heard – each speaking alternately.)

FIRST AND SECOND BLIND MEN   Take that . . . take this . . . filthy . . . scabby . . . thief . . . cheat . . . pagan . . . devil . . .

(The Donkey's powerful braying is heard. The Two Blind Men stop fighting.)

FIRST BLIND MAN   A donkey!

SECOND BLIND MAN   A donkey!

In first performances this quarrel usually falls rather flat. The actors don't warm up because they are anxious not to lose their places in their books. So the quarrel goes tamely, even solemnly, and the voices intone the insults alternately in slow, deliberate rhythm. For the fight the two boys struggle with sticks in one hand and books in the other; while the need to avoid *actually* walloping each other is in the forefront of their minds. In all this stress they are very likely to miss the dramatic pause that comes as the donkey brays and truth dawns on the blind men.

Usually, in dealing with this sequence, I can start by referring back to the sharp, clear way the actors portrayed the beggars' quick tempers on the Comedian's arrival at the opening of the play. Then I point out that the quarrelsome nature of the two men needs to be conveyed just as sharply in the present passage: and then I resort to a questioning tactic, which might go like this. (I put in brackets here the substance of the answers I hope for. But, of course, a number of revisions of the question are often needed before that substance emerges):

'Why do you suppose the First Blind Man provokes the argument?'
(Because he realises that he has been made a fool of, and he wants to cover up by seeming to be cleverer than the other man.)
'And how would you describe his attitude at first?'
(Teasing or scornful or 'crowing'.)
'Now where does the Second Blind Man begin to dig his heels in?'
(When he says 'It's a cow, I tell you.')
When they begin to get *really* angry, how do we know – what should we see?'
(They start to shout, and advance on each other, and brandish their sticks.)
'And as the quarrel starts to flare up, how should their voices follow each other?'
(Quickly, with scarcely a pause.)
'Good. Now who would like to do this bit up to the point where they lash out with their sticks?'

If the first volunteers do very well, we move on to the fight directly. If they don't, I invite another pair, and another if necessary. When we reach the fight itself, the boys almost always get the point that the blind men, in their blindness, are quite out of reach of each other's blows, but the first demonstrators usually stand rooted to the stage and wave their sticks rather unconvincingly. So I go on trying to elicit sharper engagement.

'Will you all look at the stage-direction at this point, please. Why do both sticks strike *the air* to right and left? . . . Yes, that's right – because both beggars have a very shaky sense of direction, and as they step into battle they go aside from each other instead of coming together. Now what did you think of the way they struck at each other last time?'
(It was too feeble; they didn't look as though they meant it.)
'All right, let's ask them to do it again with a bit more spite. Remember, you two – each time you hurl a name you must hurl a blow with it. Off you go . . . Well, the blows were certainly fierce enough that time, but, as we all noticed, Jones and Robinson lost their place almost as soon as they began shouting the rude names at each other. It's tricky, this moment. But if the actors *do* lose the place, they can keep the spirit of the thing going by – well, can anyone tell me?'
(By *making up* insulting names as they go along.)
'Yes. Any suggestions?'
(Bandit. Stinker. Blockhead. Louse. Worm. etc. etc.)
'Fine. Fine. And when the Donkey's loud braying breaks into this flood of names, what is the effect?'
(Sudden stillness and silence. The Blind Men realise they have both been wrong.)
'Right. Now who would like to have a shot at doing the whole quarrel right through?'

Even when teaching as carefully as possible, one cannot *altogether* avoid 'producing': but this kind of procedure, through questions and invitations, does mean that most of the mental and physical activity of discovering the dramatic life of the play *belongs* to the boys, as well as to their teacher.

In this style we explore perhaps three or four short sequences in a lesson: and matters of acting technique, especially matters of timing and movement and gesture, are tackled as the need for them arises from the speech of the characters. They are not made into exercises for their own sake. Much of the teacher's work of watchfulness at first performances lies in taking properly the chances offered here. For instance, at one point in the play the Comedian persuades the Innkeeper that the Donkey has an 'almost human' cleverness, and the trick is helped along by confirmatory wags of the head and tail from the animal. The comic point is largely lost if – as often happens at first – the donkey is more or less hidden from view by the other two actors. In touching on this moment, one may have a first chance (and it is very unlikely to be one's last) to point out that in order to make the best of a scene actors must avoid huddles and 'masking'. At another time a character's late appearance at a crucial moment may lead one to suggest to all actors that in order to arrive on the scene punctually it is wise to start all entrances just *before* the stage-direction says *Enter So-and-so*; or again, a conversation that has gone flat between the characters may give one the chance to show how much difference it makes to the life of a performance if the actors lift their noses from their texts as often as possible and look each other in the eye. The point is that general advice should arise from particular happenings in performance. It is not much use declaring a list of dos-and-don'ts like 'Never stand between another actor and the audience: keep your distance from each other: don't turn your back on spectators', and so on, before any acting has occurred.

These sessions of collaborative 'rehearsal' culminate in second performances of the whole play by both Guilds. Each takes a whole period, as before, but this time the Masters of Revels redistribute the actors' rôles. I have found it unwise to delay second performances until the *whole* play has been practised. It is good – indeed, it is really vital – for the boys to feel that they managed some things in the play perfectly well under their own steam at first attempt. Sometimes, when I have waited too long before calling for second performances, the passages that have had close and sustained attention turn out to have lost all their savour. Sometimes, when I have caught something like the right moment, much *more* of the play than its 'rehearsed' passages has been engaged strongly by the imagination of actors and audience alike.

Every term Drama, undertaken in this way, has a share of the Mummery programme, along with Mime and Speeches and Poetry. We spend roughly a fortnight on a play; and sometimes there is time to do two plays in a term. Occasionally the boys have chosen to make and perform their own scripted plays; but rather more than a fortnight is needed for this. And quite often, at the end of a term, a popular way of filling two or three 'spare' lessons has been Impromptu Drama. For this, after a brief talk in council about a chosen theme or story-idea, each Guild presents a playlet to the other, with its actors improvising talk and action as they go along. About five minutes' council time is allowed, and the rest of the period is split evenly between the two groups. The results are usually spirited and entertaining, if occasionally clumsy: and, as well as having value as a creative exercise, the whole business is also useful practice for the Guilds in the art of preparing quickly and simply for a performance.

By the third term many of the boys have grown very skilful at acting with a text held open in one hand. The ablest ones can act their parts for all they are worth while keeping their place in the book through the most rapid, cut-and-thrust dialogue. The off-stage staff have usually grown fluent in the techniques of their work by this time too. So, in the portion of the third term that goes to Drama, I aim to nourish these growing talents with stronger meat. The Guilds turn from *The Curtain Rises*, where the diet is chiefly comedy and farce, to a piece of serious drama. Its title visibly staggers many of the boys when they hear it for the first time. It is *Philoctetes* by Sophocles, in a translation made by Douglas Brown specially for use in the Mummery and now generally available in The Playbook Series (C.U.P.). This version is a fine example of the way the distinctive power of Greek drama can be mediated to the imagination of schoolchildren through the power of robust English. The vigorous open verse of the translation is made for reading with the voice as well as with the eyes, and young players can make it most compelling. The direct treatment of themes of treachery and suffering, and consequent problems of honour and compromise, together with its fast-moving action and series of tense crises, make it a particularly appealing play for boys.

Briefly, the story is this.

Philoctetes was one of the heroes who embarked on the Greeks' expedition to besiege Troy. On the way there the fleet stopped at an island to visit the temple of a goddess. Philoctetes was the first to approach the temple, and as he did so he was bitten in the foot by a venomous snake, the guardian of the shrine. This wound could not be cured. It turned ulcerous and festered, rousing so much revulsion among Philoctetes' fellows on board ship that the Greek leaders, to avoid trouble, decided to abandon the wounded man on the uninhabited island of Lemnos. This disgraceful act was carried out under the command of Odysseus, while Philoctetes lay unconscious after one of his periodic outbursts of intense pain. The fleet sailed on to Troy, and the war there dragged on for the next ten years. During all that time Philoctetes was left to eke out a wretched, crippled existence, alone on Lemnos, a forgotten outcast. His sole means of survival was the extraordinary bow which he had inherited from his former friend Heracles. With this he was able to kill animals for food, for the arrows fired from it were deadly and never missed their mark.

Eventually at Troy an oracle revealed to the Greek leaders that their siege could never succeed until the bow of Heracles, and its owner, were brought to the attack. So Odysseus was sent back to Lemnos to recall Philoctetes from exile.

The action of the play starts as Odysseus lands on Lemnos with the young son of Achilles, Neoptolemus, a newcomer to the Greek forces. Odysseus is too cunning, and too frightened of Philoctetes' stored-up hatred for him, to risk meeting his former victim face to face. He goes into hiding, and leaves Neoptolemus, whom Philoctetes has never seen, to make contact and win the crippled man's confidence with a cock-and-bull story. Helped by this tale, Neoptolemus is to trick Philoctetes aboard his ship, giving him the impression that he will take him back to his homeland; but in fact the journey will end at Troy. It is a mean and deceitful plan of campaign, and inevitably it traps the young man in shame and dishonour. As he goes on he is moved more and more with pity for Philoctetes' suffering, past and present; and in the end his better nature turns against his mission, and he blurts out the truth. Stunned and outraged at finding himself a victim of Greek treachery a second time, Philoctetes utterly refuses to be persuaded to take the bow and arrows voluntarily to Troy. And he comes very close to killing his old enemy Odysseus when the latter breaks out of hiding in a last-ditch attempt to accomplish the mission by force. The situation becomes deadlocked. Philoctetes will not agree to go to Troy. Neoptolemus will not desert him yet cannot act at all, now, without betraying either his conscience or his duty to the Greek cause. Ultimately, the intervention of the deified Heracles proves to be the only way of resolving matters.

When I launch the play in class I start by telling the story in this manner, but much more fully. The reason for going into detail with this play, after deliberately avoiding doing so with the one-acters in *The Curtain Rises*, lies in the nature of Greek drama. It seems unlikely that many of the audience in Sophocles' day were hearing the story for the first time as they watched the play in the theatre. Most of them must have come to know it, or its main outlines, in the course of their upbringing – in much the same way as we today come to know the story of, say, Thomas à Becket. And *because* of this familiarity the poetry of a great dramatist can work all the more powerfully on his audience's imaginative understanding of 'the way things are'. This, for the Greek spectator, was perhaps the most 'dramatic' quality of the play, not an excitement about 'what will happen next'. And to establish among the boys some rough sort of equivalent for this receptive state of mind, I tell them the story as thoroughly as I can at the outset.

The play is too long to fit into a single forty-minute lesson (and a double one is, alas, a rare luxury on the timetable) so I divide it into episodes, each lasting twenty to twenty-five minutes and each overlapping a little with its neighbour. After one lesson spent on my story-telling and on group preparations in council, the Guilds act the play episode by episode, working alternately. This first run-through usually fills a week's lessons. Then we go on to do a kind of slow-motion exploration of the acting and staging possibilities in the manner of the earlier terms' work, but this time covering almost the entire play. The greater subtlety and sophistication of the dramatic form warrants this sustained concentration, which may last for anything from one to two weeks. During this time I aim to guide attention repeatedly to two things in particular – the expressiveness of dramatic verse (that is to say 'the way the words are meant to go and the way the words show what the characters are doing') and the rôle of the Chorus (which is filled by sailors from Neoptolemus' ship). These sailors are on the scene throughout the play, apart from the opening minutes, so their acting – and, for considerable passages, re-acting – is very important indeed: it can decide the strength or weakness of the whole performance. One of the first things that the boys acting the sailors discover is that they need a way of keeping their voices together (a Guild may put as few as three boys in its Chorus, or as many as seven). It doesn't take them long to realise that each line of verse has a rhythm of its own when spoken in 'the way the words are meant to go'; and then they find that they can make use of the slight pause at the end of the line as a sort of gathering-point if they lose step with each other. I advise Masters of Revels to appoint a Chorus-Leader whose job it is to set the speaking pace for the others and to bring them in together at the beginning of a speech with a small signal, such as a nod of the head or a wave of the hand in their midst: but this particular device becomes less and less necessary as the boys grow familiar with the play and come to feel together its inner tempi.

At the heart of the play a bout of intolerable pain from the ulcered foot overwhelms Philoctetes – an episode which depends largely on the horrified reactions of the sailors for its dramatic effectiveness. Just before losing consciousness the sick man gives his famous bow to Neoptolemus for safe keeping until the pain is over. It is a gesture of total trust in the young man. The sailors, while sharing Neoptolemus' pity for the sleeping Philoctetes, are quick to see a practical opportunity of completing their mission:

PHILOCTETES   O earth receive me, dying as I am
  I can stand no longer.
NEOPTOLEMUS   I think he will sleep, now.
  His head sinks. And sweat, do you see,
  Breaks out all over him. A dark bloodstream
  Pulses from his heel. We will leave him
  And sleep will take him more easily.
SAILORS   Come gentle sleep, stranger to sorrow and pain:
  Grant him your peace
  Lighten his darkness
  Heal his anguish.
Philoctetes sleeps.
  Think sir: what is your next move?
  You see how things stand.
  Now's your time: why wait?
  Do it while you can. Take your opportunity
  It may not come twice.
NEOPTOLEMUS   True, he lies there unconscious.
  But it's himself we need.
  We'd have bungled the operation – and by fraud, at that.
SAILORS   Leave that to the gods. Talk quietly.
  Sick men sleep lightly, fitfully.
  How can we move him? Confine yourself to that.
  Take the prize while you can.

At their first venture, most Guild-Choruses usually make a reasonable distinction between 'Come gentle sleep...' and 'Think sir: what is your next move?...' The first passage goes slowly, gently, like an incantation; the second is altogether more urgent and rapid. But the boys' timing and movement is invariably too hurried to catch all the feeling that the lines carry. So, when our slow-motion exploration reaches this sequence of the play, I try first to sharpen the felt moments. I point out that Philoctetes is not fully asleep until the stage-direction is reached, so the sailors speak warily, as well as with pity, while they invoke sleep all in unison. Then I suggest that the next lines, where the Chorus seizes the chance to speak frankly, are excellent ones for distributing to single voices in the group. The Leader decides who shall say what, and the boys soon catch the knack of following on from each other without awkward pauses. When 'cutting in' occurs by accident, it helps to convey the sailors' sense of anxiety. We practise saying the lines in whispers ('Sick men sleep lightly...') while keeping them sharp and clear. And the question 'What happens when Neoptolemus says "We will leave him..."?' directs attention to the way the words show what the characters are doing. It is usually decided that Neoptolemus goes, some distance off as he finishes speaking, and the sailors gather first round the body of Philoctetes, to check that he is soundly asleep, and then hurry to cluster round Neoptolemus. Trying all this out, using *ad hoc* groups of actors, as in the previous term, may take up a third to a half of a lesson; and by calling frequently for new groups of volunteers, I try to make this kind of work an active participation in the life of dramatic language – as distinct from mere drilling in techniques of choral speaking – for most of the class.

There are always a few boys who find the time spent in close attention to the Chorus-rôle dull. They need a lot of (friendly) persuasion and encouragement to take part in it effectively. But when we come to focus on such a moment as Philoctetes' attempt to shoot Odysseus (and the play offers occasions of equally high excitement at frequent intervals) everyone wants to take part.

At this point in the play Neoptolemus, who has kept possession of the bow ever since the bout of pain, offers it back to Philoctetes. The act expresses commiseration and a sense of solidarity with the lonely and wounded man who still refuses adamantly to join the Greeks at Troy. As Philoctetes reaches out to take the bow Odysseus breaks out of hiding, shouting, in a desperate attempt at a final veto.

ODYSSEUS   He must not have it! I speak for the gods,
  For the high council of the Greek army:
  I forbid you to part with it!
But Philoctetes has taken the bow, and sets his mark at Odysseus.
PHILOCTETES   Odysseus again!
ODYSSEUS   Take him!
PHILOCTETES   A costly capture, if I find my mark!
NEOPTOLEMUS   No sir, for God's sake: hold your hand.
The sailors scatter in fear; Neoptolemus restrains Philoctetes.
PHILOCTETES   Let go! Free my arm, boy. In God's name –
  Too late. You have robbed me of the kill,
  The man I hated most.
Odysseus escapes.
NEOPTOLEMUS   The kill would have brought no honour, sir,
  To either of us.

In the Guilds' first performances one of two kinds of hitch usually occurs here. Either an actor loses his place in the book at a vital moment, or everyone is so careful to keep the place that the action merely crawls along. In both cases the drama of the incident is lost.

When we reach this passage in practice-session everyone sees at once that words and action must work smoothly together. The question is how to make them do so. I hope to guide the boys into 'producing' the dramatic impetus through their comments on each other's on-the-spot attempts to act the incident. And the guidance is a matter of catching and using – and even, at times, provoking – the comments that bear directly on the life of the passage. For instance, somebody invariably points out that the books hinder the actors from maintaining the pace. 'Perhaps they could *learn* the middle bit, sir.' This is a good idea and so we *all* learn the central five lines, from 'Odysseus again!' to 'In God's name – Too late.' This only takes a few minutes to do and it enables us to go on working at the passage with one volunteer-group of actors after another. Once the words are thoroughly in mind, the whole incident comes immediately more alive on the stage, the struggle between Philoctetes and Neoptolemus being full-blooded and much more convincing.

Then there are practical matters to consider. Where should Odysseus enter from? Where should he stand on the stage to take command of things? At what point *precisely* should he run away? How do the sailors respond to the order 'Take him!'? How do they show their *fear* when they scatter? When should Neoptolemus *leave go* of Philoctetes?

One question is always settled quickly by a brief try-out of the alternatives – should the actor of Philoctetes fit a *real* arrow to the bow or should he *mime* doing this? (It is soon discovered that the latter procedure is both easier and more exciting to watch – to say nothing of the fact that it is considerably safer – since it preserves both the pace of the action and the spirit of swift deliberate vengeance. Audience and sailors find that the imagined arrow can be seen very clearly in the mind's eye.)

Finally I hope to have the tone and timing of the last four lines of this passage considered closely, so that the class can feel the connection and the difference between the quiet voices of Philoctetes and Neoptolemus.

It may take a quarter of an hour or twenty minutes to get most of what is registered in the short passage strongly felt, on the senses and in action. But such close attention is, I think, part of a genuinely 'co-operative form of dramatic production': and when, after perhaps two weeks of work of this kind, the Guilds undertake second performances (each Guild this time having a turn to do the play right through in two consecutive English periods) there is usually real development in the art the boys bring to the collective interpretation. When things have gone really well – and if the *class* suggests it – we do an after-school performance for parents and friends at the end of the summer term: and for this the actors usually choose to learn their parts.

I find this fairly intensive concern with *Philoctetes* a worthwhile part of English work for its own sake. It also sharpens the acting skills that began to develop in the one-acters of *The Curtain Rises* – to a degree that makes it possible to tackle Shakespeare with profit in the second year.

6. Shakespeare

And in particular I remember being Trebonius and so having to miss the assassination; and being, at twelve or thirteen, Lysander. We dressed ourselves in tunics and cloaks and carried metalled swords, and all that business happened very swiftly and easily in a few minutes before the proper beginning. I remember this. And I remember we carried huge volumes called 'Fifteen Plays of Shakespeare': far too cumbrous really for this duty, but having one supreme merit since denied to most schoolchildren. They were absolutely plain texts; no notes, no introductions, no summaries of characters or content of scenes: perfectly, nothing except Shakespeare's text. I was, I know, as unremarkable and unromantic a schoolboy of thirteen as could be. But the curious amalgam of excitements, nervous ordeals, splendid moments of gesture, and my treble declaiming phrased eloquence quite out of my proper sphere, this strange trance-like experience stayed with me. More, in fact, than the other ingredients of Caldwell Cook's teaching.

Douglas Brown

The conviction that children of twelve and thirteen can indeed feel, in response to the verse of the plays, this 'curious amalgam of excitements' seems to me the vital motive-power for a teacher who undertakes Shakespeare with his class in the early stages of secondary school: for with this conviction there goes a strong concern to *enable* children to reach such strange trance-like experience in the drama, both for its own sake and for the quality of interest in 'man alive' which the experience can awaken; a quality of interest which may continue to work, like a leaven, in the spirit of young people as they grow older.

Other, and more down-to-earth, motives for starting early exist in abundance. There is, for instance, the well-meaning (and often bardolatrous) wish to improve 'The Young Mind' with Shakespeare: there is the concern to prepare young people in good time for their O Level ordeals in English Literature. But good intentions such as these often entail teaching methods that deny children almost all chance of real excitements; methods that are more concerned with the text, alone, than with the drama. Any approach that treats a play-script simply as a thing to read through, rather than a thing to act, is very likely to inhibit most of the children from any real participation in imagined life beyond their proper sphere. Thus the extension-of-being which is the essentially dramatic – and supremely Shakespearean – experience is denied them. *Any* attempt at a performance in a classroom gives children a better chance of imaginative nurture (though it will frequently seem clumsy and inadequate to the adult eye) than any sit-down reading.

It is possible, even probable, that the experience by which the heart is excited into heightened sensibility by Shakespeare's phrased eloquence in our native tongue comes more readily to a young actor warming to his rôle in mid-scene than it comes to a backstage boy who peeps up from his book now and again to glimpse the action from the sidelines. And it is certain that this experience will come to *some* children only occasionally, and perhaps only very briefly. But it is *worth* far more than hours of drill and instruction in the classroom. And there are few children, if any, to whom it will never come, if the teacher can allow them and Shakespeare a fair chance together – which means trying to treat the play *as* a play and not as a reading exercise. When the proper treatment is regularly and carefully attempted, the drama will involve *all* the class in the Shakespearean experience from time to time – however primitive the 'stage' conditions may be. These occasions sometimes last for only a few seconds, sometimes they last for minutes on end: but always the teacher will notice them. A kind of spell involves the spectators with the performers, putting them at one in a new dimension where all share the imagined life, peculiarly strongly. *That* is the nurturing process. *That* is what does the best teaching of all.

In the Shakespeare lessons of my childhood there were many trance-like times when the play worked for us like this, although *we* never really noticed their beginning. We became aware of them when they had ended, usually through some technical hitch or some incongruity in the acting that suddenly ended the suspension of disbelief which had caught actors and audience up together. It is a delicate spell and I have felt it take its precarious, temporary hold of the class on many occasions in the modern Mummery, while I have sat at the back of the room, properly forgotten. Sometimes it has occurred in places where one might reasonably expect it to: in the Forum scene in *Julius Caesar*; during the trial in *The Merchant of Venice*; or at the close of the woodland sequence, Act IV Scene i, in *A Midsummer Night's Dream*: and sometimes it hasn't. Sometimes it has come in softer passages, such as that between Brutus and the drowsy Lucius on the eve of the battle at Philippi. And sometimes it has come in the places where one might reasonably have expected boy-players of twelve and thirteen, acting book-in-hand in class, to be quite unlikely to achieve it – in the love-talk of Lorenzo and Jessica at Belmont as they await the return of Portia and Nerissa, for instance: or in Hermia's decorous wrangle with Lysander over the matter of sleeping together once they have lost their way in the wood, where, as everywhere in the Shakespearean dramatic experience, there is an element that speaks directly and validly to young sensibilities (in this instance as a sense of decency in true love, functioning through manners) fused with the very element that directly addresses the adult consciousness (here as an awareness of the stirrings of sexual desire). This fusion through which the dramatic experience is kept particularly open to young life pervades the plays. It may owe something to the presence of the boy-players in the Elizabethan acting companies, as well as stemming from Shakespeare's infinite powers of reception and self-exposure, in memory, in imagination and in day-to-day existence.

Because I have often felt a whole class of boys to be caught up in the nurturing spell of Shakespeare, I am prepared to believe that *some* nurturing goes on, undetectably, for *some* of the children – a constantly changing number – almost all the time during a classroom performance; even when the class as a whole is clearly *not* carried away. So long as the effort to perform the play is being seriously upheld, imaginative participation *may* be taking place. The teacher should not expect to see outward and visible signs of it *all* the time.

The huge and cumbrous volumes of *Fifteen Plays of Shakespeare* had been jettisoned by the time I began to teach at the Perse. Instead of them, the book-store issued single-play volumes from the King's Treasuries series published by Dent, a long-established (and in some respects old-fashioned) edition that offers a clear and handy text. It was evidently prepared with exam purposes in mind, for it contains plenty of editorial matter – introduction, commentary, notes on this and that, questions and exercises – but all of this is so arranged, before and after the play itself, that it can be easily ignored. I encourage the boys to ignore it (one wants them to come to grips with Shakespeare, after all, not the attendant industry) but not to ignore the useful running glossary in the form of simple footnotes to the text. The whole book is far more compact and attractive for use with junior pupils than, say, Verity.

One year, as an experiment, I substituted for it the Penguin Shakespeare, which was in those days the nearest thing to an absolutely plain text that I knew of. (The edition has since been revised and considerably elaborated.) It had a splendidly clean page, trim and well-spaced, with characters' names printed in full, and punctuation that kept admirably close to the Folio. It was light, pleasant to hold in the hand, and the lack of line-numbers was only an occasional nuisance. But, alas, it was much less durable in schoolboy hands than any hardback edition.

In the Dent text the episode between Brutus and Lucius that I have mentioned is set out like this:

Bru. Look, Lucius, here's the book I sought for so;
I put it in the pocket of my gown.   *(Var. and Clau. lie down.*
Luc. I was sure your lordship did not give it me.
Bru. Bear with me, good boy, I am much forgetful.
Canst thou hold up thy heavy eyes awhile,
And touch thy instrument a strain or two?
Luc. Ay, my lord, an't please you.
Bru.   It does, my boy:
I trouble thee too much, but thou art willing.
Luc. It is my duty, sir.   260
Bru. I should not urge thy duty past thy might;
I know young bloods look for a time of rest.
Luc. I have slept, my lord, already.
Bru. It was well done; and thou shalt sleep again;
I will not hold thee long: if I do live,
I will be good to thee.   *(Music, and a song.*
This is a sleepy tune. O murderous slumber,
Lay'st thou thy leaden mace upon my boy,
That plays thee music? Gentle knave, good night;
I will not do thee so much wrong to wake thee: 270
If thou dost nod, thou break'st thy instrument;
I'll take it from thee; and, good boy, good night.
Let me see, let me see; is not the leaf turn'd down
Where I left reading? Here it is, I think.   *(Sits down.*
                    Enter the Ghost of Caesar.

The ghost is, of course, what interests the boys most of all when they
come to act this episode. I have watched some very impressive entries at
this point, with the acting finely supported by lights, music, costume
and staging arrangements: and such pleasing group-achievement makes
appreciative commentary on the performance very easy to give at the
end of the lesson. Sometimes, however, just *because* the Ghost of Caesar
has attracted so much of the acting company's attention, these moments
before its appearance have been under-prepared. This has chiefly shown
up not in any neglect of the necessary props and actions by the actors
of Brutus and Lucius, but in a riding rough-shod over the proper tempo.

The dramatic life of any Shakespearean scene resides as much in its
points of silence as in its words and actions; and, in the stress of performance, boys will often destroy or distort the shaping pauses. In this
scene, for instance, it has sometimes happened that the actor of Lucius,
being unable actually to play the lute (or the guitar that is usually used
as a substitute), has arranged with the Master of Music that he will
mime his playing to a suitable record. (To save embarrassment I usually
suggest leaving the song out.) If the Master of Music turns out to be late
on his cue at line 266, Lucius, after settling down to play in the pause
Brutus gives him, mimes a strum or two in dead silence, halts in distress,

and waits uncomfortably for music to arrive. Most of the audience then turn round to see what the Master of Music is up to at the gramophone, thereby adding to his confusion: and the flow of dramatic illusion breaks down completely for a few moments. It happens more frequently in this episode, though, that the actor of Brutus, overlooking the vital pause, runs straight on from 'This is a sleepy tune' to 'O murderous slumber'. This obliges Lucius to mime an almost instant and highly unconvincing slumber, with scarcely a note of music played. And matters are sometimes made worse a few lines later when Brutus, having taken the lute from Lucius, neglects to pause at the end of line 272 and put it down somewhere. However, on one occasion, when Harbage acted Lucius and Rollinson played Brutus, almost everything went right. It was one of those occasions when all of us were spell-bound.

The scene is part of a sequence which takes place in Brutus' tent and for this the Stage Managers had left the stage practically bare. The seat block had been set towards the back, near the left-hand archway to the Tiring House. In the middle of the stage with a few stools round it was one of the large rostra, serving as a table. On it stood a lighted candle in a holder, brought in earlier in the scene by Lucius, and one spotlight shone on this. No other lights were on and the overspill from this single lamp created a sense of shadowiness and night while giving enough light for the actors to read by. At the front corners of the stage two actors lay sleeping on the floor as Varro and Claudius, one to each side of the main entrance to the tent – the central gangway through the auditorium. (Entries and exits through the audience help actors *and* spectators to stronger engagement with the play.)

The performance itself was full of skill. When Rollinson reached the line 'Look, Lucius, here's the book I sought for so' he felt in the folds of his gown with the hand that held his text, which he then drew out as the book in question. Then, at the moment of lute-playing, Harbage's mime and the Master of Music's record synchronised perfectly. To play, Harbage sat on the seat block, while Rollinson sat on one of the stools, leaning heavily on the rostrum, apparently immersed in his reading: and he stayed motionless as the music slowly quietened and Lucius' head nodded. 'This is a sleepy tune.' Then as Lucius let his hand drop from his instrument the Master of Music suddenly cut off the melody in mid-phrase, causing Brutus to start, and nudging us all with the sudden hush. 'O murderous slumber, Lay'st thou thy leaden mace upon my boy, That plays thee music?' At this Brutus rose and walked softly over to the sleeping figure. 'Gentle knave, good night;... If thou dost nod, thou break'st thy instrument; I'll take it from thee;' – here he paused to gently disengage the lute (actually Rollinson's own guitar) while Lucius sank sideways till he lay the full length of the seat block. The pause

continued as Brutus quietly moved to the rostrum, put the guitar carefully down on it, and returned to Lucius. Then – a lovely and inspired
touch – he took off his cloak and spread it over the boy to keep him
warm. Only then did Rollinson bring his eyes back to his book and go
on 'and, good boy, good night'. It was a most striking and sensitive
realisation of a pause's dramatic value. And it was followed almost at
once by another. For, as Brutus went on with his silent reading, sitting
as still as a statue a couple of lines later, the Master of Lights waited a
good ten seconds and then simultaneously switched out the one spotlight and switched on the Mummery's second one, which cast a deep red
light on the right-hand archway to the Tiring House, where the Ghost
of Caesar came gliding forward in slashed and bloodstained mantle. 'How
ill this taper burns! Ha! who comes here?' Meanwhile, in total silence,
the Master of Music had changed his lute record to something eerily
orchestral, which he now brought in very softly.

But more impressive, perhaps, than the technical virtuosity of all this,
was the tone and manner of the acting. Some ten lines before the quoted
excerpt begins, Brutus remarks that Lucius speaks drowsily. Harbage
had taken due note; but he sustained this sleepiness with no great
laying-on of yawns and eye-rubbing. He adopted, rather, a faintly
drooping stance and a muted, heavy delivery which achieved a far
subtler effect. And, as Brutus, Rollinson caught beautifully the sense of
need and the affectionate concern that invest these lines:

Bru. Bear with me, good boy, I am much forgetful.
  Canst thou hold up thy heavy eyes awhile,
  And touch thy instrument a strain or two?
Luc. Ay, my lord, an't please you.
Bru.   It does, my boy:
  I trouble thee too much, but thou art willing.
Luc. It is my duty, sir.
Bru. I should not urge thy duty past thy might;
  I know young bloods look for a time of rest.

I am sure that the whole class experienced on their pulses the especial
tenderness that here transcends Brutus' notion of the duty he is owed in
the master–servant relationship. The cadences of the verse, the modula-
tions of tone between the speakers which mark their care of each other's
dignity, were perfectly registered: and the feeling of man speaking to
child was conveyed with complete imaginative conviction – in spite of
the fact that Harbage was an unusually fat lad, a good head and shoulders
taller than Rollinson's small, frail Brutus.

What really happened in this sequence was that both boys discovered
the dramatic life of verse in action, and with sensitive support from their

fellows off-stage they expressed it directly to the rest of us. So, for a while, we all saw more acutely than usual into the life of human feelings.

At such times Shakespeare teaches in the classroom more effectively than most of us, as professional teachers of English, can ever hope to do. He fulfils with our classes, then, our major and most challenging purpose – the cultivation of those resources of human sensibility without which we may become mere victims of our knowledge and formal skills.

In each term of the second year the place of Drama in the Mummery programme is filled with a play by Shakespeare: and at the very beginning of this year – the time of the promised change-round in the groups – the Guilds are transformed nominally into Shakespearean acting companies – The Queen's Men and Lord Falkland's Men in one class, The King's Men and The Earl of Leicester's Men in the other. I point out that this change reflects a real historical development in the theatre, as amateur acting by the craftsmen's Guilds yielded pride of place to that of the professional players; and I add that the boys themselves, with a whole year's experience behind them, have now become in a sense Professionals of the Mummery. And this is not mere flattery.

In fact the basic structure of the group, its offices, and the formal titles do not change, but the group-names and the distribution of personnel do. I leave the boys to decide how they should re-shuffle. Sometimes they choose to keep their first-year Guild membership and swap all the offices round; sometimes they choose to pick up completely new groups from scratch.

As soon as new Companies are established I launch them into *Julius Caesar*.

In the time available for Drama in the term (roughly a quarter of the total of Mummery lessons) it would be impossible for both Companies in each class to perform the *whole* play. So at the outset I divide it up into 'movements', each taking up to thirty minutes to act, and I get the boys to note down in their texts the points where each sequence begins and ends; points which do not always coincide with scene-divisions, and often overlap. Then I allot the movements to the Companies alternately. This procedure is familiar to the boys from their work on *Philoctetes*. To avoid disappointments, I make sure that movements overlap sufficiently at high points (like the killing of Caesar and the speech-making over the body) to allow both Companies to do them. The scheme then goes like this:

1. From the opening of I.i
    to I.ii.80 (Brutus: I do fear the people Choose Caesar for their king.)
2. From I.ii.51 (Cassius: Tell me, good Brutus, can you see your face?)
    to I.iii.40 (Cicero's exit in the storm.)

3. From I.ii.312 (Cassius' soliloquy – Well, Brutus, thou art noble.)
   to II.i.76 (Lucius' exit to usher in the faction.)
4. From II.i.43 (Brutus: The exhalations whizzing in the air
                          Give so much light that I may read by them.)
   to the end of II.i.
5. From the opening of II.ii
   to the end of II.iv.
6. From the opening of III.i
   to III.i.163 (Antony: The choice and master spirits of this age.)
7. From III.i.12 (i.e. starting *inside* the Senate-house)
   to the end of III.i.
8. From the opening of III.ii
   to III.ii.209 (Citizens: Revenge! About! Seek! Burn! Fire! Kill!
                         Slay! Let not a traitor live!)
9. From III.ii.152 (4th Citizen: Read the will; we'll hear it, Antony.)
   to the end of III.iii.
10. From the opening of IV.i
    to IV.iii.118 (the hand-shake closing Brutus' quarrel with Cassius)
11. From IV.iii.50 (Cassius: Is it come to this?)
    to the end of Act IV.
12. From the opening of V.i
    to V.iii.90 (the suicide of Titinius)
13. From V.iii.91
    to the end of Act V.

Before talking about the play itself, I spend some time emphasising the similarities between the boys' circumstances and the conditions in an Elizabethan theatre. I talk briefly about the size and shape of a playhouse of the period, and go on to stress the fact that the Mummery, although differing in design, does preserve some of the most important Elizabethan characteristics, such as an intimate scale which brings audience and performers close together, an absence of complicated scenery, and a great reliance on the imagination's power of response to the spoken word. I point out that our performances are thoroughly authentic in the matter of feminine rôles, since all Shakespeare's ladies were created expressly for boy-players. And I say that since Shakespeare's Companies had scarcely any more members than the new Second Form ones, and since all his plays have large casts, some of the boys will have to do as Elizabethan actors were expected to do and take two or three rôles in the same play when necessary – a tactic that Shakespeare made as convenient as he could for them.

With all this said, and while the accent remains on Shakespeare as a practical man of the theatre – a man making scripts to be acted from – we turn to the text itself and I spend more time indicating the way Shakespeare shows his actors what to do through what he makes his characters say about themselves and about each other. Again as a result

of their experience in *Philoctetes*, most of the boys are quick to see this;
but they don't realise, yet, how abundant and detailed these built-in
working directions can be. I feel there is no danger of over-emphasising
this aspect of Shakespeare's art. It is, after all, a mark of greatness, and
the more the boys can be encouraged to look carefully at his lines – and
not merely at the stage-directions of his later editors – for guidance about
how to do things, the better their performance will go. So, while they
scurry through their pages looking up the quotations, I refer them to
plenty of examples of Shakespeare's information to his actors: information about characters' bearing and looks ('. . . but, look you, Cassius,
The angry spot doth glow on Caesar's brow, And all the rest look like a
chidden train'; 'Good even, Casca: Brought you Caesar home? Why
are you breathless? and why stare you so?'; '. . . their hats are pluck'd
about their ears, And half their faces buried in their cloaks, . . .'; 'Cassius,
be constant: Popilius Lena speaks not of our purpose; For, look, he
smiles, and Caesar doth not change'); directions for characters' movements where these are important and need precise timing ('As they pass
by, pluck Casca by the sleeve. . .'; 'Trebonius knows his time; for, look
you, Brutus, He draws Mark Antony out of the way'; 'Speak, hands, for
me!'; 'Stoop, Romans, stoop, And let us bathe our hands in Caesar's
blood Up to the elbows, and besmear our swords!. . . Stoop then, and
wash'; 'Look you here, Here is himself, marr'd as you see, with traitors');
and clear announcements of sound effects, and such things as the weather
and the time of day, or night, as these affect the life of a scene ('What
means this shouting? I do fear the people Choose Caesar for their king';
'The exhalations whizzing in the air Give so much light that I may read
by them'; 'Peace! count the clock', 'The clock hath stricken three',
''Tis time to part'). Examples could be multiplied indefinitely. I cite
them lavishly in the hope of encouraging the boys to feel from the start
that Shakespeare's language is, so to speak, on their side; not a daunting
adversary, but a creature of co-operative intent.

For this reason too, I dwell on the point that Shakespeare used punctuation to show the reader how his verse should be spoken aloud (just
as musical expression-marks are used to show how a piece should be
played). The text of Dent's King's Treasuries edition is not as near to the
First Folio as the Penguin edition, but it is near enough to make this
point clear, as may be seen in the following comparison:

Bru. It must be by his death: and, for my part,
   I know no personal cause to spurn at him,
   But for the general. He would be crown'd:
   How that might change his nature, there's the question:
   It is the bright day that brings forth the adder;
   And that craves wary walking. Crown him? – that; –

And then, I grant, we put a sting in him,
That at his will he may do danger with.

(Dent)

BRUTUS: It must be by his death: and for my part,
I know no personal cause, to spurn at him,
But for the general. He would be crown'd:
How that might change his nature, there's the question?
It is the bright day, that brings forth the adder,
And that craves wary walking: Crown him that,
And then I grant we put a sting in him,
That at his will he may do danger with.

(Penguin)

Read aloud by an actor trained to be scrupulously attentive to the pointing given by the punctuation, these two versions would differ in their
effect. The second, where *each* of the first six lines is divided into two
units, sustains the more fitful and laborious musing, and then it releases
the point that causes Brutus most anxiety, in a sudden spurt. Un-
doubtedly it is the 'purer' version, because it comes nearer to the
Shakespearean original than the first; but only the most determined
purist, surely, would worry about what twelve-year-old performers
were missing by using the other. It is more important to help children
to see that in Shakespeare the commas, colons, full stops and so on *act*
in the lines in a variety of ways to make the small pauses that shape the
speech. So we look together, carefully, at several short passages like this
one (I find it helpful to choose them from key-moments in the play) and
we hear them severally delivered by volunteers.

The work of noting movements, pointing out some of Shakespeare's
tactics as script-writer, and exploring punctuation usually fills a whole
lesson; and I fill the next one with an introductory talk about the play
as a whole – sketching the kind of drama it is, setting out the main outlines of the story, going into some of the themes in some depth, and
considering some of the chief staging problems. I found this lesson very
difficult to give satisfactorily, when I first tried it. A whole period would
go by before I had finished even telling the story, which I did rather
clumsily. So I found myself extending this introduction over another
period, and sometimes into a third, by which time the boys were growing restive, no doubt wondering whether they were ever going to get
down to the acting. I always resolved to do better with the next play
next term, but somehow could not manage to. Then I found Marchette
Chute's admirable book *Stories From Shakespeare* (Mentor Paperback)
and was able to save time and to present our play to the boys much
more vividly by reading them her version of it. All Shakespeare's plays
are included in the book, and each story is told plainly and with spirit.

Unlike the Lambs in their *Tales*, Miss Chute makes her stories follow strictly the order in which Shakespeare makes things happen in the play. She does not paraphrase characters' speeches but quotes directly from the text: and her own comments are shrewd and sparing. Her book does not do all the work needed to make this lesson a practical preface to the play-in-performance, but it helps that work enormously.

After this, in one more period of preparation, I go through the leading characters suggesting the styles of personality that might be aimed at in the acting, and pointing out what doubling or trebling of minor rôles is possible. The Masters of Revels then spend the latter part of this period deciding their casting for the play, in council with their Companies. Every boy in the class thus knows in advance of his particular responsibilities for the performance, which takes place in serial fashion during the following lessons, interrupted only by the weekly Business Period.

The second year's work always begins with *Julius Caesar*, though sometimes we break off after Act III, where the play offers a clear breathing-space, and return to do the last two Acts towards the end of term. In the middle of the next term the Companies perform *A Midsummer Night's Dream* (where one needs to be careful, but not embarrassed, in one's introductory talk about the fairies): and in the third term they do *The Merchant of Venice*. So, by the time they leave the Mummery all the boys have encountered in a direct way one of Shakespeare's tragedies (the tragedy of Brutus), a comedy, and a play with elements both tragic and comic.

Needless to say, Shakespeare performed in this style stretches the resources of the small Companies to the limit; and this very stress encourages a high degree of involvement. When performing, the boys are hard put to it to get everything done, especially in movements which involve crowd-scenes, when almost all the backstage boys are needed to fill the walk-on parts. Sometimes a shortage of actors still remains, and then a few 'extras' are borrowed from the audience. It is a challenging business to make provision in a few minutes at the start of the lesson for all the stage-arrangement, lighting, dress and sound effects needed. And the Master of Revels is often confronted with the last-minute problem of a leading player's absence from school. The level of success in each movement depends directly on the degree to which each individual's effort helps the group-effort – and the degree of co-operation can become very high indeed. When not performing, the boys' whole attention to the play can be of a kind proper to a critical audience, and a rival company of players.

There is no time for formal rehearsal in class. Instead the boys do some quite voluntary preparation in their own time when one of 'their' movements is due. Most of the actors read through their part at least once before the day; and most of the backstage boys plan ahead carefully. There is, however, *one* exception to this no-rehearsal habit. It occurs in *Julius Caesar* at the Capitol scene (III.i). From Caesar's opening remark to the Soothsayer until Trebonius' return after the murder, the stage directions implied in the actors' lines are so highly concentrated that even the most skilful boys find them hard to keep up with. So, between the performances of Movements 5 and 6, I spend a period conducting a preliminary run-through in a sort of acted discussion with the class, choosing boys at random from both Companies to play the parts. I then put a ban on exact copies of this rehearsal being presented as the Companies' own performances of Movements 6 and 7. This is the only episode in any of the three plays where I have found such direct assistance called for. By the time they reach another big scene, like the trial in *The Merchant of Venice* or, earlier, the play of Pyramus and Thisbe in *A Midsummer Night's Dream*, the boys have learned enough from their experience to be able to cope under their own steam – though they often recognise in the endeavours of Peter Quince's acting company certain piquant resemblances to their own.

Of course, most performances are not as fine as Harbage's and Rollinson's. Most movements sag or stagger for some of the time (though they very rarely do so throughout); and there are several ways in which one can help things along without taking matters out of the boys' hands. One way is to cut the text judiciously before the play is embarked upon. This I disapprove of in principle and resort to in practice (though I have never found it necessary in *Julius Caesar*). I cut *A Midsummer Night's Dream* by about a quarter, not in a bowdlerizing spirit but simply to by-pass some of the more static passages such as Titania's long speech on the forgeries of jealousy and some of the lengthier verbal traceries and elaborations-on-a-theme in the lovers' exchanges. Similarly in *The Merchant of Venice* I cut Laban's sheep, a bit of Morocco, some of the holding-forth by both Portia and Bassanio in the casket scene, and all of III.v.

One may also help things along through one's remarks immediately before, and immediately *after*, a sequence. I speak to the class for two or three minutes only, before a performance. During that time I hope to sharpen the acting group's sense of the special characteristics of their movement, without giving them detailed instructions about what to do. With Movement 11 of *Julius Caesar*, for instance, I would point out that the sequence begins and ends in excitement, starting at the height of the quarrel between Brutus and Cassius and ending with Brutus disturbed and tense after the departure of the ghost; that in the middle section the mood is quieter but there is much coming and going, so actors must keep alert to their cues for entrances and exits; that a slow, measured pace is as important, in giving the ghost impact, as the effects of light and music. Then I would leave the boys to it. *After* the lesson, in the few minutes remaining when everything has been put back in order and the players are back in their seats, I aim to isolate two or three points for admiration – from all the work, not just the actors' contribution. Such things as a sensible stage-arrangement, or resourcefulness with costumes, or a wise choice and timing of music might be picked out here: and always they are picked out because they have helped the group to express Shakespeare's purpose as it is indicated by the language of the script. Praise is earned in the realisation of the dramatic word. I make it a habit on these occasions to call upon the spectators' support with frequent turns of phrase like 'I expect you all noticed how well...' or 'Such-and-such was particularly well done, wasn't it, because...'; a tactic which sustains morale among performers and audience alike.

Two simple conventions sometimes enable me to help a sagging performance while it is going on. The first is a general acceptance of my invisibility on the rare occasions when I creep on to the stage for a moment. It is occasionally necessary to do this to sort out some severely tangled grouping (by moving an actor's position or by whispering some brief advice) when the boys' stage-sense is not working well. The actors don't stop acting, the spectators ignore me, and so a major disruption of the scene is avoided. The second convention helps us through sticky patches of language. If an actor is stuck over a word or phrase I call out the line for him from the back of the room, and he carries on from where I leave off. It is an arrangement that everyone easily gets used to.

Needless to say, there are moments in all Mummery performances of Shakespeare when the meaning of the language totally escapes actors and audience (as it does, often enough, in the professional theatre). I certainly don't rejoice in this fact; but it strikes me as foolish for a teacher to worry too much about it. Flashes of incomprehension do no actual damage to children, and scarcely ever deprive them of the essential drama of a scene. For instance, though the boys have never grasped the import of every phrase in the latter stages of Brutus' soliloquy in his orchard (the opening is quoted earlier in this chapter) they have never failed to grasp immediately what issue it is that Brutus is concerned with.

If the teaching–learning circumstances are truly providing the class with an *experience* of the play, the children will ask their teacher about anything *vital* that they do not understand: and it is best to leave them to do this. I believe teachers should answer questions as fully and clearly as they can: I don't believe they should ask too many, at least not those of an 'individual appreciation test' variety; for being interrogated is not an experience that many people relish.

Shakespeare in class should be an experience for the children, not an ordeal; but, however helpful the conditions may be, all the children will never relish the experience all the time. What matters is that access to the dramatic life of the play, and not just access to the verbal meaning of the text, should be kept open for and by the class. That matters most of all. So I don't worry too much when Shakespeare's phrased eloquence on the Mummery stage doesn't seem to produce very much of a spell – so long as strong spells still occur on occasions. I would worry, though, if a group of actors saw no reason to try to make a passage such as this an energetic and 'entertaining' spectacle:

Dem. I say I love thee more than he can do.
Lys. If thou say so, withdraw, and prove it too.
Dem. Quick, come!
Her.   Lysander, whereto tends all this?
Lys. Away, you Ethiope!
Dem.   No, no; he'll –
Seem to break loose; take on as you would follow,
But yet come not. You are a tame man, go!
Lys. Hang off, thou cat, thou burr! Vile thing, let loose,
Or I will shake thee from me like a serpent!
Her. Why are you grown so rude? What change is this?
Sweet love, –
Lys.   Thy love! out, tawny Tartar, out!
Out, loathed medicine! hated potion, hence!
Her. Do you not jest?
Hel.   Yes, sooth; and so do you.

– though I shouldn't be *surprised* if the actors stumbled once or twice.

And I would worry if the spirits of the class failed to be in any way 'attentive', as Jessica's spirits are, while Lorenzo explains:

                    . . . therefore the poet
Did feign that Orpheus drew trees, stones, and floods;
Since nought so stockish, hard, and full of rage,
But music for the time doth change his nature.
The man that hath no music in himself,
Nor is not moved with concord of sweet sounds,
Is fit for treasons, stratagems, and spoils;
The motions of his spirit are dull as night,
And his affections dark as Erebus:
Let no such man be trusted. Mark the music.

For, in its context and with the support of a Mummery's resources, the music of these lines should touch the class, even when the reading is so flat that no-one is exactly entranced. Some classes have been more spellbound than others at this point, but none has failed to 'mark the music' along with the lovers. If this passage left the boys cold, I should think that they were probably missing, for most of the time, the essential quality in Shakespeare. It is a greater thing than simple enjoyment. It has sometimes led the boys to ask for more Shakespeare than I can find time for in the programme.

7. Mime

Yet it is the personal, inward movement, which cannot be seen, shaping something from experience as so far understood, it is this movement, which is the sign of life and giver of growth. Perhaps drama and mime are unsurpassed as vehicles of nurture for the growing self. In *Story of a School* Mr Stone writes, 'In the story of Arthur and the Knights of the Round Table, I gave the Archbishop a gold tinsel crown with which to crown Arthur. Of his own desire, he preferred to crown Arthur with an imaginary crown. It was, he said, a much better crown than the one I had given him.' I think the boy had reached the secret of art, even though he spoke no words and his miming may not have been remarkable.

From Free Writing by Dora Pym

More than fifty years ago Caldwell Cook regarded mime as a major vehicle of nurture in his work. 'Miming, the language of gesture, is as old-established a form of expression as any other language', he writes in the eighth chapter of *The Play Way*, 'and it can be made of much educational value.' He is at pains to point out that such value will only be realised when the teacher is in earnest and alert and careful. 'A teacher who is not alive to the beauty of gesture will probably not be alive to the value of expressive movement at all, and will in consequence be unlikely to introduce miming in his classes. But there may be some who will try miming either "for the fun of the thing" or at the request of a principal, without previously having realised that as much seriousness and care is required in the practice of expressive movement as in music or speaking.' Seriousness and care in the teaching are just as important today, especially in the early stages of mime work, when the teacher's manner will make or break any chance of later success. Young secondary schoolchildren are inclined to be more sceptical about mime, as an activity belonging to English, than about any other aspect of the subject. They do not *immediately* sense its potential force as an art form and as a means of communication.

I find it difficult to write helpfully about procedure here, because so much depends on instinct in particular situations: but generally this is the way I go about things.

I start, towards the end of each First Form's first term, by referring briefly to Mummers' plays, harlequinades, pantomime and charades as a way of showing that Mime is no new-fangled idea but an art with a long and popular tradition behind it. Then, for a few moments, I reminisce, going back to the time when I was a first-year boy in the school. One day the Sadler's Wells Ballet Company came to town on tour. The leading male dancer knew one of our teachers, who showed him round the school, and when they came upon our class doing English in the old Mummery, he gave us an impromptu talk about his art. I remember that he showed us a lot of its basic 'vocabulary' – the language of gesture that seemed to be not so much dancing as signs and feelings in movement: and, most vividly of all, I remember that he showed us the whole story of *Swan Lake* through Mime, all on his own, without doing anything that struck me as remotely like ballet dancing. (I stress this last point heavily, to re-assure those boys who have begun to suspect that they are going to be asked to do something sickening like pirouetting round the room on tiptoe. In fact, my real purpose in telling this story is to make a first gentle raid on their reserves of scepticism.)

A teacher's personal reminiscences, if they are brief and pointed, may be useful in the classroom; they are not likely to be so otherwise. So I move on quickly to a more active style of introduction, expressing in gesture to the class a number of simple meanings – 'you', 'me', 'yes', 'no', 'come here', 'I am angry', 'I grieve', 'you make me laugh', and so on. I go from statement-gesture to feeling-gesture quite at random at this stage. I do each piece of mime two or three times, with a running commentary something like this:

Now, watch this next one carefully... Well, what did that mean?... Yes – 'I am angry'. I'll do it again... and you can see that really it's in two parts. Look...'I' – see how I'm pointing at my chest with a sweep of my whole arm and hand, not just a flick of the wrist and one finger...and 'am angry'...now, there's a lot at work in this, look: clenched fists quivering in front, and rising up; face grim and frowning; whole body leaning forward to show that I really mean it. I can even make these boys cower away... see!

The boys near me either jump with surprise in their seats, and then giggle, or else, foreseeing my approach a split second in advance, play up with mock fear and an indulgent grin. Either way the lesson is helped along; and with any luck some of those who were left cold by my reminiscing will begin to thaw.

I think this is a reasonable way to start. One is making clear one's own enthusiasm for this mode of expression, and one's confidence in it. The children are not being asked to do something that one is not prepared to do oneself. But the teacher has to be careful not to do too much demonstration or the class will start to rely on copying him, instead of

realising from what he does the means of miming effectively for themselves.

So by the time we are halfway through this first lesson in Mime I hope
to be watching the boys' own efforts. They spread out all over the
Mummery and for a short time everybody at once has a shot at the
simple statements or feelings that I propose – 'Look out!', 'Have pity',
'I will kill you', 'Give it to me', 'I am afraid', and so on – until self-
consciousness is on the wane. Then, with a kind of benevolent tyranny
that ignores official Guild functions, I pick an individual – or a succession of two or three – to express each new idea while the rest of us
watch. It is important, I find, to avoid lingering over the weaker efforts
at this stage. Some boys can turn a given idea into clear formal gesture
at their first or second attempt. Others can't – and 'going on' about their
efforts will only make them feel pilloried. By changing the 'victim' frequently I hope to minimise discomfort for the less able boys, and I hope
to come more rapidly on those with a strong natural gift for miming. In
every class, year after year, there are some boys who – in effect – need
no teaching at all about how-to-do-it. How this comes about I do not
know; perhaps they are, simply, born mimers, and *they* will really teach
the others how to do it, if one can make use of them tactfully. With
luck, one or two of them will be among the 'victims' in this first lesson.

On one occasion, for instance, Jones mimed 'Have pity' very sensitively. I said something like this to the class:

Now that was a *fine* way of doing it, because it was so very clear. You couldn't mistake
the fact that he was pleading, could you? He looked so wretched. You could see it in
his eyes, and in the drawn lines of his face. But the rest of him showed it too – the way
he sank down so slowly to his knees and lifted his hands with the fingers stretched out
wide so that you could feel the emptiness between them. And he took plenty of time;
that was another very good thing about it. He didn't rush the end when he clasped his
hands and bowed his head low. You see, he was doing 'Have pity' with his whole self,
not just with his face or just with his arms. Can we see you do it again please, Jones?

To Jones it all probably came quite naturally and he seemed rather
surprised at my making so much fuss about it; but this kind of appraisal
of skilful miming can help to release skill in other boys. Sometimes when
the room has cleared at the end of the lesson, two or three boys have
been left behind, quite absorbed for a moment in trying out some of the
things we have done.

We go on in this way for the next two or three lessons: and sometimes
I devote the first of these exclusively to descriptive mime. As subjects
we take things like digging a deep hole, lifting down a heavy pot from
a high shelf, taking the coal scuttle, filling it, and bringing it back,
advancing in the teeth of a gale, being an old man crossing the road –

simple, limited actions that involve performers and spectators in a concern for *accuracy*. If the imaginary spade seems to vanish into thin air as soon as the digger pauses for a rest, or if the stiff old gentleman turns into a nimble eleven-year-old just before reaching the far kerb, then the mime won't do – as the audience will probably, quite rightly, exclaim. The request to make the gesture-language sharper and more convincing, without being finicky, is a challenge that many of the boys take up eagerly, and with some quick success. If, however, successive volunteers fail to manage any great improvement, it is not worth spending half the period hammering away at the same action in the pursuit of an absolute accuracy. Sometimes I offer an attempt of my own, and move briskly on to a new theme; sometimes I ask one of the born mimers to try, if I have been fortunate and discovered them by this time. One has to be careful though – or Jones may get branded as a 'favourite' through no fault of his own. On several occasions I have stupidly called on the gifted boys' services too often and too blatantly. Everyone suffered. The less able boys grew disgruntled, the able ones grew embarrassed and reluctant, and I grew exasperated.

If all goes well, though, I often change tack at the next lesson and concentrate on expressive mime and the conveying of emotions and states of feeling. This is a convenient point at which to introduce music into proceedings: *and music is really essential to the achievement of art in miming later on*. The Masters of Music take it in turns to choose a record and play us a short extract from it, and after each hearing I call for volunteers to offer a mime while the music is played again. Some boys can work superbly in the abstract like this. Moved simply by the music, they can make vivid in line and gesture and motion such feelings as happiness, uneasiness, pride or sorrow, without any narrative support. But *most* of them find it easier and more congenial to create an imaginary situation around the mood they find in the music. So one who finds, say, happiness will perhaps mime the pleasure of receiving and unwrapping and admiring an unexpected gift; another, interpreting uneasiness, may light a firework and wait tensely for it to explode – or investigate with great caution its failure to do so; another, sensing pomp and swagger, may turn himself into a haughty dandy strolling down the street. Often these efforts turn out to be very amusing, more or less intentionally; and we all have a good laugh. Spontaneous fun, from time to time, is very helpful to a working atmosphere; but if comic antics become the main business of the meeting, as it were, they impede nurture.

Once music has been recruited to the cause, I try to keep it in the work as much as possible. It helps mimers to submerge themselves in their adopted rôles, and it helps spectators to become involved – though the boys themselves do not always realise this until their first reasonably successful attempt at a complete scene or story. Until such time, the Masters of Music take it in turns to select music and operate the gramophone as we move from one small venture to another. (And in this way they also extend their working knowledge of the record collection.)

We attempt brief mimes of situations in which two or three actors have to work together; and it is at this point that I usually hand over the choice of mimers to the Masters of Revels, inviting them to select from the whole Guild, not just from the Master Players. I suggest subjects like 'busy pickpocket', 'good news' or 'bad news', 'prisoners longing to escape (and perhaps succeeding)', 'sudden fright', 'the return of the wounded soldier', 'tired shopkeeper' and so on: and after each attempt I offer brief comments on what was well done.

I always praise any piece of mime that is done *slowly*, with gestures that are ample. The need in this activity is to swell out gesture till its scale grows larger than talk and becomes a kind of poetic diction-in-movement. It is difficult to explain this need to children in words, but relatively easy to *show* them what is meant when a born mimer can be called upon. Boys who are shy, or nervous, or not very gifted, will at first be inclined to rush, to draw in the scale of their movement, to jerk and look awkward; and they need every encouragement to take their time. The teacher needs patience. The simple sign-language with which the work begins is not developed into a disciplined art-form overnight, and the weaker children's progress towards fluency is sometimes *very* gradual. The most useful advice to give them is often 'Try to slow your miming down so as to make the gestures last longer and look bigger; and try to use more than just your face and your hands.' But advice by itself rarely does the trick. The impulses that lead a boy to discover how to mime well come chiefly from within him (as a part of 'the personal inward movement...which is the sign of life and giver of growth') and partly from working with others who hold the gift more intuitively. There is no formula by which the teacher can *ensure* that these impulses will work. He can only try to provide conditions that will encourage them. I hope the class will have acquired enough liking for mime after four or five periods of progressive limbering-up in the way I have described to make the effort to render a story worthwhile.

On several occasions I have used Malory's tale of the death of King Arthur for this purpose.

In the first few minutes of the lesson I quickly summarise the circumstances that bring King Arthur from the field of his last battle, fatally wounded in the head and attended only by Sir Lucan and Sir Bedivere, to rest at a small chapel. Then, quite slowly and deliberately, I read the fifth chapter of the last book of *Le Morte d'Arthur* (usually from the

3-2

handy and clear Everyman edition) – 'How King Arthur commanded to cast his sword Excalibur into the water, and how he was delivered to ladies in a barge.' The story of Sir Lucan's death, Sir Bedivere's thrice-repeated journey to the lakeside with Excalibur, his reluctance to cast the sword away and his wonder, when eventually he does so, at the miraculous hand that rises from the water to catch it; and, finally, King Arthur's departure and Sir Bedivere's desolation – all this, expressed in Malory's robust and measured prose, invariably takes strong hold on the boys' imagination. Being First-formers, many of them relish the vivid opening –

Then Sir Lucan took up the king the one part, and Sir Bedivere the other part, and in the lifting the king swooned; and Sir Lucan fell in a swoon with the lift, that the part of his guts fell out of his body, and therewith the noble knight's heart brast. And when the king awoke, he beheld Sir Lucan, how he lay foaming at the mouth, and part of his guts lay at his feet.

– and some are clearly disappointed to find that such stark details do not continue in the story: but most of them, caught by Malory's language and half-remembering the tale from earlier years, are absorbed to the very end.

After this reading I propose that the Guilds should attempt a performance in mime at the next lesson, and we move on to a discussion about this. It might go thus:

C.P. The *events* of the story are probably very clear in your minds now. Your *mind's eye* will be very important when we come to mime the story. It will let us *see* what we can't actually *do*. Obviously, we can't really float a barge in here (by which Sir Thomas Malory probably meant a sort of low-lying open boat, by the way); and we can't throw a real sword around the room. In fact, that sword and the hand that rises from the water to catch it are likely to be much more impressive if we *imagine* them than if we arrange for them really to appear. Remember how Excalibur, 'that noble sword', is described; 'the pommel and the haft was all of precious stones'. It must have been quite heavy to carry, and Sir Bedivere would certainly have treated it with great care and reverence on the way to the lakeside. Incidentally, has anyone any ideas about *where* we might imagine the lake to be in here?

FIELDER Sir, off the side of the stage.

C.P. Well...yes...but that solid wall there, just in front of Sir Bedivere's nose – it's going to be a bit hard for the audience to ignore or imagine away, isn't it?

HENFORD What about our part of the room, sir?

C.P. Ah, now I think that's better. Like that, when Sir Bedivere comes to the lakeside he could be at the front of the stage, facing us, and then we could see clearly what he felt about throwing...

DENNING (a Stage Manager) Yes, and we could have a little platform where your desk is, to be the boat for him to put the king in, sir.

C.P. Yes. Good. That platform could be there all through the performance. But what about the three grieving ladies in the boat, the three queens?

DENNING   Er...they'd have to come to the boat through the audience...when it was supposed to be arriving at the shore...at the right time, sir.

(I can see that Soames, a Master of Revels, is looking worried, and I suddenly realise that this is the first time that the Guilds have had to cope with women's rôles. No doubt he foresees difficulties. He puts up his hand.)

SOAMES   Sir, do we *have* to have three queens?

C.P.   Perhaps not three. It might make the boat a bit crowded; and besides, the Tiring Men may find it hard to find mourning costumes for all three. No, I think two will be quite enough – and if the Tiring Men are stuck they will find some long lengths of dark material that may be useful, right at the bottom of the props cupboard.

LOVEDAY (a Tiring Man)   Sir, do we have to do anything about Sir Lucan's guts?

(My mind goes back to an occasion a year or two ago when, during preparations for miming the story, I overheard one lad earnestly suggesting that Sir Lucan should keep under his tunic a bundle of old rope splashed with red paint, and let it drop at the appropriate moment. There indeed was a conscientious Tiring Man, though his wise Master of Revels gently but firmly turned down the suggestion.)

C.P.   Well, whatever substitute you might contrive for real guts would be difficult for Sir Lucan to deal with on stage, and he needs to be fairly uncluttered to mime well. So I think this detail about Sir Lucan's death is another one that is best seen with our mind's eye. It's important too, of course, not to make this part of the performance funny by mistake; and there would be some risk of that happening if we go messing about with artificial innards. Er, yes, Peters?

PETERS   Sir, whereabouts in the story will we actually start?

C.P.   Where I began reading – when the three wounded knights reach the little chapel where King Arthur can rest.

PETERS   Well that means that Sir Lucan will die almost as soon as we begin.

C.P.   Oh yes, that's true: it's a bit of a waste to have an actor being a dead body almost the whole time, so Masters of Revels may decide to have Sir Lucan die rather later. That way he could tend King Arthur while Sir Bedivere was going to and from the lakeside. Now, let's just think of the chapel and the lakeside as far as lighting and stage arrangements are concerned...

So we go on for perhaps another quarter of an hour, combining questions, advice and practical guidance. In order to make the best use of the time I covertly steer the discussion to touch on the work of each department in the Guild. (This is not always easy to manage. Red herrings *will* crop up – 'Sir, surely we *could* have someone hiding behind a dais and putting out his hand to catch a *real* sword' – and they have to be dealt with courteously.)

In the matter of staging I try to encourage a purposeful use of different acting levels, and a sense of depth as well as breadth, through the rostra-arrangement. In this story, for instance, if the lakeside is down at the front of the stage, it is helpful to have King Arthur's resting-place raised and at the back. Discussion of this point often leads on to other matters. How can one suggest that Sir Bedivere's journeys between King Arthur and the lake cover a certain distance, without boring the audience? (The idea of having a black-out each time that Sir Bedivere sets forth – to stand for the travelling, so to speak – is not as good as it seems. It makes a jarring interruption too frequently.) What sort of music would best suggest Sir Bedivere's feelings? How can the lighting best help things along? (I hope there will be general agreement here that it should not be too bright, and should alternate appropriately between the chapel-area and the lakeside-area, and should become more mysterious as King Arthur reaches the boat that will take him into the vale of Avilion.)

When these points have had some attention, the Guilds spend the last ten or fifteen minutes of the lesson in council, planning the details of their performances. The Masters of Revels decide which member of each non-acting department shall be in overall charge of it for this occasion; and they decide which actors shall play which parts. I usually remind Stage Managers and Masters of Light to plan their work together. The Tiring Men and the Masters of Music go off to their corners to look through costumes and records. With all this going on a certain hub-bub arises inevitably. I don't object while this remains a sign of constructive mutual effort, but if the loud buzz of voices becomes a clash of outcries I do intervene. Usually, however, the boys work busily and reasonably quietly until the end of the period, only coming to me for help with specially troubling worries – 'Where can we put the rostra we don't need, sir?'; 'I'm going to be Sir Bedivere, sir, and the story says he took the king to the lake on his back, and Peters is the king, and I can't lift him off the ground.'

Before the bell goes for the end of the period I toss a coin to decide which Guild will give its performance at the next lesson; say, heads for the Merchant Taylors, tails for the Haberdashers. This time it comes down tails. The Haberdashers regard their 'win' with misgiving, for they don't feel ready to start. There is never as much time for preparation as the boys would like, but by the next lesson they will be more or less ready, with stage layout, lighting changes, actors' entry and exit points, and the general way the performance is *meant* to go known by most of the Guild.

When we next meet, I usually read the story right through a second time, as a means of warming actors and audience to their theme. Then the Haberdashers take over the lesson. I withdraw my desk to the back of the room and the boys make ready. Sometimes they take longer over this than over the whole performance, as their nervousness obstructs efficiency, but it only makes matters worse to harass them. The Merchant Taylors meanwhile put the finishing touches to plans for their own performance, or watch the Haberdasher's preparations with a critical eye.

It is impossible to describe adequately in words what a performance in mime feels like, for even as unsophisticated a version as this early effort is likely to be is a distinct non-verbal form of expression in its own right. However much it may lumber along there is invariably something to be positively admired; something more important than its faults. Most of the obvious mistakes – the sword that drops clattering from an actor's belt in an unguarded moment, the light that comes on (or goes off) at just the *wrong* time because someone was in a muddle at the switchboard, the snort that comes from the gramophone because the pick-up is lifted clumsily with the volume still turned up – these things draw quite enough attention to themselves when they happen, and in a sense they teach a lesson as they happen. If the teacher dwells on them afterwards he prolongs embarrassment unnecessarily. It is better to dwell on evidence of imaginative resourcefulness, wherever it may arise.

Light, like music, affects a mime-performance particularly strongly. I have always found it worth encouraging an experimental and adventurous use of it – a non-literal, non-realistic approach, quite different from that required for scripted drama. My advice to Masters of Lights is 'Try to support the action and mood of the story closely, *but keep your effects simple.*' This note of warning is meant as a brake on the runaway ardour that sometimes leads the boys into such subtle plans that they have little chance of carrying them out successfully. In lighting-effects fluency comes only when the operators have thoroughly mastered the layout of the switchboard. They need to be able to run their fingers over the switches during a performance, in the relative gloom of their recess, and know exactly where they are by touch. With practice some of them grow extremely good at this, but in the early stages it is best if they limit themselves to operations that involve the use of only one switch at a time.

The boys readily understand that different colours of light can endorse different kinds of dramatic feeling, but sometimes they try to support the mood of the story *so* closely that the light seems never still. Naturally this distracts players and audience, and dramatic feeling is lost, not heightened. So, repeatedly, I urge lighting teams to attend to the chief turns and developments in the story (it's up to *them* to decide what these are) and not to try to cover everything. Quite often, before a full performance, they will make a lighting cue-sheet and pin it up near their switchboard, and hold a quick briefing-session with the actors to remind them of the main lighting changes, especially if there are any sudden black-outs (which have to be held long enough for actors not appearing in the next scene to feel their way off the stage in quiet and safety).

By the end of a fortnight's work on the Mime of King Arthur I hope to find the Guilds' lighting going almost as smoothly and effectively as that which helped to make a particular performance stick very clearly in my memory.

In this, the resting-place for King Arthur was a small raised area at the back of the stage, a little to one side. When the King spoke to Sir Bedivere, before and after each of the knight's three journeys with Excalibur, this area was lit by a single orange lamp overhead. Each time that Sir Bedivere left the King, he left by going into the Tiring House through the left-hand archway; and as he did so the soft orange light went out and a cold, hard light (one green and one white bulb in the lower pair of sockets) came on at the left-hand front corner of the stage. King Arthur and Sir Lucan 'froze' in tableau as Sir Bedivere emerged from the Tiring House by the right-hand archway and crossed the stage diagonally towards the bleak light. In this way most of his journey had taken place in our minds' eye during his brief passage out of sight, and the story had effectively changed location without a break. The lighting-change was reversed for each of Sir Bedivere's return journeys, and the lakeside light returned for a fourth time as he and Sir Lucan set out finally, supporting the wounded king between them. Just as the group, with great effort, reached the middle of the stage, Sir Lucan sank dying to the ground; and there for a few moments the King and Sir Bedivere mourned for him. Then, as they rose to continue their journey, the lakeside light went out and the two spotlights, each with a blue filter, lit up the two smaller rostra which made the low boat in front of the stage. It was a mysterious, other-worldly light, and while King Arthur, leaning heavily on Sir Bedivere's shoulder, advanced painfully, almost inch by inch, towards it, three shrouded, sorrowing figures moved slowly into it from the back of the auditorium. They knelt at the three sides of the barge and received the King as he was gently laid to rest among them. Very slowly, the grief-stricken Sir Bedivere fell to one knee, took the outstretched hand of his master for the last time, and buried his face in his hands. All remained quite still. First one spotlight went out; then, after a slight pause, the other. And the music faded slowly away in the darkness. A moment after it had gone altogether the house lights came back on.

In this performance the Master of Lights had both attended to the chief turns and developments in the story and managed his cues with considerable skill. Earlier, in a practice-session devoted to the opening part of the story, I had praised the way he had lit the king's resting-place and the lakeside, for the contrasting suggestions it made felt – shelter at the chapel, and the bleakness at the lakeside. So it was hardly surprising that he repeated it for the Guild's final effort. The dramatic blue lighting for the end was a new stroke. He did so well by planning carefully and not being too ambitious. At the switchboard he used five switches only: and at several points where he might have been tempted to do more with the lights – as at the death of Sir Lucan – he rested content and left them to the actors. It was an achievement of imaginative tact as well as technical expertise.

The music had also been a notable success. I always advise Masters of Music against attempting too many changes of record during a performance. The purpose of the music is broadly a mood-setting one; it is not expected that actors should synchronise every movement with it. Where the overall mood of a story remains fairly constant – as it did here – a single disc replayed several times is often more effective than a succession of three or four different ones. This Guild's Master of Music had chosen one record only – Bach's Air on a G String – and its slow, solemn measure served mimers and audience excellently. And the performance was graced by an 'accidental' felicity. While King Arthur, Sir Bedivere and the three queens were all approaching the boat, the gramophone pick-up arm arrived at the middle of the record. For a few moments there was complete silence. King Arthur was laid gently to rest in the care of the kneeling ladies. Slowly, he was settled there, amidst their forlorn attention. When he was lying peacefully the music returned, very much more softly than before. The Master of Music had not, of course, foreseen that his record would end just at this point; but he made the most of the necessary break. He faded the music out just before the needle reached the run-off track, and carefully brought the pick-up back to the outer edge of the record. He set it down gently, and waited until King Arthur stretched out his hand to Sir Bedivere before turning up the volume control. Again artistic tact had combined with practical skill.

So, after this performance, I made admiring comment particularly on the work of the boys in charge of lights and music.

But in fact this Guild did almost everything impressively on this occasion. Their preparations were quickly over, with lights arranged, stage set, music ready, and actors dressed and waiting to begin within five minutes of the start of the lesson. The Stage Managers' setting left the entrances and exits clear, and served the actors' needs well. There were side steps up to King Arthur's raised area, and just in front of this the throne block provided a slightly lower level for Sir Lucan to rest on: and there was easy access to the barge from all sides. The Masters of the Tiring House had not loaded the actors with too many props – no spears-in-hand or swords-in-belt, just tunics, belts and cloaks, with a crown for the King. (One of the Tiring Men, not satisfied with the old and battered one he found in the props cupboard, had fashioned a new one from stiff card and silver paper decorated with fruit gum jewels.) The knights wore some of the Tiring House armour – short tunics made from hessian strips painted with silver gilt. And the miming itself was deeply felt, with the actors taking their time and growing thoroughly attuned to each other's performances.

The directness, the intensity, of feeling in this mime was the achievement of the Guild as a whole. It was the evidence of the extension of imaginative sympathy and of insight into the story which the boys had made since their first attempt to mime the tale right through.

I usually ask the Guilds to attempt to mime the whole story as soon as they have heard me read it for the first time: and most first attempts – even in later terms when classes are more experienced – are fairly empty affairs. The actors will rush on, taking whole phases of the action and feeling in the story more or less for granted. This is only to be expected, for the art of remembering *and* miming comes slowly to children. But, as I have said, there is invariably something in even the most hollow-seeming effort for one to admire and take as a starting-point. For instance, when the Merchant Taylors followed the Haberdashers' very first, and rather limp, attempt at the Mime of King Arthur there seemed to be little imaginative *experience* among them till we reached the moment when the King angrily rebukes Sir Bedivere on his second return from the lakeside. In Malory the king's speech runs 'Ah, traitor untrue, now hast thou betrayed me twice. Who would have weened that, thou that hast been to me so lief and dear? and thou art named a noble knight, and would betray me for the richness of a sword. But now go again lightly, for thy long tarrying putteth me in great jeopardy of my life for I have taken cold. And but if thou do now as I bid thee, if ever I may see thee, I shall slay thee with mine own hands; for thou wouldst for my rich sword see me dead.' The boy who played King Arthur for the Haberdashers had simply gone through the motions of 'I am angry' and 'Go back' at this point; but the actor from the Merchant Taylors lingered over it, quite losing himself in the part for a time. Verbalised, I suppose his movement and gesture would read like this – 'I – am angry – very angry – with you. – You – hurt me on the heart – I – am your king – and you – speak – to me – no-truth! – My head-wound – gives me great pain – and this is your fault. – Go back. – Throw Excalibur. – Watch carefully – and return here – and tell me – what you see – or – I will kill you – with my own hands.' These were the boy's mime-actions, but in trying to catch them in print I am reminded of the truth of a paragraph in Caldwell Cook's chapter on Mime:

The description of gesture is a thankless task, because gesture chiefly exists to save description. Words, in any case, are cumbrous to explain movement. A simple wave of the hand may be talked about for a whole paragraph, and still not be made visible. An action may express hope, desire, anger, fear, despair. But the attempt to describe in words the feeling as shown in the action is hopeless.

So I shall not persist. Suffice it to say that nothing else in either Guild's first performance came near to matching this moment.

At the next lesson with the class I recalled this impressive piece of miming and read again the lines from Malory to which it corresponded. Then we discussed all that the passage contained besides anger (or 'I am angry'). We discovered anguish – 'Who would have weened that...'; and shock and suspicion – '...and would betray me for the richness of a sword'; and pain – '...for thy long tarrying putteth me in great jeopardy of my life for I have taken cold'; and threat – 'I shall slay thee with mine own hands.' By this I do not mean that we went through the text phrase by phrase making a list of emotional qualities, but that these were the feelings that the boys lighted upon as the discussion went along. As they found more and more in the words of the passage, I asked for volunteers – anybody from either Guild – to turn what had been discovered into the language of action and gesture; to *do* it for us.

In this procedure there is useful opportunity to teach the importance of fullness in the scale of gesture and to encourage a sense of due tempo in movements. One does not need to use every volunteer, of course, nor to give each one an equal span of attention. One tries to pick out and develop the most sensitive aspects of what the boys do. This may mean that, in order to sharpen or amplify a point about gesture and to draw the class's attention to its particular power, one copies a boy's miming for a moment oneself, or asks him to repeat it with some modification. It may mean moving on to a new volunteer quickly after a meagre effort; or it may mean dwelling on a boy's attempt just *because* there is a chance of dispelling the meagreness by doing so. Whatever the case, the teacher should always try to acknowledge a boy's effort with a 'Thank you' and a definite comment, however brief. He should never reject with words that imply 'That was hopeless – look at me, this is how it is done properly.' In Mime there is no simple proper way, no mere formula for the teacher to apply.

So we explored King Arthur's wrath at Sir Bedivere's second failure to cast away Excalibur. Then we considered how the king's anger here differed in tone from his reaction to Sir Bedivere's *first* return from the lakeside – 'That is untruly said of thee, said the king, therefore go thou lightly again and do my commandment: as thou art to me lief and dear, spare not, but throw it in' – and how this different, earlier tone might be rendered in mime-terms. Then we went on to discuss how Sir Bedivere's white lie – 'I saw nothing but waves and wind' – could be best expressed in gesture; and this brought us to Sir Bedivere's bearing during each of his journeys, his feelings as he went the first time, the second and the third, and the way these feelings might show.

In this approach the class and the teacher together carry out a slow-motion exploration of the story, episode by episode, and it may be five or six lessons before the thing as a whole is performed again. In these interim periods the Guilds work without costume, and occasionally without music when a specific detail is getting close attention; but I invite music as often as I possibly can in these lessons, for by supplying it in brief 'gobbets' the Masters of Music grow more familiar with the records at their disposal and become more adroit in handling them. In the same way Masters of Lights improve their skill with the equipment by providing quite simple makeshift lighting. There always comes a point in the work where the lighting becomes the subject of concentrated attention in its own right; and until we reach that point a rough-and-ready line does no harm – indeed, it is essential if the miming itself is to be kept at the centre of concern.

When enough seems to have been gained from this sustained, close concern with the experience of the story, I ask for a fresh full-length performance from the Guilds. It is not always easy to judge when the moment is ripe for this, but if it is roughly right second performances are almost bound to be considerably better than first ones (though the boys invariably forget some of the finer points of what they have discovered; and audiences notice these 'flaws', which often arise from the excitement of the moment). The Masters of Revels draw up a fresh cast of actors for these second attempts, so that the leading parts are not monopolised. The return of full costume usually brings to the actors a sharp release of further powers of identification with their rôles; and everyone responds to the power in such effects of lighting and music as I described earlier. It is usually clear that confidence and talents are progressing.

When Mime takes its turn in the Mummery programme again, in the boys' second term, much of the skill they had acquired seems lost. But, more often than not, it returns quickly in a refresher assignment; and sometimes this may usefully be a further performance of the previous term's story. Good miming requires a presence of mind as well as a strength of feeling, and this blend does not come easily to everybody: so there can be a real advantage in doing again a 'known' piece. Through Mime children can come to 'know' a range of literature – from epic, from legend, from myth – which it would be difficult to bring alive at such a pitch, and with only limited time available, in any other way.

In first-year classes we have sometimes made mime-versions of the tale of Theseus and the Minotaur, or the tale of Orpheus and Eurydice (starting from Rex Warner's excellent re-telling of these myths in *Men and Gods*). Sometimes we have taken episodes from Homer, such as The Return of Odysseus and the Slaying of the Suitors; or The Duel of

Hector and Achilles. For the latter I start by reading the duel scene from Book XXII of *The Iliad* in E. V. Rieu's Penguin translation. To make a second scene I narrate an improvisation of my own on the phased bringing of news to Priam as he waits in his palace – an accumulation of grief, with messengers whirling in circles as they re-enact the circling of Troy, first in the chase after Hector and then in the defilement of his dead body. (As well as the notion of sacrilege, this brings into discussion the significance of the gods in Homer, and their equivalent in modern turns of speech and outlook – 'Fate decreed', 'as luck would have it', and so on. This, like a notion of the meaning behind the arrival of the grieving queens at the end of the Mime of King Arthur, is vital to the acted experience.) For the third scene I read two sequences from the last book of *The Iliad* – Priam's visit by night to Achilles in his camp, and the concession of Hector's body. All the extracts from Homer get modified in discussion to make a mimeable outline, and we work episode by episode, each Guild taking a turn at each full scene before we move on to the next. Sometimes – but rarely before the third or fourth term – we have turned to Greek drama and made the play of *Antigone* or *Agamemnon* into a mime-form which, by this stage, deserves to be called dance-drama.

To make a change in matter and style we have sometimes read extracts from Dickens' *Christmas Carol* and transferred the ideas, of the wrongdoer and of the dream-sequence that brings about his conversion, to young and modern life. This has sometimes produced some striking results, with most inventive dream-sequences, particularly when the substitute-figure for Scrooge has been the Teenage Bully.

Another melodramatic mime that has always gone well at any stage of the first or second year has been The Silver Crucifix – an adaptation of an even more stagey piece called The Angelus described in *Leap to Life* by John Wiles, a stimulating account of Alan Garrard's pioneering work in dance-drama. Our version goes thus, in a roughly Spanish setting, roughly in the late nineteenth century. A band of gipsy robbers waits in the late evening for the approach of a coach they intend to attack. Young Carlos, a mere lad, holds the watch with his elder brother, Miguel. When they sight the coach the leader of the band, Pablo, chooses Miguel, his best friend, to help him carry out the actual robbery. The rest of the gang wait for their return, a little anxiously. Soon the two men return, carrying between them a heavy sack of valuable booty. Pablo shares out the spoils among the gang and the men react variously; some are pleased, others are sullen and discontented with their share. Eventually Pablo brings out a silver crucifix, which all the men instantly covet, semi-superstitiously. Miguel lays particular claim to it as his reward for having helped carry out the robbery, but Pablo rebuffs him, and takes the crucifix for himself. Though he bitterly resents this, Miguel does not dare to challenge his leader openly for possession. He turns away, humiliated, and uneasiness spreads through the band. Everyone has eyes only for the crucifix and for the two men who have come to the brink of quarrel. Pablo orders the whole gang to settle for the night. He puts the crucifix carefully beside his own pillow. Carlos resumes the watch and the men fall slowly asleep. But Miguel does not sleep. He waits and watches. When all is still, he rises, goes over to take his brother's place on guard, and sends the boy to rest. But Carlos is suspicious, and he too covertly watches. After a few moments he sees Miguel go stealthily over to Pablo and take the crucifix from his pillow-side. Carlos starts up and, in a flash, the gang and Pablo are awake and alert. Miguel is caught red-handed. A savage fist-fight for the crucifix breaks out between the two friends, encircled by the gang. At length Pablo regains possession and holds it high. Miguel recoils, and draws out his knife. There is a second brief phase of fighting, more tense and dangerous. Then Carlos, in anguish, rushes in to restrain his brother, and is himself accidentally wounded. He sinks to the ground: the knife falls: the two fighters back away: the rest of the gang draw round Carlos and support him. He appears to be dying, and as Pablo and Miguel face each other with the boy between them, they realise the tragedy that their greed and pride have brought about. Then their enmity drops away. Pablo slowly approaches and puts the silver crucifix – now become the symbol of sorrow and repentance – into Carlos' hands. Even more slowly Miguel draws near, joins the kneeling group and helps to support his unconscious brother.

There is some value in including a romantic and spectacular piece such as this somewhere in one's mime-programme. There are superb miming opportunities for the gang, both as a group and as individuals. The boys can make the fight very thrilling with a little planning and control. They grasp the need for this when they see how quickly an unplanned effort degenerates into a tiresome piece of untidy wrestling. In building up the fight and in achieving the necessary changes of pace and tension during the whole mime, even the least able actors acquire a sense of the combination of intense feeling and conscious skill which informs successful art.

If all goes well, I hope that classes will be attempting Shakespearean tragedy in dance-drama form by the fifth or sixth term. Here I start with a sort of improvised narration, lasting a period, which partly tells the story, partly interprets the play, and partly guides towards mime. Then the Companies work on one scene at a time. The scene-list for *Macbeth*, which we take as far as the murder of Duncan (off-stage, as in the play) concentrating especially on the experience of Macbeth and his wife immediately before and immediately after the killing, would go like this:

1. Witches' dance – entry of Macbeth and Banquo – the predictions – witches vanish – the two men stumble on through fog.

2. Duncan and his attendants survey the battlefield – entry of Macbeth and Banquo – greetings – promotion of Macbeth – Duncan decides to visit Macbeth – dispatch of messenger – exit of Macbeth – tableau on battlefield again.

3. Lady Macbeth reads the letter – arrival of messenger, who gives his news and goes – resolution of Lady Macbeth – arrival of Macbeth – first temptation scene – exit of Macbeth – arrival of Duncan – ceremonial entry of royal party into castle, ushered in by Lady Macbeth.

4. Macbeth alone – vision of dagger – entry of Lady Macbeth – second temptation scene – exit of Lady Macbeth – Macbeth in shadows watches Duncan, then Banquo and Fleance, and finally a servant, pass – then he follows, to do the murder.

5. Entry of Lady Macbeth, alone and in fear – re-entry of Macbeth – 'Why did you bring these daggers from the place?' – eventual exit of Lady Macbeth to complete the deed – Macbeth, still, staring at his hands.

In making this bare outline into a narration for the introductory period, I would try to keep in contact with the verse of the play as much as possible by reading briefly and frequently from the text. This, for instance, would be the style in which I would hope to deal with the first part of the third scene:

Meanwhile, at Macbeth's castle, Lady Macbeth has received her husband's letter and the news of what has happened, and when we first see her she is walking alone, very slowly, reading that letter with close, careful attention. She reads of his meeting with the witches –

'They met me in the day of success: and I have learn'd by the perfect'st report, they have more in them, than mortal knowledge. When I burnt in desire to question them further, they made themselves air, into which they vanish'd.'

– and although Macbeth was deeply disturbed by this encounter with supernatural creatures, as we have seen, his wife reads of it now without a tremor. She is surprisingly calm as she broods over this news. When she finds that the witches' second promise has already been fulfilled, that Macbeth now *is* Thane of Cawdor, she lifts her eyes from the paper for a moment, as though thinking hard about the future. Then she reads the rest of the letter quickly. It says –

'This have I thought good to deliver thee (my dearest partner of greatness) that thou mightst not lose the dues of rejoicing by being ignorant of what greatness is promis'd thee. Lay it to thy heart and farewell.'

She does indeed lay to her heart the greatness promised. As she puts the letter aside, her thoughts fasten on that promise; but they do not contain 'the dues of rejoicing' – at least, not the kind of rejoicing you or I might find in ourselves. Something else fills her heart. It is a grim and dreadful determination. Her first comment on the letter is –

'Glamis thou art, and Cawdor, *and shalt be*
What thou art promis'd:'

– and her mind turns at once to the most direct way of ensuring that the witches' third promise will come true. She does not flinch at all at the thought of murder, but she suspects that Macbeth will.

'. . . yet I do fear thy nature,
It is too full o' th' milk of human kindness,
To catch the nearest way.'

There is no milk of human kindness, no gentleness, in Lady Macbeth: and she despises it in her husband. She knows that she must drive it out of him if she is to achieve her grim purpose. Suddenly her still, brooding mood breaks. She paces impatiently to and fro, peering in the direction that Macbeth must come from, longing for his presence – not with love, but in the desire to fill him with her own determination 'to catch the nearest way' to the crown. In what she says, he seems to be more her *victim* than her husband.

> 'Hie thee hither,
> That I may pour my spirits in thine ear,
> And chastise with the valour of my tongue
> All that impedes thee from the golden round,
> Which Fate and metaphysical aid doth seem
> To have thee crown'd withal.'

As if in answer to her impatience, a figure hurries in – not Macbeth but the breathless messenger from the battlefield. He enters so suddenly that Lady Macbeth is startled for a moment, but his news stirs her even more – 'The King comes here tonight.' At first she can hardly believe it, but the messenger assures her that it is true, and he adds that Macbeth is on his way, coming home ahead of the king. At that, Lady Macbeth dismisses the servant curtly. She sees that Fate has brought her the perfect opportunity to catch the nearest way to the throne. Left alone, she does a very terrible thing. Deliberately, she calls upon the forces that have nourished her thoughts of murder – the forces of evil, cruelty and darkness – she calls on them to take possession of her utterly, to fill her from head to foot with direst cruelty, so that she cannot feel any instinctive tenderness or touch of conscience, any urging of human kindness. 'Come you spirits' she says

> 'Come you spirits,
> That tend on mortal thoughts, unsex me here,
> And fill me from the crown to the toe, top-full
> Of direst cruelty: make thick my blood,
> Stop up th'access and passage to remorse,
> That no compunctious visitings of Nature
> Shake my fell purpose...'

Not simply 'make me cruel', you notice, but 'unsex me here': that is to say she wants to be a completely *un*natural creature – and she puts this very clearly and definitely; 'make thick my blood', 'fill me from the crown to the toe, top-full Of direst cruelty'. She has a great relish for evil and her mind goes straight to the killing. Her next words make it quite plain just how Duncan will be murdered.

> 'Come thick Night,
> And pall thee in the dunnest smoke of Hell,
> That my keen knife see not the wound it makes,
> Nor Heaven peep through the blanket of the dark
> To cry, hold, hold.'

And on these words of darkness and murder, Macbeth enters. It is as though his arrival were heralded by these things. His wife greets him, and in her greeting she moves quickly from his present glory to his future greatness –

> 'Great Glamis, worthy Cawdor,
> *Greater than both, by the all-hail hereafter.'*

She does not waste time on any great show of affection or joy on his return from battle, alive and victorious; nor does he. Both are filled with one thought only, and Macbeth comes straight out with it. But it is Lady Macbeth who takes it on, further than he dares to think.

'*Macbeth.* My dearest love,
        Duncan comes here tonight.
Lady Macbeth. And when goes hence?
        Macbeth. Tomorrow, as he purposes.
Lady Macbeth. O never,
        Shall sun that morrow see.'

Macbeth, you see, hesitates to speak what is in his mind, but his wife now has a formidable strength and she takes charge of the situation. She jumps at their chance of killing the king, without a tremor, as though her blood really has been made thick in answer to her prayer. She advises him to do as she is doing – 'Look like th'innocent flower, But *be* the serpent under't.' And she lures him on by showing him that she will not only be his ready accomplice, she will make all the practical arrangements for what she simply calls 'the business'.

        'He that's coming,
Must be provided for: and you shall put
This night's great business into my dispatch.'

It is, perhaps, the shock of finding this cold and deep relish for wickedness in the woman he loves best, together with the horror of finding himself contemplating the murder of his king – who trusts him completely – that makes Macbeth answer falteringly, as though playing for time. 'We will speak further', he says: but his wife has already begun to dominate him, fatally. The contrast between her undaunted mettle and his uneasiness should show clearly in the miming here. It comes out strongly in the way Lady Macbeth dismisses his answer with just a hint – she will make more of it later on – that he is weak and afraid.

        'Only look up clear:
To alter favour, ever is to fear:
Leave all the rest to me.'

With that she hustles Macbeth from the scene, for she hears Duncan and his courtiers approaching: and she waits, as quietly and calmly as when she first appeared, to receive the king into the castle from which he will never emerge alive.

In proposing the mime to the class through this style of narration, I aim to convey a fair amount of the dramatic meaning in the blank verse, without attending to every line. (If the reader cares to look up Act I Scene v in the text, he can decide for himself how much else ought to have been included – or, perhaps, excluded.) Needless to say, when quotations are introduced in the course of this approach the more they can be rendered as full-flavoured acted speech, and not just read out flatly, the better. In *Macbeth* this is particularly important, for instance, with the 'dagger' soliloquy which, if read with feeling and without a break, can take root remarkably strongly in the boys' imagination. In the dance-drama this passage fills the place taken by 'If it were done, when 'tis done . . .' in the play, and the 'second temptation scene' is based on the rest of Act I Scene vii. By drawing liberally on the verse of the play from the outset, and by bringing the boys back to it frequently during the ensuing scene-by-scene work, I hope to have the miming as much Shakespeare-inspired and as little teacher-directed as possible.

I generally turn to Shakespearean tragedy for the last one or two mime-undertakings of the second year, because some boys can take imaginative possession of his drama, or of some elements of it, more *directly* in this medium than in book-in-hand performance. It would be difficult to act *Hamlet* from the text, for instance, with the Second Form; but a treatment of themes in dance-drama, based in part on Robert Helpmann's memorable ballet version, has often had the class intensely involved. This brief scenario suggests fairly plainly what parts of the play I read from in the course of the opening narration.

The dance-drama starts where Shakespeare's play ends, and enacts first the scene in which Hamlet and Laertes duel with foils before the whole court, the scene of catastrophe. Laertes, having treacherously selected his foil with the poisoned tip, finds himself unable to harm Hamlet with it during the fencing bouts. In desperation, and urged on by Claudius, he attacks the Prince from behind. Hamlet, infuriated, turns on Laertes, obliges him to change weapons, and kills him at the very moment when Queen Gertrude's death reveals Claudius' second treachery – the poisoned drink intended for Hamlet. With his last strength, Hamlet sweeps to vengeance and falls back, dying.

At this moment, as life ebbs, Time stands still. Mysteriously, all the figures around Hamlet, first the living and then the dead, withdraw from his presence until he is quite alone. Then the drama enacts, in the disordered sequence of dream-vision, some of the memories and phantasms that haunt the Prince's last moments of consciousness, evoking some of the distresses too deep for understanding that obstructed decisive action earlier and brought tragedy upon so many.

First, the Gravedigger approaches, and digs away briskly and cheerily. Hamlet watches from the shadows, fascinated yet appalled, as he turns up Yorick's skull. Then this vision fades and the Prince meets again, on the spot which had been the grave a moment before, the ghost of his father. He listens to its tale and hears, first, the false, public account of the king's death by snake-bite, then, the truth. With that the ghost vanishes and its place is taken by the figure of Claudius himself. Hamlet, recalling the apparent elusiveness of his prey, re-lives the frustrating opportunity for killing him at his prayers. Finally, the visions culminate in a nightmare return to the duel itself. But this time all does not take place precisely as before, for the figure most immediately associated with death – the Gravedigger – confuses itself in Hamlet's mind with his adversary Laertes. At the start of each fencing bout the Gravedigger takes the place of Laertes; and he wins each encounter, laying about him with great swashing blows of his spade. As each bout ends, with the umpire declaring the hits against Hamlet, the Gravedigger vanishes and Laertes returns. Yet this nightmare belongs only to Hamlet: all the court, and even his friend Horatio, see nothing strange or peculiar, and they are at a loss to understand his distress. Then, as before, Laertes makes his treacherous attack on the Prince; and the sequence of catastrophe recurs, bringing the drama back full circle to Hamlet's dying fall. There the outer world, which Hamlet's dying consciousness had taken leave of, returns. Time continues: and Horatio receives the dying prince.

I expect many readers will regard my procedure with Mime as unsatisfactory, in whole or in part. From time to time visitors have commented on the apparent lack of improvisation in the programme. In fact, the work I have described in this chapter is improvised by the boys to a greater extent than my account may suggest. (This is another respect in which 'the attempt to describe in words the feeling as shown in the action is hopeless'.) But by Improvisation visitors have usually meant making-up-the-whole-story (as against interpreting-a-given-tale) and I try to find at least three or four periods in each mime-season for the Guilds and Companies to do this. But I regard the kind of work I have concentrated on in this chapter as more important.

Any teacher's job is to make the most of his pupil's abilities. In trying to do that, a teacher of English through Drama must try to do more than draw out spontaneous and unselfconscious personal feeling in free expression.

I have sometimes heard teachers assert, quite seriously, that it is not worth their while trying to do Literature with their pupils because they (the children) 'can't take it'. This seems to me a very questionable kind of assertion. Those who make it are often very proud of what these same children achieve in creative improvisation: and if the children can achieve admirable things in this way, then *they have a capacity for literature*. And Mime is a *particularly* apt means of exploiting it among those who cannot read confidently enough to act well with a book in their hands. Some of the boys I referred to earlier as 'born mimers' have been just such children, and the inclusion of Mime in the English programme has given them, and others, chances of an imaginative extension of being, chances of satisfaction, even pride, in their own creative achievement, that might never have come to them through the subject's other modes of engagement. The point is that children who do not yet read or write easily can be just as *involved* in Literature that they *hear or see* as their most literate fellows.

When I was a boy in the Second Form, there was a large picture of the storm scene from *King Lear*, with figures three feet high, stencilled on one wall of the Mummery. One day Douglas Brown told us the story of the first part of the play, stopping just before the blinding of Gloucester. He concentrated on the third act as material for our dance-drama, reading us many extracts and linking them together with his own comments and explanations. About a fortnight later, our Company watched the other's final performance and I still remember how we were gripped by Lear's progression into madness. We saw him rage at the thunder and lightning that crashed and flashed about him; we felt his brief, kindly concern for his Fool; we watched him shelter Poor Tom and cling close to his side; and we saw, finally, how he arraigned his invisible daughters in a crazy, lumbering, slow-motion display before the bewildered gaze of his motley crew of 'false justicers'. I was certainly not the only boy on that occasion to whom something of the woe and wonder in great tragedy came home. At the end, when the house lights came on, there was a long pause before we remembered to clap. And after many mimed performances in the new Mummery I have found the class coming back to itself slowly like this from that trance-like state in which – to use Mill's words on the Imagination – one human being enters into the mind and circumstances of another. Eleven or twelve is certainly not too early an age for children to begin to 'take' something of the peculiar power of Literature.

Unless we *show* children in school that a past Literature is alive in their present, is both accessible and meaningful *now*, is there *for them* in ways that have nothing to do with the ways of examinations, we have little ground for being surprised or dismayed at their lack of interest in culture – beyond the superficialities of television-culture – when they grow up.

One morning, as I was walking back to the staff room at playtime, I caught sight of two boys – Burton and Loveday – playing at the far side of the yard. Two periods earlier that morning their Company had performed the mime of *Hamlet* right through for the first time. The actors had not done very well, though the Master of Lights had treated the nightmare duel very impressively. He flashed his variously coloured lamps continually during each bout, imposing a restless, lurching sense of disturbance upon the scene; then, when the Gravedigger vanished, steady light returned. Burton had been the Master of Music and had fitted the records to each sequence very sensibly, with violent, surging music for the duel, a jaunty tune for the Gravedigger, something quietly sinister for the Ghost. Loveday had been one of the Tiring Men. Now they were playing out the nightmare duel for themselves. Their respective rôles were quite clear. Burton fenced with a ruler, while Loveday slashed with a hockey stick. They had not noticed me and I should, I suppose, have gone across and stopped them before they hurt each other. But I was too pleased – pleased that the Mime they had seen was still, in a way, teaching them. I left them to it (and fortunately no injury occurred).

Such moments do much to make up for all the times when things do not go well at all; when one knows that one has hindered or damaged by interfering too much or in the wrong way; when the boys have been moody, unsettled, careless or unresponsive to suggestion; when depression sets in among us all because everyone can see that there is no progress; when one's ideas of how to cope with the teaching situation are temporarily exhausted and one wonders whether it is all worth the trouble.

Mime is certainly no *less* subject to weaknesses and failures than any of the other enterprises proper to English with junior classes. But it is certainly not *more* so. I think it deserves a place in the curriculum.

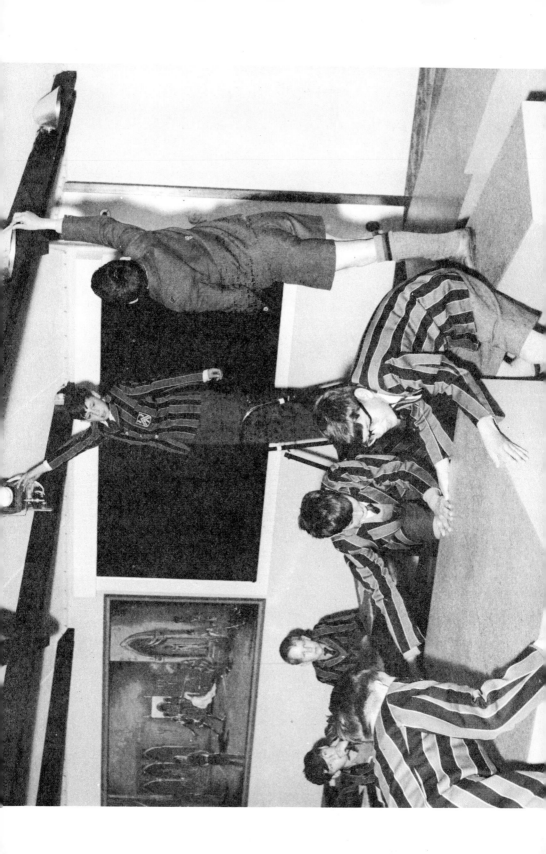

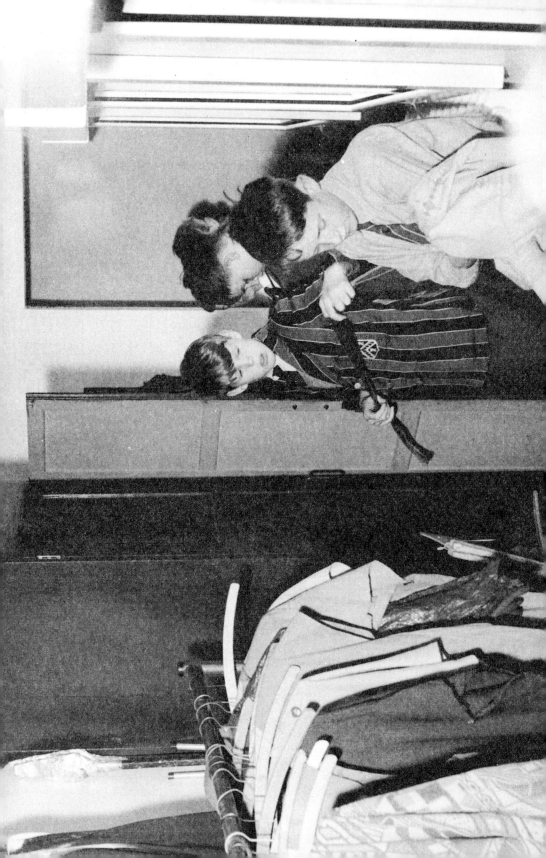

8. Speeches

A good moral, my lord; it is not enough to speak, but to speak true.

Lysander

The Master of Music hurries in and busies himself with the gramophone. As the rest of Form 2A assembles a lively piece by Handel fills the room. Today it is The King's Men's turn to conduct a session of Speeches. When the class is settled, the music fades slowly away.

'Well, as you see, the room is all ready for the King's Men. 2 Alpha were doing Speeches last period, so we can make a start without further ado. Will this morning's officers come to the back, please; and perhaps one of you will give a hand with my desk?'

The desk is shifted down the centre gangway to the back of the auditorium, turned round and joined to the last row of the King's Men. Three boys come and stand in front of it. They face the stage and wait. One of them is in front of the other two. He holds a small card on which he has written the speakers' names and the titles of their speeches. He is the Chairman for today. It is just two minutes since the Master of Music entered the room, and the session begins.

We all stand up as the three boys advance. They mount the stage, and take their places. The settle is on a low rostrum in the middle and towards the back; the two thrones are nearer the front, one at each side. The Chairman goes to the settle, turns to face us, and glances round the room to make sure that all is in order before he speaks.

'I declare this session of Speeches open.'

Everyone except the Chairman sits down. He waits for the rustle and shuffle to stop.

'It is my pleasure to introduce Mr Porter who will speak to us on Ivory.'

As the Chairman sits, Porter rises from the audience and takes his place on the stage behind the Speaker's Box. This is a little wooden cupboard on legs, carved in oak to match the thrones; it stands about waist-high and has a flat top. Porter takes his time. He is a quiet, capable lad, a little shy: he was recently elected to be Master of the Revels, and at the moment he is rather nervous. From one pocket he takes a sheet of exercise-book paper on which his notes are written. He smooths this flat on top of the box, then holds his hands a little stiffly at his sides. The officer nearest to him stands waiting for the start of the speech, when he will turn over a small egg-timer on one corner of the box. Porter takes a deep breath and turns briefly to the Chairman.

Mr Chairman. Gentlemen. Today it is my great pleasure to speak to you on the subject of Ivory.

Ivory comes mainly from elephants, but it is also comes from the teeth of the hippopotamus, walrus, narwhal, wild boar and from the fossils of prehistoric animals such as mammoths. Mostly the best ivory comes from elephant tusks and there are forty thousand elephants killed a year for their ivory. True ivory comes only from the tusks of the elephant which are seven feet long and weigh fifty to two hundred pounds or more a pair. Ivory is so valuable that none of it is ever wasted. Sacks of the cuttings and the shavings are used for inlay work and the dust is used for polishing and making Indian ink.

It's a confident start. He speaks slowly and steadily in a voice that is clear and strong. He hardly glances at his notes.

The Sudan are the leading suppliers for ivory buttons made from nuts. This is a sort of vegetable ivory. In the large islands north of Asia many fossils...fossil remains...of ivory are found. These are the tusks of mammoths and there are so many that at least a hundred pairs of tusks are sent to the mar...markets a year. Walrus are hunted for their hides, oil, flesh and for their ivory tusks. The ivory tusks are enormous canine teeth which are used for biting, digging for food and climbing.

There is a long pause. Porter's next point has slipped out of his mind. He looks carefully through his notes for help. The audience remains silent and quite still, as though holding its breath. Then Porter is off again – though perhaps, in the stress of the moment, he has jumped too far ahead in his notes.

The Ancient Cretans carved exquisite figures in ivory. The Japanese are the best ivory carvers in the world and can make a procession of elephants march out of one tusk all joined together.

Several boys swap wry grins on hearing that. I take out a pencil and jot the sentence down for possible reference at the end of the period. Perhaps it is the sight of us reacting in this way that makes Porter stumble as he goes on.

Zanzibar, a small island off the coast of East Africa, is the main port in the world for ivory, and will remi...and will remain so while ivory is still in Africa. African ivor... el...elephant tusks...are better quality and size than the Indian and are therefore the best in the world.

By now the shortcomings in the style of this speech are clear, but the material is certainly at Porter's fingertips. He has probably spent longer than the two homework periods of half an hour each on its preparation.

He takes another look at his notes to steady himself; then he goes on, looking his audience solemnly in the eye.

The use of ivory can be traced to prehistoric times. King Solomon made a great throne of ivory and there are still examples of inlaid Egyptian ivory. In the British Museum there are many Assyrian ivory carvings made in Nineveh about a thousand years before Christ. In Ancient Greece ivory was used for carving, sculpture, and for luxurious objects. Gothic ivory sculptures of the thirteenth and fourteenth centuries are very beautiful and they made ivory mail cases, jewel caskets and other articles with scenes from real life, in which their costume can be seen.

While I scribble 'Encyclopedia undigested' on my note-pad, the sand in the egg-timer runs out. The official who set it going rings a tiny handbell. Three-and-a-half minutes, the minimum acceptable duration for a speech, have passed. The bell informs the speaker of the fact. Porter jumps a little at the sound of the bell, then smiles. He knows now that the end of his speech will come at a respectable distance after the bell (and well before the timekeeper's final deadline, two-and-a-half more minutes away, when he will ring again and insist that the speaker comes to a halt, finished or not). Porter feels more or less home and dry.

Ivory is very sensa...sensitive to sudden changes in the temperature and ivory can be divided into two groups – hard and soft. Hard is more glassy and transparent, and harder to saw. The soft ivory contains more moisture than the hard and therefore stands changes in the climate and temperature better. From ivory are made billiard balls, piano keys, combs, brushware, knife handles, paper cutters, chessmen, dice...and many other things. Three billiard balls can be made from one elephant's tooth. Ivory is so flexible that excellent riding whips can be made from one tusk. On this point, Mr Chairman, Gentlemen, I would like to end my speech.

The Chairman rises. If he is as surprised as I am at Porter's abrupt ending, he does not show it.

'Are there any questions Gentlemen wish to put?'

Several hands streak up simultaneously. To ensure that this part of the session is not too prolonged no more than two questions are permitted by the Chairman after each speech. He calls first on a boy from Lord Falkland's Men.

'Mr Westgrove.'

Westgrove stands up. Hands go down.

'Mr Porter, what is a narwhal?'

'It's a whale with a long tusk...with a long tooth...or tusk.'

'Thank you.'

Westgrove sits down. The hands go up again. Again the Chairman chooses to turn to Lord Falkland's Men.

'Mr Goode.'

'Mr Porter, which is the more expensive of the two, the harder or the softer ivory?'

'I'm afraid I couldn't tell you that, Mr Goode.'

'Thank you, Mr Porter.'

Although this exchange of 'Misters' is, in some sense, artificial, it is none the less a genuine politeness. The boys take to it readily and it is upheld in every session of Speeches.

The Chairman rises again.

'You will wish me to express your thanks, as well as my own, to Mr Porter. Thank you, sir.'

While we applaud, Porter bows slightly, first to the Chairman and then to us. Then he turns and goes briskly into the Tiring House. Every speaker waits in there, secluded from possible embarrassment, while the Timekeeper takes down the marks we award his effort.

'Your marks, please, gentlemen. First, for Style. Three? Four? Five?'

A couple of hands are lifted. The Timekeeper barely pauses.

'Six?'

About half a dozen hands go up.

'Seven?'

A forest of hands, and the Timekeeper writes down 7 in his notebook. This is a fair mark (out of 10), I think. In choosing what to award for Style, the boys are considering – I hope – such things as the speaker's manner of expression, the degree of clarity and confidence in the way he spoke, his stance at the box, his decorum. Porter spoke carefully and steadily, in a clear voice, without any distracting fidgeting. 7-out-of-10 indicates that the speech was competent but had little distinctive quality.

The Timekeeper calls next for a mark for Interest, in the same way. This time he goes to 8, only to see that the majority vote was clearly for 7, which he duly records as the mark. Judging Interest involves the boys in considering the speaker's handling of his topic and the extent to which his speech 'held together' (and thereby held our attention). In these respects, Porter's speech offered facts rather like items in a catalogue, his conclusion was a mere breaking-off, and his even, regular intonation suggested that his own interest in Ivory was more academic than passionate.

The Timekeeper continues briskly.

'Thirdly, for Independence. Two? Three? Four?...Five?...'

Here the boys have to assess how independent of his notes the speaker has been. If no notes at all have been used, the Timekeeper does not call for a mark but records 10-out-of-10 as a matter of course. To Porter the boys award 6, which strikes me as slightly less than fair, since he used his notes sensibly to regain his poise on the occasions when he really needed them. At other times his glances at the paper were brief reassurances, not dire necessities.

'And lastly, your mark please, sir?'

'Seven-and-a-half.'

As usual, I declare my mark very softly; it's not supposed to filter into the Tiring House. Porter, having heard the Timekeeper call for it, emerges a moment later and returns to his place in the auditorium. He flashes a quick smile of relief at his neighbours, as the Chairman stands to introduce the next speaker.

'It is my pleasure to introduce Mr Himble, who will speak to us on The Opening of the Audley End Model Railway.'

As Himble walks to the box, the class stirs in anticipation. He is a new boy in 2A this term, a friendly, chubby boy who beams as broadly when he is puzzled, or in trouble, as he does when he is pleased. Every other boy in the class gave a speech in each term last year: Himble has had to pick up the whole idea from some brief explanations of mine one lunch-time, and from the various (and probably garbled) accounts of the experience that his friends have given him; and, of course, from watching the sessions of Speeches that the class has been conducting in the last four days.

He looks confident, anyhow, striding to the blackboard just behind the box and drawing the rough outline of a locomotive, with two groups of four circles making the wheels down the side. Now he turns, with a beam, to face us. He holds his notes tightly by the edges and starts firmly on the opening conventions.

'Mr Chairman. Gentlemen. Today it gives me great pleasure to speak to you on the Opening of the Audley End Model Railway.'

For a moment there is silence, then his eyes swoop down to the page.

The Audley End Estate... Audley End was a... The Audley End Estate was once a royal residence and... but since then it has been in the hands of the Lord Braybrooke who has kept it for quite a few years and... until just recently it was taken over by the National Trust.

He looks up, beams again, and pauses to steady himself after this unsettled beginning. I glance at the third officer on the stage. He holds a small wooden hammer in one hand, poised ready to knock on the arm of his chair, and he is known officially as Mr Hammer. He is not looking at me but concentrating on what Himble is saying.

The National Trust only took over the mansion but Lord Braybrooke has kept most of the estate. His son is a keen... railway enthusiast and... he decided that with the grounds he would... on the grounds he would build a model railway. This model railway runs for about half a mile and the gauge is ten inches. On it there are two engines. One is... is diesel, run by diesel power, which is called the Western Thunderer; the other, which is a four-four-O steam-engine (you will see what four-four-O means... from my diagram)...

Here he lets go of his notes with one hand to give a quick wave at the blackboard; but in doing so he loses his place.

...is powered by steam...and I'm afraid I can't remember its name. On... The... opening took place on Saturday 16th and it was opened by Stirling Moss...who said, among other things, that...since he had now finished with racing cars, he now went on to the rather more tame subject of model railways...

There are three short raps from Mr Hammer. He exercises his function firmly but in a gentle tone.

'Will Mr Speaker kindly not leave such long gaps between the sentences?'

The courteous way of putting it suggests a certain sympathy. It is a tactful gesture, too, to have waited thus long before interrupting. He has remembered that this is Himble's first speech and has given him a chance to mend matters himself before striking: but to little avail. Himble looks across at him, blushes, grins ruefully, but is not able to oblige.

...First...um...before any visitors...er...er, before any paying visitors were allowed on the line, the...the friends of Lord Braybrooke had their turn. And...they ...er...er...drank champagne, among other things, and had a number of rides. Stirling Moss drove the steam engine for about three rides and then one of the...other people took over... The crew of the train...er...consisted of the driver, who was dressed in British Railways uniform, and on one train a guard was dressed in British Railways uniform. There was a guard on the other train, but he wasn't dressed in the... in the uniform...

He is stuck, in a muddle – and the little bell rings, at last. A sigh of sympathy comes from somewhere in the auditorium. The end of the ordeal is near. But although Himble glances gratefully at the Timekeeper, he seems to have dried up completely. The silence stretches on and on; and after about half a minute Mr Hammer strikes again. Rap, rap, rap.

'Will Mr Speaker please kindly try to make his speech a bit more fluent?'

Alas, it is asking for the impossible. Himble scans his notes feverishly, growing redder and redder as the pause continues. I am about to intervene, as a last resort, and suggest that he closes the speech by simply telling Mr Chairman that he has reached the end, when he finds at last a way out of the crisis. Abandoning the crumpled notes, he fashions a conclusion out of the one thing that comes clearly to mind.

The cost of the trip was...um...two shillings for adults and six...and a shilling for children below sixteen. When I had my shilling's worth I...I went with a number of other people and we all tried to crowd into one seat, and it was rather difficult, and I had a very uncomfortable shilling ride. On this point, Mr Chairman, Gentlemen, I would like to end my speech.

The evident relief with which he comes to a halt causes a quiet titter in the room; but the Chairman rises with unshaken dignity.

'Are there any questions Gentlemen wish to put?'

The first questioner forgets to address the speaker as 'Mr Himble' or

'Mr Speaker'. He is promptly rapped by Mr Hammer for lack of etiquette, and sits down with the question unasked. While others fare more successfully, I jot down – 'Remember that notes should be *clearly* set out, for the sake of speaker *and* listener!'

'You will wish me to express your thanks as well as my own to Mr Himble. Thank you, sir.'

There is a short round of applause that seems to be offered in a consoling spirit to a fellow who has had a trying time. His speech is marked very dispassionately, however. It is voted 4 for Style, 3 for Interest, and 4 for Independence. I make some allowance for it being Himble's first effort, and give it 6 which, judging by the gasps of surprise around me, is rather too charitable, in the boys' opinion.

The next speaker's name is Henford and his subject is Human Torpedoes. His notes are very extensive. I can see that they cover two full sides in small, close-packed writing: not quite a verbatim version of his speech, but almost, I should think. He glances down at them after every three or four sentences, and speaks rapidly, with much self-assurance.

Mr Chairman. Gentlemen. Today it is my great pleasure to speak to you on Human Torpedoes.

A human torpedo was approximately the same size as a normal twenty-one-inch torpedo, but it was driven by electric batteries.

I quietly note this fascinating fact, for comparison later with Porter's procession of marching elephants.

It had joy-stick control for rudder and hydro-planes, and pump mechanisms and compressed air supplies for emptying and filling its tanks. There were two crew. Number One of them drove and navigated from the forward of the two seating positions. Number Two helped negotiate nets and secured the detachable war-head to the target. The first human torpedo was a wooden mock-up. It was named Cassidy. It was taken to a lock in Portsmouth Harbour, a sheltered stretch of water about thirty feet deep. It was unmounted from a lorry several sizes too small. Next day canvas screens were placed around the head of the lock. Two officers struggled into lightweight diving suits, and forced on their nose clips and gripped tight onto their mouthpieces. The oxygen breathing apparatus was then fitted and their instructions were to open the vents on the main bal... on the ballast tank and let Cassidy sink slowly to the bottom. But, this all sounded very simple, but it just wouldn't work. Cassidy refused to dive. Perhaps she – he – saw no reason for leaving the surface, or maybe it was because of his extreme youth which made him obstinate. Anyway, he refused to dive. So pounds and pounds of...of lead were nailed to his...er...body. Anyway, he had to give up the long struggle, and sank to the bottom. His riders then saw what were to become familiar sights: seaweed, rock and mud. When the first – the real prototypes were produced, they worked excellently. They had a compass and other luminous dials, among them a pressure gauge to...and deck gauge, added in the way of equipment.

The first attack by these vessels ended up in failure. It was an attempt on the *Tirpitz*. Two chariots were lashed to the upper deck of a cargo vessel named *Arthur*, an ex-fishing vessel, under the command of the legendary Lief Larsen, of the Royal Norwegian

Navy Special Service Unit. On October 26th 1942 they set sail. After two days of rough weather they saw land on 28th at mid-day. But twenty miles from the coast the engines broke down. As they were being mended a German plane was sighted and this was the only piece of excitement during their journey. This...the chariots were then secured underneath the hull by means of ropes. *Arthur* was then stripped of its wireless set and all cigarette packets bearing British names were thrown overboard. When the engine was repaired...er...then the engine broke down again. It was repaired with the help of a secret agent and a blacksmith. After being searched by a German patrol, a noise was heard – and the propellor was fouled. A diver was sent to investigate. They found... The diver found that the human torpedoes had gone. So the attempt could not be made.

An attack was made on Palermo harbour from Malta...with the chariots based on Malta. This was a... This...attack was a complete success, one vessel being sunk, one badly damaged, and four possibly damaged. Then they went to La Spezia in the north of Italy. There one large cruiser, the *Bolgano*, was sunk. Later, in 1944, they went to Singapore and attacked two merchant ships. These were both sunk; and at this point, Mr Chairman, Gentlemen, I would like to end my speech.

Like the merchant ships, my spirits have sunk. It was a clumsy speech, relying heavily on the phrasing and vocabulary of a book or magazine that Henford has recently read. Important pieces of narrative-information were omitted, damaging clarity and continuity: and the torpedoes' successes received very meagre and matter-of-fact treatment. Yet Henford (who can be very lazy) has never before tried as hard as this with a speech. He spoke it carefully, deliberately keeping his natural tendency to gabble in check.

He answers questions simply and directly.

'Mr Henford, what is a chariot?'

'It is the other name given to a human torpedo, Mr Soames.'

'Thank you.'

'Mr Henford, about how much does a human torpedo weigh?'

'I think it was about 600 pounds, Mr Banton.'

'Thank you, Mr Henford.'

The questions themselves point to one major weakness in the speech – the lack of clear explanation, stemming from Henford's inadequate 'realisation' of his subject in his own imagination. He has been beguiled, rather, by some of the devices of sophisticated journalism in his source, such as the jocular play with personification when the wooden torpedo is tested, or the glib expressions that make an easy turn of phrase a substitute for genuine feeling – 'His riders then saw what were to become familiar sights'; '...under the command of the legendary Lief Larsen.' On the other hand, he has spoken on a subject that he obviously enjoyed reading about, and he itemised the technical equipment of the torpedo with a relish that Porter never showed.

There is no point in forbidding boys to draw on their reading-matter in their speeches; but they do need encouragement to treat the subject in their own way. Henford's story was offered to his audience without

4

much imagination of his own, or any clear line, as the garbled account of the attempt on the *Tirpitz* showed; yet he seemed to have made some effort to give the speech a beginning-middle-end form corresponding to Specifications–Testing–Performance.

I am not at all sure what to say about his speech at the end of the lesson. Henford is clearly pleased with it and thinks he has done well; and it was certainly more fluent, more assured in delivery, than any he has given before. He may, justifiably, expect some reference to it in my appraisal of the session at the end of the period. But too much praise will leave him smug and unlikely to try harder next time, and too much criticism will leave him piqued and disposed to fall back on his minimal effort. Meanwhile, the boys have voted their marks – 7 for Style, 6 for Interest, and 6 for Independence. I award 6, and I am still wondering what comment I shall make, when the next speaker is introduced.

'It is my pleasure to introduce Mr Hales, who will speak to us on PQ 17.'

Hales is a pleasant, conscientious, neat and rather stolid boy, bigger than most of the others. Speeches Sessions are a great trial to him, though he has always done reasonably well. At home he reads about the Second World War, avidly.

'Mr Chairman. Gentlemen. Today it is my great pleasure to speak to you on PQ 17.'

(There are two purposes behind this practice of repeating the title of the speech. As a piece of etiquette it gives those members of the audience who may not have heard the Chairman clearly a second chance: and it gives a timid speaker the support of a firm opening line.)

This was one of the convoys run to North Russia in the last war. But perhaps before per...proceeding with PQ 17 I should give a bree...brief sketch of the events that led up to the running of this convoy. In 1939 Poland and East Europe was invaded by Germany, and Britain and France declared war on Germany. Then the Low Countries were invaded and the Russo-German alliance broken when Germany invaded Russia in 1941. Britain was asked to send help. Her British High Command faced a dilemma. They could send help by two routes. One, the land route through Turkey, or two, the convoy route from the North of Scotland to Murmansk in the polar inlet in North Russia. They decided on the latter route. The convoys were to carry mainly aircraft and tanks, the two weapons in which the Russian forces were most lacking. The first five convoys incurred no losses, perhaps due to bad German intelligence or to the...fact that the Germans believed that Russia would go before their Blitzkrieg before Britain's help could be of any use. The sixth convoy lost twenty-five per cent of its vessels. This was only three vessels – which isn't such a great amount. There followed several more convoys. And then came PQ 17. This was the most disastrous convoy run to North Russia in the last war, and perhaps the most disastrous of *all* the convoys run in the last war. It comprised thirty-six merchantmen. Twenty-two of them American, twelve British, and two Panamanian. It had the largest escort so far – thirteen ships. It was the thirteenth convoy to run, and it sailed on Friday 13th June 1942. Going for the first few days was smooth, then when they neared the Luftwaffe (or German Air Force) bases in Norway several attacks were incurred by torpedo bombers, with no losses. Then a lone Junkers 88, carrying a torpedo, tor...pedoed a freighter. The vessel was immobilised, so the crew were taken off and the vessel sunk. There followed several attacks by bombers and torpedo planes with the loss of two more merchantmen and one frigate.

Then early one morning the Admiralty received the signal from an Air Force base in the Shetlands that, after flying a reconnaissance over Trondheim Fjord, the German battleship *Tirpitz* was seen to be missing. She had been anchored in this fjord for the past two months. The Admiralty, believing the *Tirpitz* was out to raid the convoy, panicked. They ordered the escort to run and the convoy to scatter. In fact the *Tirpitz* had gone a few miles further down the Norwegian coast for slight repairs. But the convoy scattered, later gathering in small groups, proceeding to Murmansk in this manner.

For the last few moments Hales has been glancing anxiously at the egg-timer, though he has scarcely lifted his nose from his brief but vital notes hitherto. Now, the little bell tinkles, and some of the strained expression goes from his face.

Many ships were sunk by aircraft and U-boats, but the loss of life wasn't very great. Commodore Dowding, senior officer of the convoy, wrote in his report, 'Not a successful convoy.' He was right. Seven merchantmen, out of the thirty-six that started, completed the journey. Here, Mr Chairman, Gentlemen, I end my speech.

It is a piece of very good luck to have this speech coming straight after Henford's. Both have offered accounts of hazardous naval operations in the last war, so I can conveniently cast comments in the form of a comparison, pointing out the more effective communication in Hales' treatment of his subject. Doing this should give his morale a deserved boost, while giving counsel to Henford inoffensively. I admire the way Hales has selected and ordered the material so as to make the speech unfold briskly and clearly. The beginning was well defined in the brief sketch of the war-situation that gave rise to the convoy: the middle narrative section was developed straightforwardly with some engaging touches, such as the cluster of coincidental thirteens and the description of the *Tirpitz*'s disappearance: and the conclusion was given point by the deliberate understatement. There seem to be no loose ends, and when Mr Chairman calls for questions none are asked.

I suspect that Hales prepared this speech by writing it out like a composition, and then practising and practising the delivery till most of it was memorised: then, not being confident enough to speak with no notes at all, and knowing he would be nervous with the whole class watching him, he probably made a short summary to take to the box with him. All this amounts to very thorough and conscientious preparation, but as a method it turns the whole business of giving a talk into a heavier imposition on a boy's time and nervous energy than really it ought to be. I cannot prevent boys from composing their speeches in this way if they choose to, but I try not to encourage them to it.

'Your marks please Gentlemen...'

The boys are a little hard on this speech, I think. They give it 7 for Style, 7 for Interest and 4 for Independence. I give it 8.

By my watch there are eight minutes of the period left: time for one more speech. Mr Chairman rises.

'It is my pleasure to introduce Mr Grain who will speak to us on The First Tay Bridge.'

Grain is probably the most intelligent boy in the class, and he is a little younger than most of the others. He is small, alert, unassuming, gentle; and neither adulated nor scorned by his fellows. He steps quickly up to the box and is off at a spanking pace before the Timekeeper has even begun to turn the egg-timer. He speaks crisply: and uses no notes.

Mr Chairman. Gentlemen. Today I would like to speak to you on The First Tay Bridge. The North British Railway, whose line served the East coast of Scotland north of Edinburgh, was twice divided by deep inlets, the wind-swept waters of the Firths of Forth and Tay. On reaching each of these, a passenger bound for Dundee or further north would have to leave the comfort of his train and transfer to a ferry-boat crossing. So several suggestions were put forward for a bridge across the Tay: but Parliament had first to agree. This took from 1864 to 1870, so great was the opposition. Eventually though, in 1871, the railway company placed a contract with a building firm to construct in three years, at the cost of £172,000, a bridge over the Tay estuary from St Fort to Magdalen-green in Dundee – a distance of nearly two miles. The designer was Thomas Bouch. Born in 1822 in Cumberland he had already designed such notable structures as the Redheugh viaduct in Newcastle, so there was good reason for his design being chosen. Test borings had shown that the Tay had a rocky bed. Bouch therefore intended his bridge to be supported by numerous masonry piers, 200 feet apart; but when fourteen of these piers had been constructed the test borings were found to have been inaccurate, and so as to lighten the weight on the foundations, as the bed was softer, Bouch reduced the number of piers, while increasing their distance apart to about 250 feet. As a clearance of 88 feet was required by the authorities for ships passing up the Firth, the railway ran on a rising gradient from one bank towards the centre, where it was level for a while, then on a downward gradient to the other side. Whereas most of the bridge was of the deck-bridge type – that is to say the railway ran along on top of the girders – the high-girders as they were called in the centre were of the through-bridge type, where needless to say the railway ran *through* the girders.

Work continued at a steady pace but by 1873 it was evident that time and cost for completion had been vastly underestimated. The work was eventually completed in 1877. The bridge had cost £300,000 and the lives of twenty workmen. To test it, six locomotives coupled together, a load of over 420 tons, were run across at 40 miles an hour. This satisfied the Board of Trade inspector but he nevertheless imposed a speed limit of 25 miles an hour for trains crossing the bridge. On May 31st 1878 the bridge was officially opened with all the usual Victorian junketings deemed appropriate for such an occasion.

(Ripe expression such as this turns up from time to time in speeches. It is not often the boy's own choice of words, but in Grain's case I feel it may be, for he is a precocious child who enjoys occasional verbal pomposities. Others sometimes include phrases from their reading because the ring of the language impresses them. Both cases show a willingness to make a venture with vocabulary, and I have no wish to discourage that. The trouble is that often – perhaps more often than not – the language is a piece of grandiose or trite or hackneyed phrasing, or some slick jargon; which I have no wish to encourage. But since the twelve-year-old ear does not easily recognise the expression as any of these things, direct criticism of it probably does more harm than good, by giving a boy the uncomfortable impression that what sounds grand to him is likely to be 'wrong' somehow. So I make no direct attack on rhetorical indulgence, whether it is second-hand or not. When it is obviously a close and prolonged 'crib', I do criticise the mere borrowing, as a lack of enterprise on the speaker's part. Otherwise I make little fuss, but try to praise straight, telling and vigorous speech as often as possible.)

The little bell tinkles, but Grain does not falter for an instant.

A train ran across from St Fort into Dundee where it was greeted by crowds, bands and flags; and a sumptuous feast was held in Dundee Town Hall. A few weeks later Queen Victoria herself crossed the bridge, and just over a year later Bouch was knighted. His bridge was in regular use for just eighteen months until December 28th 1879.

On this stormy winter's night the 5.20 slow train, awaiting ferry passengers from the Forth, was not headed by the usual small tank engine, as this had broken down, but by the much heavier weekly express engine, Number 224. When the train of five coaches and a brake van reached St Fort station at seven o'clock, a seventy-mile-an-hour gale was blowing up the Firth with relentless fury. This was one of the strongest ever known in the area, and the signalman at St Fort had to crawl on all fours to reach Number 224 to hand the staff for the single-line workings to the driver. When a previous train had passed through at 5.20, he had noticed sparks flying from its wheels, so now with another man he watched carefully to see if this phenomenon would be repeated. It was – and just as the train's tail-light disappeared into the distance along the girders there was a brilliant flash; then nothing but darkness and the roar of the gale. The suspicious signalman tried to block his instruments, but found they were dead. Then with his companion he tried to walk out onto the bridge, but they were driven back by the gale – which isn't at all surprising. Then together they went down onto the shore and – in a brief moment of moonlight – saw that the high girders in the centre – had gone.

Another man, named Maxwell, who chanced to be looking out of his window on the north shore, also saw this. He saw three separate streams of fire falling from the bridge. At first he thought it was the fireman cleaning out his fire and sending hot clinker into the Tay, but then he realised that the train's lights had disappeared. Inquisitively he fixed a telescope on the bridge and saw that the high girders had disappeared. He immediately ran to the New Tay station to give the alarm and the signalman and foreman there tried together to walk out onto the bridge. Although buffeted by the gale they persisted, and came back with confirmation that the high girders had collapsed. The fate of the train, however, remained obscure.

While the few signalmen at St Fort prayed that it had crossed in time and was now in Dundee, the officials in Dundee hoped that it had stopped and was now back in St Fort. But reports of mail bags washed ashore and a salvaged destination board disturbed them very much. The ferry *Dundee* was sent to investigate and pick up possible survivors, but she came back with just a story of twelve collapsed piers and a confusion of twisted girders in the water.

An official enquiry was held at Dundee, at which Sir Thomas Bouch tried to put forward an explanation. According to him, the rear part of the train had been derailed while crossing the deck-spans and on reaching the high girders it had fouled them, thus bringing them down. This explanation, however, was rejected. Later on divers salvaged the train, little damaged, and it was brought back into active service on the railway, where it stayed till 1919.

It took a very long time to persuade the suspic...superstitious railwaymen to drive Number 224 across the new bridge which had now been constructed a little further west, but eventually, twenty-nine years later, on December 28th 1908, the anniversary of the disaster, she safely hauled the down-mail train into Dundee...

For the second time the Timekeeper rings his bell. Six minutes have gone past since Grain began, and a prompt ending to the speech is now compulsory.

...across the bridge that still spans the Tay today. And there, Mr Chairman, Gentlemen, I would like to end my speech.

He concludes with a relieved smile that clearly says 'There, I just got it all in in time!' The class has listened spellbound, and when Mr Chairman calls for questions, many hands are raised.

'Mr Seale.'

'Mr Grain, has anyone thought of the real reason for the bridge collapsing?'

'Well, they think it was partly due to the fact that Bouch in his design didn't make any allowance for the heavy winds; partly to bad workmanship. As a matter of fact, it was later discovered that cracks in the girders and in the supports had been botched up with Beaumontage. I think this is a composition of melted iron borings, beeswax and lampblack. Quite insufficient.'

'Thank you, Mr Grain.'

'Mr Denning.'

'Mr Grain, are there any remains of the old Tay Bridge?'

'The stumps can just be seen at low water now.'

'Thank you, Mr Grain.'

I have transcribed the words of Grain's speech, but print does not render his dramatic delivery. His tone shifted subtly as the story unfolded, moving from a plain, drily informative manner at the start, through emphasis on each freshly disturbing fact about the fatal 'stormy winter's night', to build the excitement gradually to the climax when the girders were first seen to be gone, a moment that he shaped with careful dramatic pauses ('...they went down onto the shore and – in a brief moment of moonlight – saw that the high girders in the centre – had gone.'). It was a real tour-de-force, and the class acknowledge it with thunderous applause when the Chairman thanks Grain. There is excitement in the air as the Timekeeper steps up to ask for marks.

'Your marks please, Gentlemen. First, for Style. Six?' (He knows there is little point in starting any lower.)

No hands are raised.

'Seven?...Eight?'

Still no hands.

'Nine?'

Two or three hands only. The Timekeeper gapes a little.

'Ten?'

All the remaining hands shoot up. The Timekeeper grins at the sheer scale of this gesture of approval. Then when 10 is voted equally firmly for Interest, and recorded as a matter of course for Independence since Grain used no notes at all, we are on the border of a sensation.

'And your mark please, Sir?'

It is not a moment for quibbling – I too award 10, and the gasps and whispers of wonderment at this clean sweep of full marks go on until Grain, looking very red and somewhat breathless, has returned to his seat. Then the Chairman rises and waits for silence.

'I declare this session of Speeches adjourned.'

We all stand while the three officials come down from the stage and walk to the back of the room, and formalities come to an end. I ask the boys to sit down; the three officers return to their places among The King's Men; and I move my desk to face the class from the front again. There is about one minute of the period left, so my summing-up is very compressed.

That session was the very first in which a speaker from any class has scored four tens. So I do congratulate you, Grain. I expect all of you noticed how thoroughly this speech had been prepared. Grain had a lot of facts and figures at his fingertips; but notice that he always worked them into the speech in a way that helped to make the *story* more interesting. This business of choosing the right details and using them wisely is extremely important in speeches that tell some kind of story – as four of the five speeches did this morning. In this respect I think Hales' speech was also very well put together, though he did not make it *sound* quite as stirring as Grain did.

Outside the end-of-lesson bell rings. The boys stir at once.

Before you go, I have two more important things to say about this session. First, I think it was very well conducted by the officers: and here I will mention Mr Hammer in particular. As you know, it is always a mark of a successful Speeches Session if Mr Hammer has very little to do, as was the case today. But in this session, when action *was* needed, Mr Hammer took it both efficiently *and* tactfully – by not rapping too soon or too often, for instance, during the second speech this morning which was, remember, a first effort.

And the second important thing is this: you probably noticed that the first four speakers all used notes, and some seemed to have laid those notes out better than others.

Do remember that – as I think I have said before – the best notes are always set out so clearly that you can find your place in them straight away at a single glance.

Right, off you go.

While the room is clearing there is a cluster of boys round the Time-keeper's chair, where the mark-book lies open. I always let the speakers look up their score after a session, if they wish to. Today they are surrounded by a gaggle of their friends, curious to see the maximum score in black and white, and loud in admiration of Grain's speech.

'Cor that was *super*, Grainy.'

'Yeh. How d'you manage to remember it all so well?'

'I bet nobody'll beat *that* mark for a long while, anyway.'

'You didn't half go fast, G. I liked the bit where the girders went best.'

'Yes, that was fabulous.'

As the throng moves away to the next lesson, I notice that Himble and Henford are joining in this chorus. Though they were not directly mentioned, both of them, and Porter, may have drawn an inference or two from my brief closing comments on the session. Or they may not. One can only hope for the best. My remarks *may* lead Porter to notice the catalogue-element in his own speech, *may* persuade Himble to produce a clearer set of notes for his next speech, *may* suggest to Henford that his story could have been presented more successfully, *may* encourage Hales to enliven his delivery, *may* make some of the class more aware of some aspects of the art of oral composition. But it is likely that the boys' personal impressions of the speeches, and in particular their memories of the outstandingly good one, will do more effective teaching.

On the whole it is best for comments on speeches, like comments on drama, to be short and pointed towards successful achievement: and this may mean leaving a lot unmentioned. Most of the jottings on my note-pad, along with my intended comparison between the speeches of Henford and Hales, were abandoned this morning, and I don't expect I shall return to them at the beginning of 2 A's next English lesson, since the occasion for them will have lost its bloom. One can speechify too much about Speeches.

Occasionally the three Officers (who are appointed afresh for each Session of Speeches by the Master of Revels) show a less consistent poise than the trio in the lesson recorded here. Otherwise this session – with the exception of Grain's speech – is fairly typical, in standard and conduct, of the work in oral composition at the opening of the boys' second year. By this stage the class is thoroughly familiar with Speeches procedure – a procedure which deliberately cultivates the notion of a propriety in public address. Its strong stresses on formal courtesies, on the due decorum and etiquette for the occasion, help to form social consciousness. Through these stresses each member of the class is kept for a time distinctly aware of the means of order, and of his particular position in sustaining it. Such consciousness does not occur naturally and instinctively to all of us and, beyond school, the conditions of contemporary life offer young people many inducements (not to say incitements) to alien allegiances.

The etiquette enables the boys to demonstrate that they can conduct quite a specialised piece of civil intercourse with dignity and independence. With it they run their own affair from beginning to end. I only interrupt to rescue speakers who occasionally dry up even more disastrously than Himble did, and – *very* occasionally – to rebuke naughty, larking behaviour. Boys are not angels and sometimes a member of the audience will try to put a speaker off his stride by pulling faces at him or catching his eye with distracting, clandestine signals. When this sort of thing occurs, I try to reprimand it at the time of giving my mark to the Timekeeper, in order to disrupt procedure as little as possible; but on one or two occasions an unusually daring Mr Hammer has taken this stern duty upon himself and interrupted the speaker to call a nuisance to order – courageous action for the common weal!

Some time after this session I decided to suppress the office of Mr Hammer. As well as looking out for breaches of general etiquette, he had also watched for weaknesses of style during the speeches, weaknesses such as lazy, feeble language (slang, fractured grammar, too chatty colloquialisms) or too many 'ums' and 'ers' or gaps in the middle of sentences. His job was to rap if he found any of these faults becoming persistent, and to ask the speaker to correct them (though he was always expected to be charitable in the opening phase of any speech). I eventually realised that the very presence of Mr Hammer, even if he remained quite silent, mightily increased the nervousness of many of the less confident speakers.

For a time I resorted to Caldwell Cook's practice of having the hammer passed round the audience, each boy handing it to his neighbour after he had used it once. Unfortunately this practice made a timid speaker feel that the whole class was a hostile tribunal, whereas only *one* of his fellows had previously concentrated on his faults. So the abandonment of the hammer caused much relief.

Yet even with it gone, the task of delivering a speech remains something of an ordeal for most boys; and *because* it offers a stiffish challenge there is, for most of them, a sense of substantial achievement in meeting it, a sense of having coped with something difficult. This satisfaction for the individual, however slight, is endorsed by the rest of the class, since every boy shares the speaker's 'ordeal' to some extent, not only by undergoing it personally when his turn to give a speech comes round, but by his involvement with every speaker he listens to. (I think, for instance, of the anxiety we shared with Himble during that long silence when he was stuck for words; or the way we were all rapt at the moment when the missing girders of the Tay Bridge were shown to our mind's eye.)

In giving a speech that lasts for the minimum acceptable time and accords with customary procedure, the individual is, as it were, fulfilling his dues to the community. If, through nervousness, laziness or accident, a boy falls well short of the three-and-a-half minute deadline with his speech, I ask him to revise it and give it again. If he falls short again I make no more demands; the temporary discomfort of failing to meet a challenge that the rest of the class has met is enough for him to have at heart. But 'short measure' is rare after the sessions of the first two terms.

In the boys' first term it usually takes me a whole period to explain all the whys and wherefores of Speeches. In this introduction I urge the courtesies as much as possible, pointing out that the formal wording involved in beginning and ending a speech, in putting a question, in calling for marks, and especially in conducting the session as Chairman, expresses a politeness that is not only proper but useful to the occasion.

In giving advice about how to make a speech I stress that the boys can choose their subject completely freely. This they don't at first believe – 'Sir, can I *really* give a speech on Chinese Tortures?' – and then when they do some strange choices are made. I have learned to show no alarm or impatience when subjects such as 'The Case for Fascism' or 'How to Make a Raspberry Sandwich' are announced. (In fact, the latter speech turned out to be highly entertaining. It was given with a solemn, dead-pan air and went into well-nigh clinical detail; but some would-be imitators did not fare so happily later on. Comic speeches need very careful and thorough preparation. Nothing is duller than the funny talk that isn't.) The only way I limit the boys' freedom of choice is to warn them against the inevitable dullness that will arise if they merely tell the class what everyone knows perfectly well already.

I suggest that speakers should try to give their speech clear form by making a definite beginning, middle and end, and I point out some of the ways in which a good speaker should show consideration for his audience – by speaking clearly enough for all to hear without strain, for instance, and by looking them in the eye for most of the time and trying not to fidget, even if he feels nervous. I explain how to mark a speech, how to assess Style, Interest and Independence. Then, by way of summing it all up, I do a demonstration speech on the subject of 'Making a Speech'.

At the end of this introductory lesson I ask the boys to spend their next two homework periods preparing their first speech; and after that the first sessions begin, conducted by each Guild in turn, lesson by lesson, with the speakers taking their turn alphabetically or anti-alphabetically. In these early sessions the class really learns how it all works. In the First Form the maximum length for a speech is fixed at four-and-a-half minutes, in the Second at six minutes. The *minimum* acceptable length remains at three-and-a-half minutes for both years, it being as hard for some boys to fill this time out well as it is for some others to fit what they have to say into nearly twice the span. In the first terms the Chairmen carry, as an aid to memory, a small card with the formal wording of the various announcements typed on it. Most Chairmen have dispensed with this by the start of the second year. And by the end of the second year most speakers have dispensed with notes.

In the matter of marking I advise the class to use at first a scale that runs from 4 for a very weak speech to 9 for an extremely good one. In the session that I have transcribed here I think that most of the boys' marks were fair; if, as sometimes happens, they are notably unfair I adjust my own mark to restore a balance. Periodically I give brief reminders about how to mark for Style and Interest, for the habit of voting for marks encourages alert listening only so long as the boys keep a clear idea of what to look out for.

Like any lesson that depends completely on sustained collaboration, a session of speeches can easily go limp. There are many reasons why speakers may be dull – nervousness, lack of talent, idleness; and an audience that suffers two or three poor speeches in succession can grow quite restless and inattentive. The etiquette of the session may then seem a tedious business to all and sundry, and the teacher will probably feel more depressed than anybody. At such times it is more than usually important that he should not *show* disappointment or irritation by breaking into the formalities and making a fuss, for by doing so he is most likely to accelerate the impending disgruntlement with the whole 'Speeches idea'. Fortunately, if he sits tight, the session will usually bring itself out of the doldrums – all it needs is one able speaker with an intriguing topic. I have never been in a session where *all* the speeches have been really dull.

A session of speeches conducted like this depends, in a variety of ways, on trust, which *may* be abused (as trust may in all human affairs). For instance, a speaker may betray our faith in his integrity by taking his speech (or the major part of it) from a chapter of a book or an article in a magazine, more or less word for word. Very occasionally I have been quite sure that this has happened, and sometimes I have been fairly sure.

But unless one *is* quite sure (say, by actually recognising the source of the piece) there is a great risk in accusing the speaker of 'cheating'. On the occasions when I have done this, speaking to the boy alone after the lesson, I have been wrong as often as right – to our mutual embarrassment. And when my more-in-sorrow-than-in-anger suspicions *have* proved right, the boy's evident woe at being caught out has usually proved far more acute than I would have wished it to be.

In most cases it is simply impossible to discover to what degree a speech 'borrowed' from a book has been the result of imaginative laziness and to what degree it has resulted from fear – fear of not being able to meet the challenge. The more the teacher probes, the more upsetting the interview will probably be, and the harder the boy's *next* speech is likely to become for him. It is wrong to stir children's fear and guilt in a classroom, so I accept the risk of undetected abuses of trust occurring from time to time. In any case, in a class of boys almost all of whom do *some* reading for pleasure at home, a number of speeches in every term are sure to draw on that reading, if a free choice of subject is allowed. It strikes me as improper for a teacher of English to appear to object to this. Most of the speakers in this morning's session must have consulted various pieces of printed matter that caught their interest, in order to prepare their speeches. Such elementary gestures of research strike me as something to be glad of. If, in the process, a *little* plagiarism creeps in from time to time, I don't think a great deal of harm is done. Plenty of education, in matters of oral communication and matters of individual and social poise, occurs even so.

9. Poetry

Poets learn from poets. Ben Jonson approves the doctrine of the Ancients that *Imitatio* is the third requisite in a poet: 'Not as a creature that swallows what it takes in, crude, raw and undigested: but that feeds with an appetite and hath a stomach to concoct, divide and turn all into nourishment.'

From 'Shakespeare the Poet' by George Rylands in
A Companion to Shakespeare Studies, edited by
H. Granville Barker and G. B. Harrison

The notes on Poetry that Douglas Brown made for me just before he left the Perse read as follows:

This is the field in which my own ideas and methods have changed most from year to year. I shall only record the things I am most confident about.

I think that we ought to pay due attention to the much advertised 'responsiveness' of the young to poetry, and make it pay. *But* I think, too, what I don't find in the books about English teaching, that we oughtn't to fool ourselves or our pupils about the actual place poetry takes in our lives: it is marginal. It may be important; I agree myself with Pound – the very life of the language is at stake. But I don't read poetry more than marginally myself (say a tenth of all my reading. And that may be generous, but would just be true if it includes poetic drama) and therefore I am not prepared to teach English as though poetry were central. It becomes, of course, more nearly central for VI Form level and scholarship specialists; a field of chosen study. But that's different. Forms I and II contain at most 2 or 3 such persons, or say, generously, half a dozen.

Therefore I argue for presenting poetry in this 'marginal' way; giving it a slightly short ration of a quarter (drama, mime, speeches, being the other quarters) of the two-thirds occupied by Mummery work (business period and reading and homework being the other third).

I argue, secondly, for a series of study-in-depth, rather than the usual anthology approaches. The library is the place for these, and there are several good ones there, and the boys can dabble in Poets Tonguery when they have nothing better to do. But I think it is much more important to leave some distinct impressions of certain sorts of poetry, than to pursue mixed grills through five-sixths of school life – and I am sorry to say that is becoming the drill everywhere.

So I take Ballads; Lawrence's Birds, Beasts and Flowers; Waley and Pound's Chinese Verse; Biblical and Heroic songs and laments; and Blank Pentameter in Wordsworth, Thomas (Edward), Frost and Muir for description of man in nature: and explore these fairly well. Explore by having readings, on stage, with adjusted lighting, by myself, by chosen and prepared readers, or both. I go for repetition, at intervals, of the same poems – up to 3 or 4 hearings. And I converse (not merely talk) about issues of technique, method, expression-rightness, and so on, informally. Each fresh undertaking, I make clear at the outset, is going to lead to composition in the same style – here is a practical and deeper reason for attention.

In addition I sometimes set aside a period for me to read a chosen programme of verse: usually including one longish narrative poem. And each time we have a fortnight of verse, I include a period during which each boy reads a passage of his own choice from anywhere, of between 8 and 14 lines, as finely as he can. (These readings I sometimes make the gesture of marking. But I don't do anything with the marks.) My contribution has been spasmodic; theirs invariable – i.e. 3 times a year.

I incorporate mime into the handling of balladry with Sir Patrick Spens and The Blind Harper, the latter as a solo. I find the boys – given a session of periods of mime behind them – able to invent the relevant narrative sequence of mime for Sir P. excellently. But you must limit dramatis personae, and have some doubling. Sometimes I add choral and solo production of the ballad itself; sometimes a single reader from the miming Guild, from among the audience. The new Mummery lends itself well to experiment in the matter of location of reciting groups during a mime.

Once or twice in the two years I try for tableau productions of short lyrics; and at least once in the series of D. H. Lawrence readings we have a *production* of the reading of *Bat*, with lighting and music in full.

This is the sort of thing. The field is wide open for further experiment. In the summer term of Year 1 I neglect verse on the grounds that *Philoctetes* covers the need. If ever you feel during the second year that you are not doing enough (and remain unpersuaded by my Paragraph 2 above) recollect that all your drama is Shakespearean and most of it in superb verse.

This was not quite the way we did poetry when I was a boy in the Mummery, for in those early days our teacher had not fixed his general bearings so clearly. Then, we dipped about together in the Guild Verse Book. This was a duplicated anthology containing some thirty to forty poems. It included, I remember, a number of pieces by Walter de la Mare and these were, for a time, my personal favourites. Douglas Brown had not arranged the poems in any particular order, though altogether they ranged over a number of different themes, such as 'the feel of the seasons', 'the mysterious and the magical', and 'creatures common and uncommon'.

When we turned to poetry in the term's programme of classwork, the Guilds presented short Verse Sessions, consisting of four or five poems on a particular theme from the book. Our themes were usually suggested by Douglas Brown, but we were left to choose the poetry for ourselves. I don't think we *had* to choose exclusively from the Verse Book, but we generally did. Sometimes both Guilds would include the same poem in their choice, and such overlapping never seemed to matter very much. What *did* matter was that each Verse Session was a full-blown Guild *performance*, with lighting, music and costume, along with mime, tableau, grouped and solo voices, to heighten the impact of the spoken word. These were no periods of mere reading aloud.

Each Verse Session kept the Guilds busy for two or three lessons, discussing, 'casting', planning, practising, before the actual presentation of the four or five selected poems. Of necessity, everyone in each Guild was involved in these arrangements. At some point Douglas Brown would read us some poetry on our theme from a source outside the Verse Book – one long poem, perhaps, or several shorter ones. Whatever kind of poem he chose, serious or gay, rhymed or free, he read it always with a care for the way the poet was speaking, a relish for the just sense and cadence of the word, which was, I realise now, a piece of good teaching in itself – a demonstration of what poetry *is*.

I remember also that at this stage of term our class usually spent a period or two in the school library, browsing in anthologies. At the start of these lessons we had five minutes to rummage round the Poetry shelves and pick out any collections that looked interesting at a quick glance between the covers. Then we settled down to read to ourselves for the next half-hour. We could sit anywhere we liked – on the floor, on the radiators, on the window sills, at the tables, anywhere – but we weren't allowed to talk. Five minutes before the end of the lesson we returned our books to their proper places or filled out a borrower's ticket at the teacher's desk. Though I rarely borrowed a book on these occasions, poetry not being the part of English that I liked most, I enjoyed the peaceful time.

This was the way that poetry went in those days. The chief difference from Douglas Brown's later method lay in the status then afforded to the anthology approach, and in the lack of special focus on 'some distinct impressions of certain sorts of poetry'. I think we once composed some short pieces in ballad style, after reading and talking about some poems from a little blue textbook called *Ballads Ancient and Modern* (which the school issues to the First Forms to this day) but I don't remember any special venture with Lawrentian free verse, or Chinese Verse, or Blank Pentameter. We must have run across examples of all these, but we never dwelt on them or attempted to write poems in the same style ourselves.

Douglas Brown's notes on principles and procedure were distilled from his teaching experience during thirteen years. When I found myself faced with the task of teaching poetry in the Mummery I followed his suggested methods closely at first, because I had little idea what else to do. Years later, I still teach poetry largely along these 'inherited' lines, because I have found that they work, although they reflect a view of poetry's place in the teaching of English which is currently unfashionable.

In the narrower sense of the term – the sense that defines the literary form as distinct from drama and the novel – poetry does indeed fill a marginal place in my actual cultural life, as it does in the actual cultural lives of most of the English teachers I know well. Furthermore, it fills a marginal place in the world which the children we teach will live in as adults. Outside the teaching profession and the education industry, only a very small part of our society is involved, at all, in poetry. A fragment of the reading public cares for it. A few publishers, only, are concerned to print it. The BBC does what it can and gives it a little attention. A few periodicals cater for those with a specialist interest, whose zeal is often intense; but the sphere of their influence in contemporary culture is tiny. The fact is that the novel (or narrative) and drama, as styles of literature, claim a far greater degree of the adult community's attention. Yet school English syllabuses frequently place a stress upon formal poetry which would imply just the opposite: and *many* young people find that the implication is false to the world about them long before they leave school. I think it is much to their advantage, and ours, that as teachers we should accept 'the facts of literature' as they pertain to adult life.

If we accept this much about the place of poetry in its narrow sense, we ought also to accept the bearing that poetry in the wider sense has on the way we teach – the poetry that is not simply a literary Kind but a quality that may work through *all* the forms of literature. Such poetry makes the greatest of our drama both exciting and permanently relevant; the most enduring and majestic of our stories live in it; and strictly speaking it is the proper term for that heightened prose, perfectly articulate and impossible to paraphrase, in which the greatest novels have their being. (For 'poetry' once signified, simply, *making* with words; *all* making, especially stories; and something of that sticks in the wider sense of the term today.) A concern for poetry in *this* sense, for the potency of the creative word to celebrate the true action of human experience, needs surely to fill not a marginal, but a central place, in the actual cultural life of teachers of English. The stronger the concern the more we are likely to care for relationships between the various aspects of our subject.

On the other hand, our taste for poetry in the narrower sense of the term is *bound* to be partial. The field is too vast, the other obligations claiming our energy and attention as teachers are too many, for matters to be otherwise. Taste involves partiality, by definition. It involves, too, a delight and respect that stay alert. It does not find everything 'interesting' merely. Though one's taste may shift, may expand or contract, may make sudden surprising leaps as one grows older, it can properly care for only a limited number of sorts of poetry at any one time.

So, although so much current practice puts things all the other way round, I feel that in teaching poetry in secondary school, at all levels, we should aim to give a place in the *foreground* to distinct encounters with distinct creative spirits, where our own most vital, or still sensitive, interests are strongly engaged, and a place in the *background* to anthologies. As I see it, the rôle of collections of mixed poetry should be a strictly supplementary one. As miscellanies for the library shelves, available for silent reading, for the pleasures of browsing or as sources of material for recitals around a chosen theme, anthologies are useful. But as *foundations*, as teaching instruments, they do damage. They encourage the idea that poetry is a mixture of oddments. They propose to show what variety poetry can offer, and too often leave only a blurred impression of nothing but variety. They tantalise with snippets, and move on too promptly from what may delight or disturb or impress or excite to something different. They foster an attitude of lucky dip in place of taste. And, most damaging of all, they prevent our pupils from experiencing what Wordsworth rightly teaches us is the very character and function of a poet – the fact that 'he is a man speaking to men'.

In the poetry we care for most it is, surely, the note of a distinct being, speaking to us in a specialness of experience, that rouses the delight and respect which may enhance our own capacities for living. This particular connection, this peculiar kind of speaking between selves, is what makes a poet matter to us: but it is not a connection that happens automatically. We earn it in a sustained response of active imagination. If, in our way of teaching children during their growing years, we do not give them the opportunity, and the time and the encouragement, to earn it for themselves – the chance of experiencing the distinctness of now one, now another *kind* of poetry or *voice of a poet* with real attention (by which I do not mean to suggest anything that in any way resembles drilled conning of a set book for examination purposes) – then we have little right to be disappointed if they treat poetry with indifference or aversion when they leave us.

It may be objected that what I am urging restricts pupils' acquaintance with poems and poetry too severely; that *because* the time available for teaching poetry is so limited it is all the more important that we instil both a liking and a sense of its range and riches; that there must be a certain abundance of choice offered before a taste can truly be formed.

Certainly we must aim to make a liking for poetry result from our lessons. But a lesson-*habit* of fleeting and superficial contacts with assorted *kinds* of poem strikes me as a poor way of aiming. There is liking and liking: a kind which is a simple readiness to be entertained, and a kind which engages growth in consciousness. This latter seems to me most likely to arise in children when they are concerned with a small body of work. For such 'liking' is both an experience *and* an art – an art of receiving, an art of grasping life felt in the action of words. It is an art which depends, like any other, upon powers of discernment, and which needs, like any other, to be *learned*. Young artists learn, and their skill grows, from close and careful attention to a small repertoire: and in our pupils' experience of poetry such attention seems to me to be the best means of giving taste a chance to develop as time goes on.

In some terms I have given poetry as much Mummery time as Drama or Mime or Speeches, in others slightly less, according to circumstances. Once or twice I have left it out of the *Philoctetes* term in the first year. And occasionally in the second year, when there has been real point in letting a class spend longer on Shakespeare than I had planned (that is, when things have either gone unusually well or unusually badly) I have given (other) poetry short measure. But in a normal term we spend two to three weeks, a sequence of ten or a dozen lessons, involved in Poetry. This sequence has seemed to work most effectively when it has included the following components, usually in the following order.

First, a period in which I read to the class a programme of verse of my own choice: second, a library period for browsing: third, a period in which each boy reads aloud a short passage of poetry that he has chosen for himself: then several lessons during which each Guild prepares and presents its Verse Session: and finally a period spent in preliminaries for the do-it-yourself homework assignment. Overall this sequence aims to keep to the fore the notion of a poet as a man *speaking* to men.

In starting by reading a programme of verse myself I hope to warm up some enthusiasm. The success of the tactic depends, of course, on not overdoing it. Too forced a display, too much 'style' in the reading, will simply discomfort the captive audience with an uneasy sense of one's self-indulgence. Yet one has to try to read with all the feeling that the poem's words register, with heart but not in frenzy. Though the right 'voice' is sometimes hard to hit, it is always more than a *merely* natural one that is needed. Possibly it comes right more easily when we try to read *slowly* enough – a good deal more slowly, at any rate, than is the rule in many public recitals nowadays, where the poetry simply goes too fast to be heard with a real understanding.

Spaced out at intervals in the programme for this lesson, I include several examples of the particular kind of poetry that I want the boys' attention to focus on during the next two weeks. And since thirty-five minutes is a long time to ask the class to sit listening attentively without any text, I try to keep interest alert by doing at least one longish poem in a 'staged' version with adjusted lighting and mime-gesture where appropriate; by including at least one poem with a refrain for all to join in; by pausing to chat about the poems from time to time; and by always including a humorous poem or two. At the end of this period I tell the class that each boy's own choice of poem will be needed for the lesson *after* next; so everybody has a reasonable chance to prepare for it.

We all spend the *next* lesson in the library, browsing in the way I used to do as a child. The boys are not bound to choose their poetry for the following lesson during this time, but in fact many of them do. The period is partly intended, in fact, to give a chance for preparation to those boys who don't wish to spend more time on poetry than is 'officially' required. It is intended, also, to show that poetry, however else one may take it, is valid as a personal and *private* experience, an experience of discovery and enjoyment, carrying no further obligation than that of pleasing oneself. I hope to imply this much by reading poetry silently to myself throughout this period (and being clearly seen to be reading it) even when a heavy backlog of marking or preparation for other lessons is urgently pressing. What the teacher *does* matters quite as much as what the teacher *says* in all aspects of English – but especially in this one.

For the boys' reading of their own choice of verse we sometimes need a period, sometimes a period and a half. We push all the desks round the four sides of the auditorium, facing outwards; and we seat ourselves facing inwards. The Guild arrangement is thus dispensed with, the teacher is simply one of the people in the circle, and the atmosphere stays informal and easy. Sometimes we read in order round the circle, sometimes we go alphabetically or anti-alphabetically through the class, each reader announcing for himself the title of his piece and the name of the poet. Deliberately I give no advice on Elocution (beyond a general reminder at the outset to speak up and not to rush) nor do I ever give marks to the readers, since the occasion is no kind of test.

Sometimes the same poem turns up twice, by chance, in which case I try to make some useful comment comparing the two renderings: and in the early days many of the boys (perhaps even a third of the class) choose to read nonsense verse or the like. The licence to read aloud what they think is not, somehow, 'proper' poetry is what some of them enjoy more than anything else. Yet few choose to read comic verse *every* term, though there is nothing to stop them from doing so. The taste simply seems to shift as time goes on.

It happens quite often that one or two of the boys choose examples of the distinct kind of poetry that I want everybody's attention to come to concentrate on later. If this happens I try to follow one of them with my only contribution to this session, a re-reading of one of the pieces of the same kind from the initial lesson. In this way the chosen poetic 'kind' can quietly take root in the lessons. In a term when I wanted to focus on the traditional Ballad, for instance, the boys had heard by the end of the third lesson *Sir Patrick Spens* (twice; I read it once in the first lesson and again in the third), *The Demon Lover* (in the first lesson), a version of *Barbara Allen* and a short piece from *The Ancient Mariner* (both read by boys in the third lesson), and *The Highwayman* by Alfred Noyes, which, being a 'stagey' piece, became my staged effort in the first lesson. This latter poem is not, admittedly, a traditional ballad, and – unlike the Coleridge – it does not adopt the metre of one; but its narrative style is related enough to that of ballads to make it worth an encounter. It strikes me as melodramatic, sentimental, even – in places – nasty; but with the Mummery in darkness except for a patch of 'moonlight' to read by, and a reading voice catching up the swashbuckling verve in rhythm and image ('And he rode with a jewelled twinkle, His pistol butts a-twinkle, His rapier hilt a-twinkle, under the jewelled sky') it can rouse considerable enthusiasm for poetry. Its manner took hold of Salter's 'ear' so exceptionally firmly on this occasion, in fact, that he wasn't free of it when writing his own ballad some three weeks later (see chapter 11, p. 208). By that time the class had heard *The Demon Lover* a couple of times more in Verse Sessions, had also read together *The Wife of Usher's Well* and *The Lochmaben Harper*, had worked up a full-scale mime to go with further readings of *Sir Patrick Spens*, and had written *The Beggar and the Hermit*, a ballad in traditional style which the whole form put together line by line one day:

> The beggar walked a-through the wood.
>   The wind did howl and rage.
> He sheltered in a hollow tree
>   Five hundred year of age.

> In there he found a golden cup,
>   Covered with silken cloth.
> He picked it up and look'd it o'er.
>   To leave it he was loth.

> 'O I will keep this cup, I will.
>   No beggar I will be,
> I'll sell it in the nearest town.
>   Fortune has come to me.'

> He hadna gone a step, a step,
>   A step but barely four,
> When he came upon a hermit-man,
>   All ragged and so poor.

''Tis mine, that golden cup, 'tis mine.
  I stole it long ago.
So give it me or you'll not live.'
  The beggar then cried, 'No!'

(and so on, at some length.)

This composite piece was the boys' last undertaking before they wrote the *Notes for Ballad-Makers* in their exercise-books (chapter 11, page 149 and page 207). These notes were meant as a sort of *aide-mémoire*, recalling what had been realised in communal experience and discussion, when each boy came to write his own ballad – a homework assignment which I set on the same occasion.

In spite of the relative sophistication of their form, I put Ballads into the first term because most of the boys at this stage are convinced that rhyme is essential to poetry. They don't all *like* this notion very much, but it is firmly *embedded* and ballad-making is a positive and fairly enjoyable way of using it. In the same term I start to extend the sense of what poetry is by calling for a piece of open verse such as the Elegy (chapter 11, page 144 and page 206): and I hope to strengthen such a sense by calling for little or no composition in rhymed verse in the following terms.

Lawrence's poems about creatures, reptiles and birds strike me as ideal for the purpose. (There is, fortunately, no novelty about saying this nowadays.) They invariably waken responsive resources with peculiar immediacy: and the craft in the poetry, hardly apparent at first in its direct and 'earned' simplicity, quickly becomes a source of real interest.

I often start out by including *Snake, Mountain Lion* and *Man and Bat* in the programme for my opening lesson. A sufficient slowness in the reading is crucial for the first two poems, to register the unfolding awarenesses and the closing melancholies, while *Man and Bat* is a poem which fairly cries out for accompaniment in mime or gesture from the reader. At the end of the lesson one or two boys usually ask where they can find one or other of these poems, and a fair amount of seeking out goes on among the anthologies in the library at the next lesson.

After this, in the third lesson, it is fairly certain that one or two of Lawrence's other animals will be introduced in the boys' readings – and I aim to read again one of my first poems (more often than not it has been *Snake*), only this time the boys follow the words on copies of the text. After this re-reading I try to bring together the notions of what-the-poetry-does and what-the-poetry-looks-like by briefly discussing the features of a short excerpt: it might, for instance, be this one.

And as he put his head into that dreadful hole,
And as he slowly drew up, snake-easing his shoulders,
    and entered farther,
A sort of horror, a sort of protest against his withdrawing
    into that horrid black hole,
Deliberately going into the blackness, and slowly drawing
    himself after,
Overcame me now his back was turned.

I looked round, I put down my pitcher,
I picked up a clumsy log
And threw it at the water-trough with a clatter.

I think it did not hit him,
But suddenly that part of him that was left behind
    convulsed in undignified haste,
Writhed like lightning, and was gone
Into the black hole, the earth-lipped fissure in the wall-front,
At which, in the intense still noon, I stared with fascination.

What I try to convey to the boys about this is that although there is
no rhyme, and no metre, the language *is* shaped. The words feel ordinary,
but they are not slack; the expression seems to be spontaneous, but it
isn't random. The lines make steps, each being a distinct 'unit' of feeling
or description. And the pauses – the spaces on the page – are not gaps
in the poem but pivot-points where something unseen and unspoken,
but definite, occurs. The shaping is done by the poet's sense of '*that's
how it was*', alert to the memory and to the actual writing. So, in this
passage, you can feel his 'sort of horror' gathering gradually, overcom-
ing him, as the long-drawn lines move and curl their slow way (they
simply cannot be properly read at speed) towards the first pause in the
extract. During that pause the 'sort of horror...sort of protest' turns
into a decision. The poet's consciousness pivots sharply outwards and
swift, concise announcements of decisive action seem to burst with
'clatter'. The consequent pause, the moment of strained looking, is the
point where protest turns towards fascination, as the note of apologetic
relief in 'I think it did not hit him' acknowledges.

Exposition of this sort is what I hope to draw from the poetry with
the boys – though not entirely in this style of language. It would be a
matter, rather, of reading a few lines aloud and then aiming to elicit
consideration of the way they *work*.

For the next few periods both Guilds will prepare, and then present,
their Verse Sessions. I give the class a theme – which in this case might
be 'Creatures and Humans' or 'Meeting Animals' – and ask each Guild
to include two or three examples of the chosen Kind in their programme
of six or eight poems. I urge the boys to avoid presenting all the poems
in the same style: and I try to help them with their ideas without impos-

ing my own. The final decisions on which poems shall go into the programme, in which order, and in what style of performance, are taken by
the Masters of Revels in council with the whole Guild.

These periods tend to be filled with discussion and general bustle, for
there is a lot to arrange: general stage-setting, music to accompany or
link the poems, mime and movement for some of them, costumes where
needed, a lighting scheme – all this as well as the fundamental business
of deciding who will read the poems (a task not exclusively reserved for
the Master Players) and then giving the performers a chance to practise.
From all the varied activity a fair degree of group co-ordination somehow emerges, and after two or three periods each Guild uses a whole
lesson to present its performance to the other. In the course of all this
work the boys will find themselves attending, several times over, to at
least three or four animal poems by Lawrence: in this sense, *his* voice
will be the main one in the proceedings, and it is through the repeated
contact with it, the growing familiarity, that the boys really begin to
know what manner of man it is, what specialness of human *being*, that
is speaking to them.

This becomes apparent in quite uncomplicated performances. I
remember, for instance, a simple but moving rendering of *Mountain
Lion* by four boys. Two were the Mexicans, carrying an imaginary lion
between them slung from a real staff across their shoulders: the other
two were the poet and his companion. The poet read the whole poem
except for the Spanish phrases; the companion asked 'Que tiene, amigo?';
one of the Mexicans replied 'León'; and the companion commented
later, 'Hermoso es!' They read from copies of the poem, and mimed as
they went along, the two Englishmen starting from the back of the
auditorium and the two Mexicans coming from the Tiring House in the
first pause of the poem. They mimed chiefly in the pauses, doing briefly
but carefully the hesitation, the meeting, the 'smiling foolishly', the
lifting of the dead lion's head, the parting. Some of the rostra were piled
high at the back of the stage, and when the meeting was over the boy
who was Lawrence climbed to the top and there discovered in mime the
lion's lair, while his companion stayed watching him from stage level.

The whole performance was done in bright white light, and some
solemn music played quietly at the end. Although one of the actors had
had nothing at all to say, and two more next to nothing, the experience
of the poem had been *made* by all four, and *shared* by the whole class.
The two lads who spoke the Spanish had gone to some pains to get the
pronunciation right, but in the event it was not the accent that impressed
us all but the *tone* of the words, which caught the shades of feeling
behind the language – the uneasiness in the matter-of-fact question,
'Que tiene, amigo?'; the embarrassment in the bold answer, 'León –';

and the admiration fused with regret in the comment on the dead creature, once the distinction of its beauty had been fully taken, 'Hermoso
es!' Lawrence spoke as strongly at these points as anywhere else in the
poem.

Catching the creatureliness, in words that define sharply while they
carry the true tenor of the observer's feelings, this is the essential art
in the composition of these poems. In the lesson that follows the second
of the Guild Verse Sessions I try to draw attention to it, not by giving
notes but by discussing some more extracts and then asking the boys to
write their own poems on the spot. For discussion purposes the following two extracts, from *Baby Tortoise* and *Fish*, are among those that have
proved most useful (though I have not dwelt on either poem *as a whole*
in class).

> You know what it is to be born alone,
> Baby tortoise!
>
> The first day to heave your feet little by little from the shell,
> Not yet awake,
> And remain lapsed on earth,
> Not quite alive.
>
> A tiny, fragile, half-animate bean.
> To open your tiny beak-mouth, that looks as if it would never open,
> Like some iron door;
> To lift the upper hawk-beak from the lower base
> And reach your skinny little neck
> And take your first bite at some dim bit of herbage,
> Alone, small insect,
> Tiny bright-eye,
> Slow one.

> I have waited with a long rod
> And suddenly pulled a gold-and-greenish, lucent fish from below,
> And had him fly like a halo round my head,
> Lunging in the air on the line.
>
> Unhooked his gorping, water-horny mouth,
> And seen his horror-tilted eye,
> His red-gold, water-precious, mirror-flat bright eye;
> And felt him beat in my hand, with his mucous, leaping life-throb.

When I talk with the boys about these passages, I start from the
apparently free flow of the verse, where the poet seems to be setting
down his impressions even as they are arising. In this free-flowing
manner we seem to come specially close both to the living man and to
the creature he responds to. I suggest that this close feeling springs from
two simultaneous kinds of acuteness in Lawrence's way of *looking*. He

looks hard enough to find the wonder and distinction of the creature's being, particularly when he moves over into its nature for a moment and, so to speak, sees things from its angle ('The first day to *heave* your feet little by little from the shell...And take your first bite at some *dim* bit of herbage'; 'And seen his *horror*-tilted eye...'). And he looks hard enough into language to find the words that will keep his meaning really sharp – sometimes in a sudden deft stroke ('...what it is *to be born alone*...': '...And had him *fly like a halo round my head*...'), sometimes in an accumulation of facets ('A tiny, fragile, half-animate bean': '...his gorping, water-horny mouth...'). The bright eye of the fish is distinctly different from the bright eye of the tortoise. Both are acutely evoked, and the acuteness is fruitful discussion-ground in class – and, as part of it, Lawrence's way of making two words into a single new one by using a hyphen is often considered. Is 'water-horny', for instance, simply the sum of 'watery' and 'horny', or something more? And how does a tortoise have a 'beak-mouth'?

After spending just over half the lesson in this sort of discussion, I ask the boys to use the last fifteen minutes or so to write their own animal poems, on the spot. Before they start, I suggest a possible title or two. I remind them that each line should make a 'step' and it may be of any length. I remark again on the fact that spaces between lines indicate something which happens but is not announced – like a shift of viewpoint or a move from 'observing' to 'feeling'. And that is all.

. Usually, as the writing gets into its stride, the silence in the room takes on a sort of concentrated charge. Each boy grows absorbed in his own 'looking'. By the time the bell goes most of them have written something with some substance in it, though few, if any, have finished. Sometimes one or two are actually reluctant to break off.

Here are two typical fifteen-minute poems from such a session. I had offered 'Ladybird' as an optional title.

> I was writing in my room.
> Suddenly a sound.
> No bigger than a water-drop.
> There! On my book.
> Red! Something red was moving across my book.
> It was a Ladybird, with all six wire-thin legs ponding at my book.
> It post-box red was covered with black spots
> Seven! Little drops of ink in a sea of blood.
> But why did it come here.
> To land in the baren wilderness of my book.
> He stopped, and looked round with pin prick eyes.
> The red case opened and out came two wings.
> Beautiful like lace.
> Transparent.

> I met an earwig
> A small, long, scab of shining shell;
> With its petty pincer raised in defiance of me.
>
> I could have killed it with my thumb-nail,
> But why should I?
>
> Its tiny head, with two small-jointed feelers,
> Waved uncertainly.
>
> How many earwigs are there like this one?
> A million million?
> More?
>
> Each complete in itself,
> Each a mirror-image of the next.

Clearly this verse is still in a fairly rough state; and much in the lines is 'derivative'. One can find, for instance, echoes of the staccato style of *Man and Bat* and the note of half-indignant wonder from *Snake* ('There! On my book. Red! Something red was moving across my book'). One can find the undertone of compassion, as it informs *Baby Tortoise* and *Fish* – indeed, as it informs *all* the animal poetry of Lawrence ('But why did it come here. To land in the baren wilderness of my book'). One can find a straight legacy from the experience of *Snake* ('I could have killed it with my thumb-nail, But why should I?'). And the *format* of the voice on the page – in matters of line-division, pausing, epithet-formation, and so on – is obviously 'borrowed' from Lawrence.

But of course it is not any apparent expertise in borrowing that makes these brief, unfinished pieces admirable. They deserve respect, rather, for *what the derived format has helped to release in the individual writers* – an acuteness, a delicacy with senses and feelings, in the apprehension of personal, remembered experience. As a specific example of this I might cite the first writer's deft economy in simultaneously recording and measuring this ladybird's arrival –

> Suddenly a sound.
> No bigger than a water-drop.
> There! On my book.

– or the way he catches the little surprise of seeing its wings, the suddenness modulating into an arrested, close-up attention –

> The red case opened and out came two wings.
> Beautiful like lace.
> Transparent.

The second writer's attention goes further than this –

> A small, long, scab of shining shell;
> With its petty pincer raised in defiance of me.

In his poem the creature is observed with precision (how exactly right, for example, is that word 'scab'), but its pettiness is acknowledged along with its 'otherness'. That is to say, its *status* is appreciated as well as its form; and the effect is to keep the writer's sympathy restrained to a *hint* in the description. In its spaces as well as in its lines, this poem is aware of how ordinary the insect is while showing respect for its particularity – respect that has grown near to, but not quite committed to, a tone of wonder by the time the lines break off –

> How many earwigs are there like this one?
> A million million?
> More?
>
> Each complete in itself,
> Each a mirror-image of the next.

In these last two lines, that register so gently the mystery of natural plenitude and design perceived in one insect ('mirror-image' catches a remarkable, if not fearful, symmetry), the acuteness belongs entirely to the boy: it is not something mechanically or fortuitously derived from playing with Lawrence's way with words. In both poems, in fact, the boys have 'looked' and 'made' for themselves. Written in some sense after a model, both poems are also works of creative sensibility.

I do not think it is fanciful to see in these two boys' 'ad hoc' poetry a personal coming-to-life in the word, roused by the life in the words of Lawrence. When a boy composes at his best in this way, he does indeed write 'not as a creature that swallows what it takes in, crude, raw and undigested: but that feeds with an appetite and hath a stomach to concoct, divide and turn all into nourishment': and 'Imitatio' is then something that quite transcends pastiche or parody.

In order to strike while the iron is hot, after the lesson in which these first efforts are made I ask for a complete Animal Poem from each boy as his next English homework. I leave the choice of subject open, but urge them to choose an animal they have really *met*, as opposed to one they have merely seen. As a result poems like these are often handed in.

A Frog

There was a rustling in the long, damp grass.
A swishing.
And silence.
Another swish, and there, sitting on the grass,
Was a frog.

He sat gulping, as if in deep meditation.
He stared, wide-eyed, unblinking,
With his glass-flat eyes,
Black in the centre, surrounded by white tinted with gold.
He gulped, his sides wobbling,

With his fish-belly-white underside resting on the ground.

He seemed somehow unreal.
As if to reassure myself,
I touched him.

He leapt, on to the palm of my other hand,
Like a blob of wet, palpitating dough.

His eyes were fish-like,
Covered by a fine network of golden lines, hair thin.
His back was olive green.
Dotted haphazardly about on it were black spots,
Raised up from his pitted skin.

His webbed feet strike cold on the palm of my hand.

He is an outcast in the world,
One of the most despised of creatures.
Yet to me he is somehow one of the most beautiful.
His lips are ruler-straight,
Giving him a permanent grin.
He is like a creature from the past,
A link with the times of huge reptiles,
All long dead.

His eyes are fascinating;
Though flat, they seem strangely intelligent,
Looking out at the world with a laugh.

With a power-packed jerk from his hind legs, he leaps,
Leaps into the water,
Escapes from the giant horror of dry land,
And is gone.

Hamster

Eyes.
Two eyes, deep-brown jewels
Emerging from a snow-white nest.
A nest, his bed.
The Hamster.

The cage, his home,
The world he knows so well,
His only world.
Perhaps he longs for Freedom,
The yellow-patched forest of grass.

Then should I take off the lid and say,
'Now, go'?
But no, he lingers as if some invisible thread held him back,
Back into the dark shadow of his cage.

Why does he not leap out?
Right out of his metal prison?
Food.
Food – his daily measure of seed,
Black-white seeds,
That he holds with unmoving stillness in his hands,
Almost human hands,
Daintily poised, so as not to miss a morsel.

Grain-filled cheeks with wisely-stored nourishment for lean, meagre times
Bulging beneath his ears,
A Lilliput lion grimace.

At night,
When all is dark,
An ominous creak breaks the stillness,
The creak of the wheel turning round,
As the nimble Dwarf treads on the rungs of the endless ladder;
An acrobatic feat.

Suddenly a minute bear grips tree-like cage bars
In an alien forest.
I am near, a comforter
Peering into his small world –
A secret understanding between his and our race.

In both of these pieces there are fairly obvious weak spots (for example, that too-good-to-be-true leap of the frog when touched, or the tautology of the hamster's 'unmoving stillness'); in both there are some momentary – and probably unconscious – echoes of expressions in the poems of Lawrence that I have referred to. Such weak spots and echoes strike me as small matters, minor consequences of 'feeding with an appetite'. Far more important (because it generally occurs in the poem of each member of the class to a significant extent) is the fact that catching in words the 'creatureliness' of their chosen animal has involved these writers (as it involved Lawrence) in meeting it with their own 'kindness' – in the dual and Shakespearean sense of that word. In such a process of creative sensibility lies the kind of nourishment that Ben Jonson speaks of.

In another term Chinese Verse, in the translations of Ezra Pound and Arthur Waley, will be our 'certain sort of poetry'. It is a particularly engaging verse-form for young readers and writers, for reasons that can, I hope, be fairly readily reduced from *Notes for Chinese Verse* (chapter 11, p. 195).

General procedure in the sequence of lessons is much the same as that which I have described, except that I encourage the use of *tableau* as a performing medium in the Guild Verse Sessions. Tableau is appropriate to the picture-making element in this poetry, and effective work in it involves the whole Guild organisation and most of the Mummery's technical resources. The 'dreary sorrow at the North Gate' in Pound's superb translation of Rihaku, for instance, can become an even more powerful presence when the impact of the voice – or better still, voices – is supported by a bare stage-setting, a few figures carefully poised and costumed, a well-adjusted light or two, and a quiet musical fade-in.

Lament of the Frontier Guard

By the North Gate the wind blows full of sand,
Lonely from the beginning of time until now!

Trees fall, the grass grows yellow with autumn.
I climb the towers and towers to watch out the barbarous land:

Desolate castle, the sky, the wide desert.
There is no wall left to this village.
Bones white with a thousand frosts,
High heaps, covered with trees and grass;

Who brought this to pass?
Who has brought the flaming imperial anger?
Who has brought the army with drums and with kettle drums?

Barbarous kings.

A gracious spring, turned to blood-ravenous autumn,
A turmoil of wars-men, spread over the middle kingdom,
Three hundred and sixty thousand,
And sorrow, sorrow like rain.
Sorrow to go, and sorrow, sorrow returning.
Desolate, desolate fields,
And no children of warfare upon them,
No longer the men for offence and defence.

Ah, how shall you know the dreary sorrow at the North Gate
With Rihaku's name forgotten
And we guardsmen, fed to the tigers.

There can be much advantage in having a poem like this delivered by several single voices. (In fact the poem as it is here printed has been prepared for such a reading, the spaces in its layout being a liberty taken with Pound's original after a discussion in class.) The class can be contained 'within' the poem, in a near-literal way, if the readers are spread in the shadows that surround actors and audience: the rise and fall in mood, the inner shifts of feeling, can be the more clearly pointed: and readers and listeners alike can be helped to grasp the way in which this kind of poetry is shaped in sharp-minted impressions and images.

The abundance of excellent translations by Arthur Waley makes it easy to choose a fine example as focus for teacher-guided discussion –

from which *Notes for Chinese Verse* arise. On different occasions I have used for this purpose *Fighting South of the Ramparts, Plucking the Rushes* (which is also the title of an admirable collection of Chinese verse, edited by David Holbrook and published by Heinemann – all that a teacher needs), *At Fifteen I Went With The Army, The Little Cart, The Red Cockatoo*, or this –

The Herd Boy

> In the southern village the boy who minds the ox
> With his naked feet stands on the ox's back.
> Through the hole in his coat the river wind blows;
> Through his broken hat the mountain rain pours.
> On the long dyke he seemed to be far away;
> In the narrow lane suddenly we were face to face.
>
> The boy is home and the ox is back in its stall;
> And a dark smoke oozes through the thatched roof.

Here, the distinguishing feature of this kind of poetry – the way the language makes pictures 'that hint at feelings or situations', conveying them 'in a kind of picture-shorthand' – is very clear. It is perhaps at its most impressive in the fifth and sixth lines, and in the closing two, with the 'line' of silence connecting them. Almost all the craft that *Notes for Chinese Verse* point out appears here, especially the 'distinct rhythm' in each line and the way 'the choice of words is all-important'. The boys are quick to grasp, for instance, how the sense of exposure in the third and fourth lines of the poem accumulates force from the repeated sentence-shape; or how the situation is held in the balance by the pattern of 'On the long dyke...far away / In the narrow lane...face to face'. Similarly they can all feel how language is being 'exact and delicate' in the slight thrust given to the word 'suddenly', or in the way the verb 'oozes through' spreads itself in the last line.

In following up discussion with a homework assignment, I give the boys the choice of composing a number of short poems or one or two longer ones. I suggest plenty of possible titles; the list for Nigel Cooper's class, for instance, ran like this – *Discovery, Awakening at Night, Defeat, Blind, Sudden Strangeness, Peace, Stargazing, Black, Forsaken, The Return, Firelight, Old Age*; but the boys are free to choose any of their own rather than these. This freedom is an important condition if they are really to catch 'moments of life that seem particularly vivid'.

Frequently, as I read the results, I come upon short pieces which, to judge from a certain abandon in such matters as handwriting and punctuation, have not cost their writers much labour; for all that, they may be genuinely poetic expressions. Nigel Cooper's *Peace* (p. 196) is a case in point. His *Venus Fly-trap* (p. 197), an unexceptional, spry little poem, with a subtle tone about its last line, probably did not take long to compose either. In such cases I don't think the lack of labour should be deplored (unless it is accompanied by really messy presentation, when it should be the *untidiness* that is rebuked). The fact is that many children can do well in this style of composition without much strain: and one ought not to seem to grumble about that.

They can do well in a variety of ways. Some, like Paterson, find the Chinese *setting* attractive, as well as the manner. He starts his poem called *The Last Resting Place of the Pirate Junk* like this –

> The wood of the junk is green, rotten and damp,
> It is holed in many places for ever;
> Dead barnacles still cling in hundreds to its sides,
> Those that live, white as snow, cling to those now dead.
> The muddy water drips, drips, from the rotting hull,
> The slimy seaweed hangs in tattered wreaths.
>
> Lin Chow remembers the junk from his boyhood:
> It was feared by all the honest men of the land,
> For its captain, Won Soo, was both cruel and wicked.
> Then it sailed with great treasure in its vast holds,
> Now in its watery holds, fishes swim, crabs dance...

There's some art in the presentation of those pastiche-Chinamen; but there's more, and greater, in the strangely elegiac language that describes the junk. How sensitively he *sees* it, without wasting a word.

Other boys adopt a Chinese setting much less blatantly. This, for instance, is how Reece realises his sense of what it is to be *Blind*.

> You see the peach blossom carpet the fertile earth.
> I do not.
> You see the elegant swans ripple the surface.
> I do not.
> For you the reeds toss and sway.
> For me the breeze whistles through the grasses.
> The kingfisher is azure, turquoise, gorgeous in its colours.
> To a blind man the kingfisher is black.
> Everything is black.

Most boys, however, leave the *settings* of Chinese verse quite alone: but its *voice* becomes an instrument of discovery for their own feelings. Dakin, for instance, reflects on *Stargazing* like this –

> The stars gleam and twinkle,
> Pinpricks of light in a black ceiling.
> The same stars shone on armour, chariots, and swords.
> Stars that form dragons, bears, giants.
> Stars, ancient, undying.
> That shone yesterday, will shine tomorrow.

Sometimes, like Soames, they choose to adopt a *persona* –

Old Age

Pipe, coat and a glass of beer
On a sunny seat by the river under the draping willows.
Children stare at me then run away.
Have they no respect for me?

More often, like Jenkins (a plump, bookish, amiable boy) they speak
straight from themselves —

Cricket

White-shirted boys with bats in hands,
White-shirted bowler with the ball in his hand,
White-shirted fielders with crouching bodies,
And I, the scorer.
Pencil in hand, content to jot down runs,
Byes,
Wides,
Boundaries,
Sixes.
Glad to be away from the flurry
And the bustle.
Glad to be away from the bowling,
Leg and off-spins.
Glad to be away from the jeers of fielders,
Cries of 'Howzat?'
I am content.

The boys' poems in this chapter are representative examples of a
response to a teaching approach which aims 'to leave some distinct
impressions of certain sorts of poetry' by leading, in each fresh undertaking, to composition in the same style – that is to say, by making
positive use of the principle of 'Imitatio'. This approach appears to confine, by presenting a model. But I believe that this is appearance only,
that the poems quoted do celebrate, creatively, real meetings with the
spirit of 'a man speaking to men', and that they vindicate the reality of
the boys' experience of poetry.

It seems to me that the process of Imitatio enabled the boys to write
more totally their own writing. It appeared to confine, but it *actually*
released – by disturbing their experience and enabling new fibres of
imaginative sensibility to stretch out.

10. Reading

Teachers of English are frequently perturbed because the books which children choose to read and enjoy are usually not the books which teachers feel it would be good for them to read. In the content of the former we find cause for concern; while our own analytic and refining experience of the latter convinces us that children who do read these ought to find rich rewards...

Does the content of books consumed by the young reader have the bad influence which older and more analytic readers assume it has? I don't know of any final, objective proof either way.

...I would like to propose a series of aphorisms which I would like to see discussed. I do not believe that they contain the entire truth, or that they contain an infallible method of leading children to a sensitive response to and enjoyment in literature, but I do think (as a devil's advocate) that they offer a new starting point for the old debate.

All else being equal:

(i) Quantity in reading is possibly more important than quality as a preparation for an ultimate sensitive response to literature, and a lasting love of reading.

(ii) Children should never be discouraged from reading anything.

(iii) Popular books, regardless of content, probably have no lasting ill-effects, if consumed in large enough quantities.

(iv) The beneficial effects of a book are in inverse proportion to the time taken to read it, e.g. a book read in two days does twice as much good as a book read in four.

From 'Popular Reading or Literature?' by O. Gaggs
in *The Use of English*, Volume 21, Number 2
(Winter 1969)

This epigraph 'tops and tails' an article which is well worth reading in full. Mr Gaggs summarises an important debate, and his own position emerges directly from his personal experience, as schoolboy and as teacher. I believe that his 'aphorisms' hold some essential truths, devil's advocacy or no.

There are no infallible methods of 'leading children to a sensitive response to and enjoyment in literature'. On the other hand there are plenty of methods that are very likely to *de*-sensitise children's responses, and as teachers we could (indeed should) strive to avoid them. We should, for instance, avoid altogether the use of Class Readers in the junior forms of secondary school. The case is put admirably plainly by

Brian Hankins in another good article in *The Use of English*, 'Enjoying Reading: Aims and Methods in the First Three Years of the Secondary School', Volume 19, Number 4 (Summer 1968). There, he writes:

One of the most damaging causes of bad teaching is the assumption that when children in school aren't taught, they don't learn. In the teaching of fiction, this assumption commonly leads to the use of Readers, the most likely consequences of which practice are, in less able pupils, an increasing sense of the unrewarding labour involved in reading anything more demanding than a comic strip and, in more able pupils, the development of keen dislikes for particular books or writers. My wife's only recently overcome dislike for George Eliot stemmed from a term's crushing boredom with *Silas Marner*, while the dislike felt by two recent fourth-year girls for *The Diary of Anne Frank* and *Shane* was the result of similar experiences in their second year. (This prompts the disturbing thought that the premature class study of a particular book is at its potentially most damaging when the book itself is good or by a good writer!)

With older classes examinations will require us to teach through Class Readers (in the form of 'set books') often enough. Such a requirement may not be wholly deplorable, for most teachers of fifth and sixth formers would feel, I am sure, that there is some potential *value*, along with the risk of damage, in *some* class study of *some* books at this stage. But nothing requires us to adopt risky tactics in the earlier years. Ideally, for children in secondary school the reading of books ought to be an experience of freedom that endures for as long as possible – freedom, that is, for the individual to *choose* and explore, to follow up personal impetuses, to indulge a 'craze' for this and then a 'craze' for that; to *use* the chances implied in Mr Gaggs' aphorisms, in fact.

In practice, I incorporate a Reading Period into the weekly English programme for all first- and second-year boys. For the First Forms this has usually been one of the English lessons that takes place outside the Mummery. For the Second Forms it's a fixed point in the weekly Mummery work which reading almost invariably fills: if work in drama or poetry or mime is at some critical stage we may use the Reading Period to push on with it, but only as an exceptional arrangement.

At the start of the first year I explain to the boys that each Reading Period will be a time set aside for private reading, so they should bring for it any book of their own choice, from a library or from home or from any other source. Any *book*, whether fiction or non-fiction – that's the point. Paperbacks, of course, are included in that category, but periodicals, papers and all kinds of magazine are not. I hasten to explain that this ban arises not because all magazines are 'bad' but because it is impossible to draw a firm line between those that it could be profitable to read in Reading Periods and those it couldn't. (In any case, the school library carries a wide range of magazines which are available to everyone every day.)

Some boys will bring, and read avidly, a different book each week:

others – including some who would probably read no books at all if Reading Period did not exist – plough steadily through a single volume for most of the term. And, of course, the teacher brings a book, and reads it to himself, like everybody else. (When one needs to convince some, if not all, of the class that reading is an activity that deserves time and some effort spent on it for its own sake, one would be foolish to do otherwise.) On average two or three boys per class per week forget to bring their books to the lesson, so I keep a supply of texts in the Mummery (Dickens, Stevenson, Buchan, Williamson and others) and lend them out. I make a fuss, by design, about the forgetfulness; but I always let the books go out on extended loan if the boys ask to keep them, to finish the story, at the end of the period. It's surprising how often boys who have started to read *A Tale of Two Cities* on these occasions *do* ask this.

Two or three times a term, in an informal, unpremeditated way, arising perhaps from curiosity or a whim of mine ('I wonder what they'd make of this . . . ?' from what I'm reading) or from a boy's comment or question ('Do you think it all really *did* happen just like that in Gerald Durrell's books?') Reading Period turns into a reading discussion. Usually we find ourselves talking about a particular genre of literature – the adventure yarn, say, or war stories (fictional and real-life) or animal books or Westerns or detective stories, historical novels, science fiction. I try to make my rôle simply a chairmanly one, never a censuring one, by joining in the discussion only to focus a point from time to time or to send things in a new direction if talk flags (as it very rarely does). People are usually eager to say what they think, and contributions range very widely, sometimes jumping from point to point with no apparent connection. Where personal 'crazes' are roused or challenged – as they repeatedly are in the very nature of this activity – feelings can run high, and discussion often tends towards debate. The Biggles series of books, for example, generally leads to a confrontation between those still ardent with enthusiasm and those whose 'craze' has worn out ('There's always a good, fast-moving story, and that's what I like.' 'It's always the same story, really.' 'The main characters go from one story to another, so you get to know them very well.' 'They're all just types!'). Sometimes I'm appealed to for an opinion in an argument, occasionally with a certain archness – 'There's nothing wrong with James Bond books, is there, Sir?' – in which case I try to sound neither evasive nor reproving; but if necessary I'll adopt a little archness of my own – 'Only if you forget what a strange kind of fairy tale they are.' (In this particular case an outcry of some kind usually follows, allowing the issues to be more plainly defined in the ensuing talk.)

So long as the teacher doesn't preach or harangue, an occasional period spent like this is a useful way of offering support to the reading habit. Such discussions (in which different people will speak up on different occasions) bring individual tastes into a social 'climate' where all – including those who contribute little or nothing vocally – can share the feeling that in reading books, and in enjoying books, and in reflecting upon books, they are doing something which is as normal a part of civilised life as talking is.

But, of course, before it can be present for any kind of social endorsement, the activity of reading is a personal and private experience. It seems to me to be proper for a teacher of English both to acknowledge and to use the individual child's privacy here – to acknowledge that the better part of it is, for the child, a kind of living that we cannot expect to *dissect*; and to use our opportunity for fostering his powers of communication and judgement through what we *can* ask him to say about it.

So, I ask each boy to keep his own Reading Diary – a notebook in which he writes a brief report on each book that he reads during his first two years in the school. Some of the boys would find this a difficult thing to do without a set pattern for the report, so when I issue the notebooks, early in the first term, I dictate a short note for the first page on 'How to Use this Diary' (title of book, author's name, brief account of the story or subject-matter, brief account of what was liked and/or disliked – a pattern that is a simple fore-runner of that used later for Book Reviewing, see p. 163 and p. 209). I aim to devote one homework period in every four or five – i.e. one every two weeks or so – to Reading Diaries, though many boys prefer to treat their diary as a sort of running assignment, writing each report as they finish each book, regardless of the 'official' homeworks. This is a very acceptable arrangement, by which, in general, they give rather more time and attention to their Reading Diaries than under the alternative scheme.

Simply as an information service, with *no* kind of syllabus-intention lurking in the background, I give out the following duplicated book-list for the boys to stick in the back of their diaries – and from time to time some of them do refer to it. It gives, like all selective lists, an indication of the compiler's personal tastes and preferences; it gives a deliberate reminder of the existence of authors from the past; and its one-title-per-author policy goes with an eye on the stock of the school library regarding further titles.

From 11 to 13: A Selected Reading List
This list is not arranged in any order of importance, but those books with their titles in capital letters are outstanding of their kind and well worth the effort of reading. Usually only one book by each author is named: if you enjoy it, you can find your own way to others.

1. Books by Older Authors
Twain: TOM SAWYER and HUCKLEBERRY FINN
Jefferies: BEVIS
Stevenson: KIDNAPPED
Marryat: Mr. Midshipman Easy
Fenimore Cooper: DEERSLAYER and THE LAST OF THE MOHICANS
Scott: The Heart of Midlothian
Dickens: A TALE OF TWO CITIES
Ballantyne: Coral Island
Collins: The Moonstone
Dumas: The Three Musketeers
Verne: 20,000 Leagues Under The Sea
London: The Call of the Wild
Fitzpatrick: Jock of the Bushveld
Haggard: Allan Quartermain
Kipling: Kim
Henty: Bonnie Prince Charlie
Masefield: BIRD OF DAWNING
Conan Doyle: The White Company
Buchan: Tales of Hannay
Hope: The Prisoner of Zenda
Conrad: Youth

2. Books by Authors of Our Own Time
Guillot: COMPANIONS OF FORTUNE
Church: The Cave
Kästner: Emil and the Detectives
Muhlenweg: BIG TIGER AND CHRISTIAN
Schmeltzer: THE LONG ARCTIC NIGHT
Corbett: Man Eater of Kumaon
Hodges: Columbus Sails
Grey Owl: Adventures of Sajo
Armstrong: Sea Change
Dawlish: Dauntless Finds Her Crew
Ransome: We Didn't Mean To Go To Sea: GREAT NORTHERN?
Sperry: The Boy Who Was Afraid
Rawlings: THE YEARLING
Welch: The Gauntlet
Harnett: THE WOOLPACK
Manfred: Timpetill
Sutcliff: THE SHIELD RING
Mayne: The World Upside Down
Trease: The Hills of Varna
Carruthers: The Forest is My Kingdom
Tomlinson: The Haunted Forest
Bell: CORDUROY
Vipont: The Lark in the Morn
Forester: The Gun
Craigie: Dark Atlantis

Wells: The Time Machine
Severn: Dream Gold
Pertwee: The Islanders
Hogg: Sealed Orders
Saville: Redshanks Warning
Seligman: Thunder Reef
Williamson: TARKA THE OTTER
Guillot: KPO THE LEOPARD
Garnett: THE FAMILY FROM ONE END STREET
Collis: Marco Polo
Mountevans: South With Scott
Morrow: The Splendid Journey
Noyce: South Col
Heyerdahl: THE KON-TIKI EXPEDITION
Mowat: People of the Deer
Doorly: The Microbe Man
Mason: Socrates, The Man Who Asked Questions
Manston: ALBERT SCHWEITZER
Grimble: A PATTERN OF ISLANDS
Durrell: The Overloaded Ark
Lorenz: King Solomon's Ring
Falkner: Moonfleet
Garfield: Devil-in-the-Fog
Pearce: TOM'S MIDNIGHT GARDEN
Southall: Ash Road
Laye: THE AFRICAN CHILD
Serraillier: The Silver Sword
Williams: Elephant Bill
Warner: MEN AND GODS
Treece: Viking's Dawn

De La Mare: Collected Rhymes
Reeves: Blackbird in the Lilac
Walsh: The Truants
Eliot: Old Possum's Book of Practical Cats
Faber: The Faber Book of Children's Verse

About twice a term I call in the Reading Diaries for a read-through, when I try to fit a marking-scheme to a set of widely differing performances (see p. 220) Some notebooks will contain twenty to thirty entries per term, others will have only three or four. It would be hopelessly misguided to try to *force* the unprolific readers into undertaking more. I try to encourage them to make the most of what they *can* do when, two or three times a year, I talk to the class as a whole about the task of keeping a Reading Diary. Then I emphasise three possible ways of 'doing well'. The first, most obviously, is to read plenty of books, with a good variety in the choice. The second is to make really interesting and attentive *comments* on the books one reads (many boys rest content with a quick outline of the story or subject-matter followed by a sentence or two to the effect that 'I thought this was a very good (bad, or indifferent) book'). And the third – particularly open to those who read little – is to keep the diary extremely neat and well-written. The three possibilities do not necessarily go together, and no one need exclude himself from virtue on all three counts (though some boys *will* manage to do so, in spite of all exhortations).

I do not hesitate to ask for extra private reading from the class if I have to be away from school or if asked to provide work for a colleague who is away, since the boys cannot do too much of it. In my opinion private reading is, in itself, a dramatic function, by which the word on the page is carried alive into the heart where powers of imaginative sympathy must inevitably be stirred into action and re-action. As Lawrence said of the novel, 'It is the way our sympathy flows and recoils that really determines our lives.' Reading (and not *only* the reading of fiction) 'exercises' the sympathetic consciousness in manifold subtleties of flow and recoil; and thereby it extends a child's very capacity for experience, it helps him, so to speak, to grow more human.

There are functional benefits, too, to be gained from the habit of private reading. As Frank Whitehead says in his fine chapter on Reading and Literature in *The Disappearing Dais*, 'Just as in earlier years the accumulated experience of listening to other people speaking enabled the child to acquire his intuitive grasp of the patterns of speech, so now for the older child the accumulated experience of reading builds up gradually an intuitive sense of the patterns and structures of the written language. Through it comes increased vocabulary, the ability to spell, to punctuate, the ability to write.'

Beyond that, I am inclined to share the 'instinctive and private conviction' of Mr Gaggs:

...The habitual book reader has been taught by the medium that every situation and every action has a multiplicity of causes and consequences. He is more likely to arrive at private and considered judgements, more likely to have the ability to make objective assessments and to be aware of subjective attitudes. He has experienced the privacy of his own mind. The non-reader is more liable to random and spontaneous behaviour and judgements, more likely to assume the popular public poses and opinions. For all of the above I have no evidence whatsoever, beyond an instinctive and private conviction that it is probably true.

11. Writing

From the outset we must make sure that the child understands what we require of him when we tell him to 'use his imagination'. There is a tendency for this phrase to be used sporadically by the teacher without there being any opportunity for the child to develop, over a period of time, his understanding of what is involved, namely, a *real mental discipline*. As he assimilates this and as his interest grows accordingly, we shall see in the classroom the beginnings of that climate of heightened awareness – of exciting mental exploration and extension of experience – that is our aim.

In order that the child may recognise and respond readily to the demand being made of him, it is important to be consistent; whether we are dealing with the purely visual aspect of imagination or with more complex sense impressions, our lessons need to have certain stable features.

From 'The First Year: The Rediscovery of the Familiar'
in *Sense and Sensitivity* by J. W. Patrick Creber

Although no two classes ever follow identical courses of written work, the programme is conceived as a developing, two-year course with 'certain stable features' apparent in the kinds of composition. To put the matter over-simply, extension of sense perception is the chief purpose behind ideas for the first year, while extension of imaginative power is the aim for the second: and, deliberately, there is a considerable overlap.

During his two years in the Mummery, Nigel Cooper's end-of-term reports regularly gave him a class-position in English somewhere between tenth and twentieth, out of thirty-one boys. His Written Work Book is as typical a one as I can find, the writing in it being – in the *strict* sense of the adverb – nicely representative of the average quality.

A transcript of his whole six terms' work follows, thus:

Rules for Written Work

1. Always leave a blank line under the heading.

2. Do not write too many words on a line.

3. Always rule off a completed piece of work.

4. Always take a fresh side for a fresh piece of work.

5. Remember the final full stop.

Notes for Explorer

1. Exploring, here, means becoming as alert as possible about the details of ordinary day-to-day doings.

2. As you think about the activities and feelings that go to make up whatever it is you are exploring, these are the questions to ask yourself (in whatever order seems helpful).

   What can I see?
   What do I hear?
   What can I smell?
   What do I taste, in reality or in imagination?

   What do I touch or feel?
   What thoughts go through my mind?

3. Don't become too absorbed in story-telling. Concentrate on discovering as much as possible.

4. Write as naturally and "speakingly" as you can. Keep the sentences mainly short, Make your words as exact as possible.

5. Start at the beginning of the activity itself and move stage by stage through it, asking yourself whichever questions seem most helpful as you go along.

6. It is best to leave the more obvious things out. Concentrate on what interests you most of all.

⑦

<u>Exploration I</u>

<u>~~Going~~ Falling Asleep</u>

I think that the best way to go to sleep,
is not counting sheep. ~~but to~~ Make sure that the
room is dark, pull the bedclothes up to your
chin, turn over, shut your eyes, and before you know
where you are, you are asleep.

As I lie in bed the shadows of the trees
outside ~~through~~ throw grotesque shadows on my
bedroom wall. Bats fly past catching insects
atracted by the light, (if I am reading). If it
is raining the water gurgles along the gutter
and trickles down the drain pipe. Usually you
can hear Screech Owls hunting mice and shrews,
their silent flight aided by downy wing feathers.
Occasionally you can hear headgehoge grunting
while ~~seach~~ searching for snails and slugs and
leaving tracks in the dewy grass. As my
bedroom faces west I can see the lovely
colours of the setting sun.

~~But~~ But eventually I fall asleep, ~~my~~ my eyes
slowly close; I am asleep

⑫

141

Exploration II

Frying a Sausage.

The liquid fat slowly ouses out from the solid lump and spreads across the pan. It reminds me of the tide coming in and sluggishly flowing across the sand. Then I drop in the sausages and stand back in case the sizzling fat splashes into my eyes. The tiny dropps of fat look like little fleas trying to jump out of the frying pan. When the sausages are brown on one side I turn them over so that they are cooked on the other side as well. When the bread (the sausages contain bread) is warmed it swells, this causes wierd contortions to project from their otherwise smooth skin. A delicious odour wafts up from the succulant sausages, they remind me of fat, sunburnt sunbathers lying on a crowded beach soaking in the suns rays. When the sausages are cooked all over, I carefully lift them out and settle down to a delicious meal of fried sausages.

(14)

142

Handwriting and Punctuation.

The Wife of Usher's Well.

There was a wife of Usher's well,
And a wealthy wife was she;
She had three stout and stalwart sons,
And sent them o'er the sea.

They hadna been a week from her,
A week but barely ane,
When word came to the carline wife
That her three sons were gane.

They hadna been a week from her,
A week but barely three,
When word came to the carline wife
That her sons she'd never see.

⑧

143

An Elegy ~~Spo~~ for King Arthur, Spoken by Sir Bedivere.

"Ah, my Lord Arthur,
What shall become of me.
Now you are gone from me,
And leave me here alone
Among mine enemies
Multitudes shall weep, my Lord, and your name
will forever be ~~~~ remembered.
Why did you ~~your son~~ kill Sir Mordred, your son?
When thou knew your life was at stake,
But alas you are now in the Vale of Avilon,
Whence no man returns
But enjoys eternal happiness.
Multitudes shall weep, my lord, and your name
will forever be remembered.
Yea, you were swifter than eagles,
And lions could not face your might;
Your cunning was greater than the leopard's
lurking in the shadows;
Your wisdom was beyond all understanding
And your courage was greater than the gods,
Multitudes shall weep, my lord, and your name
will forever be ~~rend~~ remembered."

(14)

Free Writing

A An aeroplane taking off, excitement the engines cut out, slow sea swell, going up a spiral staircase. Picture on right wall of mum. Shooting down a slope on a sledge, ~~hiccup~~ hiccup, saloon car going through the countryside. Coming to a slow stop, fanfare. Crescendo. Royalty, a dirge. Distant guns, firing rythmetically. Birds in the morning. ~~Falling~~ down endless depths. X15 breaking the flying record.

Fun and games, football, cricket, digging a hole, trumpets, crucibles, sand and glasses of water, archaeologists uncovering a mummy ~~skulls, Pr free spec~~ glasses, cars, paper, lines, Hair. Black shoes. Plastic records, magnesium oxidization, ~~red~~, orange fire, 6 blue warts, tea-cosies, a film, Scotland Yard. PC 49, Z-Cars. Television ~~bth~~ Wireless valves. A pen making circles on a piece of paper. Geometry sets. The gym

getting out of bed, getting dressed.
Breakfast. Buses. Red. Blue. Grass. An
aeroplane, landing doors blinds. black.
Harp. Lantern, pyramid, weaving. Spotlights,
fencing. Swords. The Death of King Arthur.
Lies, Bed. Chair Table Bench. School. The
cross-country. Water in the vice, Ice, cold,
snow, winter summer leaves falling. Fire
surf. Life-boats, drowning, Rockets, Guy Fawkes.
Bonfires, leaves.

Exploration III

Climbing a Tree.

The huge oak tree on which I am now precariously perched must be at least a thousand years old. I think as I haul myself up to the next thick branch. The ~~but~~ birds sing gaily, and ~~so~~ somewhere near by a late cuckoo pipes its hollow notes. An ~~unusual~~ unusual smell, not to my taste is created as my hands rub the moss off the green bark. As I heave myself over a bulbous piece of wood, deformed by fungal growths, I see ~~saw~~ a pair of large solemnly unblinking eyes gazing stolidly at me. It is ~~was~~ an owl! After what seems an age it uttered a screaming cry and silently launches itself out of its hole.

As soon as I reach the top, I look around, I am higher than any other tree in sight. The motorway in the distance looked like a piece of charcoal with ants crawling along it. After seeing my watch I will have to hurry to be home for supper so I decend ~~reminded~~ ful of the Proverb:-

"More Haste, Less Speed."

(12)

Notes for Ballad-Makers

1. The rhythm for a ballad goes like this:

    Te-Tum, te-tum, te-tum,
    Te-tar, te-tar, te-tar,
    Te-tum, te-tum, te-tum, te-tum,
    Te-tar, te-tar, te-tar,

    The first line has four feet, the second three, the third four and the fourth three. So the pattern of heavy beats goes four-three-four-three.

    You can leave out a <u>light</u> beat from any foot or you can put in a <u>light</u> beat as an extra in any foot, but you must always keep to the right number of <u>heavy</u> beats.

    They hadna sailed a league, a league,
    A league but barely three,
    Until she espied his cloven foot,
    And she wept right bitterlie

2. A strong and clear story is the first

need. It can be your own, of or from
History, or from old Legend.

3. The first need of the actual story telling
is _repetition_. Words, phrase, lines, couplets, whole,
stanzas. may be repeated. Near-repeats or
repeats with variations also add to the Ballad
efect.

4. It is most important that a large amount
of the story should be told by using the
voices of the characters in it.

5. The story must be told in separate and
distinct scenes, and most of the unexciting
parts in between are left out.

6. Rhyme: only one ~~thyme is~~ rhyme is
needed in each stanza. It comes with the
last word of the last line which matches
the last word of the second line. That is
to say only the second and fourth
rhyme.

7. To sum up: a Ballad needs the drama of distinct scenes; plenty of repetition; plenty of talk; only one ~~rhyme~~ rhyme on the last word of each stanza; and a firm rhythm with strong, clear beats

⑥

A Ballad.

The Sinking of the Nancy Lee.

Around the headland came a ship.
Its name was the "Nancy Lee".
Its captain was called Bloody Bill.
No pirate ~~was~~ worse than he.

She had three stout and stalwart masts,
And cannons five and twenty,
Below were many powder barrels,
And cannon balls a plenty.

Suddenly a shot rang out,
And splashed into the sea,
And on the port there was in sight
A ship. "The Victory."

"Run up the sails," cried Bloody Bill,
His face alive with glee,
"We'll fight this dirty English ship,
And see which one shall flee.

The captain of "The Victory."
("His name was captain Bill)
Said to his merry men, said he.
"These pirates we must kill."
_____

They hadn sailed a league, a league,
A league but barely three,
When suddenly a shot ~~sang~~ rang out,
And splashed into the sea.
_____

The Victory fired the first broad side,
The second from the "Nancy Lee,"
And ~~canon~~ cannon smoke lay all-around
As far as the eye could see.
_____

"The Victory" chased the "Nancy Lee,"
O'er many a mile and more,
Until at last she anchored off,
A far and distant shore
_____

And "The Victory" sank the "Nancy Lee."
And sank her in the sea,
And sank that Villain Bloody Bill
No pirate worse than he.

(14)

Exploration IV

Setting off a Firework.

I looked at my firework; it was a beauty, all two-and-sixpence-worth of it. I read the instructions and carefully obeyed them easing the firework the into the soft soft earth, and piling more of it around the firework's base to make sure it was upright. As I opened the box of matches, the cardboard tray made a scraping noise which set my teeth on edge. I carefully selected a match. The rest of the matches lay there like soldiers lined up in ranks. I struck the match - it b the stick snapped, so I chose another and struck it; once, twice, "Third time lucky," I thought, and struck again. The black head burst into flame. After waiting for the stick to light, I applied the flaming torch to the blue touch paper. A dull red glow moved slowly down it to the powder as I retreated. Seconds passed as I watched; suddenly a flame darted out of the top; the roaring grew in crescendo until there was a great

explosion, a large blue ball "hopped" out of
the firework. It began silently jumping high into
the air. After about seven of these jumpings it
exploded in in the air with a huge explosion.
(16)

A Description of
A Fireplace

I sat back in my chair; it was lovely sitting next to the fire after running the cross-country. The fireplace was in front of me. The ~~the~~ shiny cream tiles up the side of the fireplace glistened a mellow orange-pink ~~colur~~ colour in the rays of the setting sun. Some of the tiles on the hearth had tiny pock-mark indentations, where hot fragments of "Cleanglow" (~~our~~ the smokeless fuel we use) had "banged" out of the fire (this is caused by moisture ~~got~~ into the coke's pores and being trapped. When the coke is heated the moisture expands and blows off a piece of coke). The carpet is saved by tall fire guard which covers the fire. On the hearth tiles are: the poker, the instrument with which to take out the dis-coloured ash can, and a square brass plate on ~~legs~~ four round legs.

156

I don't know what it is or why it is there; but it is. The firebrick up the side of the grate is pink where the fire oxidizes the carbon, and black where the carbon it has formed; The cupboard to the right of the fire place is where the coke is kept, in a blue plastic hod.

I'm glad we've a fire these days; aren't you?

(13)

Exploration V

Feeding a Pet

An amusing sight met my eyes as I gazed out of the kitchen window. Tigger, our growing ~~gint~~ ginger kitten was stalking a bird. He worked his way across the lawn towards a black-bird, with his ginger tail wagging furiously in anticipation. As I called his ~~m~~ name, Tigger turned and raced towards the house. I knew what he wanted and fetched a tin of "katto meat". from the pantry, while Tigger followed - mewing at my heels. I almost tripped over him as I walked to the tin-opener. I fitted the tin into it and turned the handel. The cutting wheel slowly sliced the tin lid as Tigger rubbed against my legs.

I then emptied the tin of the ~~brow~~ brown "sludge." and gave the ~~tor~~ full ~~bowl~~ bowl to ~~the~~ Tigger who started it - purring. while eating, while I threw the empty tin away. ⑪

Hector and Achilles.

Achilles saw that Hector's body was completely covered by the fine bronze armour he had taken from the great Petroclas when he had killed him, ex accept for an opening at the gullet where the collar bones lead over from the shoulders to the neck, the easiest place to kill a man. As Hector charged him, Prince Achilles drove at this spot with his lance; the point went right through the tender flesh of Hector's neck, though the heavy bronze head did not cut his windpipe and left him able to address his conqueror. Hector came down in the dust and the great Achilles triumphed over him.

"Hector," he said, "No doubt you fancied as you stripped Petroclas that you would be safe. You never thought of me: I was too far away. You were a fool. Down by the hollow ships there was a man far better than Petroclas in reserve."

⑦

159

Words from Philoctetes.

Contingent — a share or proportion.

Brazenly — impudently

Forage — to go about and forcibly carry off food.

Dereliction — state of being abandoned

Alacrity — briskness; cheerful readiness.

Spurn — to reject with disdain.

Acquiescence — quiet absent or submission.

Exploration VI.

Visiting the Dentist, II in the Surgery.

I strode into the dentist's surgery, trying to look far braver than I felt. Butterflies were playing cricket inside me; the air around smelt clean, but dead. The nurse smiled brightly, and the dentist glanced up from writing a report on a former patient. The nurse began to wipe the small, round, moveable platform - on which reposed the dentist's shiney instruments - with some coton wool dipped in a liquid. Then she took four pink pills, and dropped them into the glass of water by my side. They spun round and round like dizzy dancers. When they ~~and~~ and gave off strings of bubbles. When they had disappeared, a ~~pink solution of~~ pink paraffin mouthwash was left. By now the dentist had finished writing, and advanced on his ~~kept~~ "helpless victim". His instruments clinked as he picked them up - a feeler and a mirror. He started

peering into my mouth and probing with
the feeler. I crossed my fingers and hoped
he would not find anything. Suddenly the
feeler caught; I had a hole. He The dentist
unhooked the drill holder, and selected a
bur from a white plastic dish. He fitted
it in and switched on. The ingenious array
of pulleys started in action and the bur
wizzed. The dentist held my mouth open and
contacted my tooth with the bur. Eights
skulled past, on the river unaware of my position. The
dentist continued intermitantly drilling while
I clu clutched the cold plastic arms of
the chair. Soon he had finished, and he
then filled the whole, was which was hot
from drilling, with a metal substance. He
then polished the filling, and I was as
good as new.   (15)

Notes for Book Reviewers

A to book review does the following things: firstly, it gives a short account of a book's contents; secondly, it offers some opinions about the book's qualities; lastly, it gives a personal judgement upon the book's worth

First Section

The first section consists of a short sketch of what the book is ~~it~~ about. It may be an outline of the story; or it may say a little about the sort of people in the story; or (if the book isn't fiction) a quick summary of the subject matter.

Keep this section very clear. It should not be more than one paragraph long.

Second Section

Section Two is the place for your

opinions about the book and your final judgement on it.

Begin this section by talking about whatever struck you most about the author's way of writing a book. Try to make your observations as detailed and exact as possible.

Everything depends upon evidence

This means that you try to support what you have said about the book with quotations or with reference to some incident or character or situation.

You may have something to say about the people in the story; about how lifelike they were, or about how convincing they seemed to your imagination.

You may have something to say about the plot of the story and how it is worked out. Or about the style of the writing and the descriptions. Or about the dialogue. Or about the atmosphere.

Try to remark upon everything that has interested you. Above all, produce your evidence.

⑦

A Book Review

The Sea-Girt Fortress

Percy F. Westerman

Sub-Lieutenant Jack Hameston aged 20 twenty years, was sailing in the eight ton ketch Domedia with Oswald Detroit aged nineteen. The former was tall and thick-set, while the later was tall and slender. They were sailing to Holland when fog set in. During the fog they sail into the German harbour at Helgoland by mistake (this was before immediately before the first world war) and are tried for being spies. They are sentenced to tree years imprisonment; naturaly they escape, but are recaptured again. The story ends up with an a very exer exciting sea battle.

I liked the authors way of describing a person or thing, when it was first seen in the story. Then when there are other scenes you can imagine it as in real life He also describes very vividly as in this piece.

"Jack Hamerton was a tall, broad-shouldered fellow of twenty years of age. He might well have been described as thick-set, for his head was set upon his square shoulders by a short, thick neck, his arms were brawny, while his legs would have caused many a professional footballer to turn green with ~~envy~~ envy."

I also liked Percy Westerman's fast, exciting scenes, and I felt that I had difficulty in keeping up with the pace of the, book, they are extremely well described, as in this passage.

"It was a large destroyer, painted a dull gray. She was travelling at close on thirty knots, dull red flames were spurting from her four squat funnels. Her decks were being swept from end to end with water, while the spray, dashing against her funnels, trailed off into wisps of steam, leaving the fore side of the smoke stacks bleached with salt."

I think the author's plot was origonal and his ingenious idias were highly successful.

(14)

Free Writing

Looping, diving, riding superbly the billowing gusts

Gliding with delicate easy grace down, down towards me a glider, silently almost hovering above the ground slowly it turned away and banked round me, & its shiney perspex ~~an~~ eye reflected the sun at me. Its tail plane and wings were in a straight line ~~from~~ ~~an~~ ~~and~~ as it slowly gathered height all the time it was silent, leaving an air of mystery about it. Rather as if a noiseless space craft from another world ~~had~~ been spying out the green land. The red shape was again ~~above~~ me, flighting like a bird in the morning sunshiene. It moved smoothly like a fish ~~too~~ through water, sedately turning like a ship in ~~no~~ hurry at all. Its long wings fough the cool breeze easily, and effortlessly it hung over the ground. Soon it banked round, slowly, and taking a fresh life from an upcurrent of air it glided ~~away~~ over the horizon.

Sights and Sounds at Evening.

I strolled down to the river in a leisurely fashion, and ~~startld~~ startled an overgrown rat. Its brown fur was plastered to its sides by the damp grass. As it scuttled ~~way~~ away it seemed to mysteriously cover the ground as I could not see its small legs. The reeds and rushes made a rustling noise, like new five-pound-notes being brushed by the wind. In the tall elm trees the wind made an irregular pulsating sound, like that of a waterfall far off. Suddenly there was a singing noise in the rails and a deisel ~~goods~~-train came round the bend. I watched its gigantic ~~wells~~ wheels. as it towered above me the wooden sleepers quaked and sank in the balast as it went on x its journey. In the river was a dead rudd lying on its side its silvery scales upwards and its tail bent downwards into the depths. In the

shallows stickelbacks, tiny in comparison
guard their nests to the death as
can be seen from the several bodies
lying mortive on the muddy bottom. They are
adorned with a phosphorescent green back
and a challenging red breast. The females
are brown and have a body distorted body
by the amount of eggs they are carrying.
Young ones that have already hatched
hang like black needles in the clear
water. Suddenly the water is disturbed
by the rain, and the noise on the leaves
sounds like an army of elves felt fet
feet; so I trudge home.

(15)

Handwriting

We have heard of the fate of wicked
men justly punished
We know of privation and torture
But we never saw suffering as this
man suffers
An innocent man.
The roar of the breakers by day, by night,
Loneliness by desolate shores
A voiceless waste for a airless invalid
How did he endure these?
To burn with fever unattended
To forage for food between bouts of pain
~~To crawl for water between~~
To crawl for water as a child might
crawl
How did he endure these?
But now in the fulness of time our
prince brings rescue
Homecoming after a swift voyage, new
hope
Return from exile.

⑥

Exploration VII.

Having a swim.

I was the first person to the edge of
the swimming-pool. The water was as smooth as
glass. The pool looked as if it was devoid of
water, and the really white tiles were a
beautiful light shade of blue deepening as the
depth increased. At the deep end the colour was
almost mediterranean blue. I dived. The water was
cold and I hunched my shoulders to prevent myself
shivering. The bottom seemed to glide past silently
and smoothly. When I came to the surface the
water seemed almost warm. Other people were
gingerly climbing in, and I swum side stroke down
to the deep end. I climbed out up the
steps and water streamed down my legs. I looked
up at the diving board above my head. It
did not look very high and I had not been
off it before. I climbed up the steps to it
and stood at the end of board. The distance
down to the water was terrifying. My heart

begant to beat faster and faster. In the
distance I heard a sarcastic voice saying,
"Take you time". I "took the plunge; literally.
It seemed an age before I hit the water,
which streaked past me. When I reached the
surface, I looked at the clock it was time to
go home. So I climbed out and toweled
my myself warm.

(14)

A Soliloquy

In the Dark.

"The darkness it presses down; it suffocates me. It is something solid and oppressing, like the folds of a huge black blanket. I hit out, my clenched fist touches nothing. There is nothing there. Just, darkness. My fingers grope out. The dry, bare floorboards have protruding nails. Why am I here? Who is my captor? Where am I? What do they want of me? ~~Whit~~ Will they keep me here long? Can I escape? If so how? If only I could shake off this uncanny dark silence. How I long for a blue sky, trees swaying in a gentle breeze, and ~~birds~~ birds singing beautifully in the green bushes. Why is this happening to me? There are millions of people to choose from, Why me? Perhaps I am dead. If I died, how? Ah! Footsteps. Closer. Closer. Closer. The noise of a key in a lock. And light!"

(14)

A Ballad.

The Train Robbery.

Up rushed a van at dead of night,
To the great railway;
To rob a train it went so fast,
Come and go what may.

They whistled to keep their spirits up,
And to while away the time;
To rob a train they waited so long,
Knowing well 'twas a terrible crime.

The train came slower, and slower still,
Until at last it stopped.
A robber said to the train driver,
"If you move, you will be shot."

They made a human chain, they did,
And took the money away;
For that night, they had robbed,
The great railway.

Next day the papers were full of it,
And for many days as well;
For two whole million pounds were gone,
They knew it very well.

The master-mind was a brilliant one,
He'd planned the raid for weeks.
He knew that no one would dare
To stay his might and sneak.

The leader, he said to his men,
"You will have two thousand or more."
But they knew within their inner hearts,
He'd reap a greater store.

For weeks and months the policemen
searched,
They searched high and low;
But nought could they find of the robbery,
Though they searched high and low.

At last a shepherd found their fort,
But they were many a mile away;
And they have not been seen again,
To this very day.

_____

Time in "Julius Caesar."

" Beware ther ides of march "

" Ay, Casca, tell us what hath chanced today that Caesar looks so sad?."

" And yesterday the bird of night did sit even at noon-day upon the market place, Hooting and shrieking."

" Comes Caesar to the Ca capitol to morrow?"

" How could I, Casca, name to thee a man most like this dreadful night, that thunders, lightens, opens graves, and roars as doth the lion in the Capitol."

" Come, Casca, you and I will yet ere day see Brutus at his house."

" Let us go, for it is after midnight. and ere day will awake him and be sure of him "

"It is not tomorrow, boy, the 'ides of March'"

"Some two months hence up hither toward the north; he first presents his fire and the high east stands as the Capitol, directly here."

"It is not for your health thus to commit your weak condition to the raw cold morning."

"He wish'd to-day our enterprise might thrive,"

"He lies tonight within seven leagues of Rome."

"I dreamt tonight that I did feast with Caesar, and things ~~unto~~ unluckily ~~did~~ charge my fantasy." ⑤

Book Reviews II.

The Axe of Bronze.

Kurt Schmeltzer.

This story concerns the work, and liesure of two villages in the late stone age. One village thinks the gods do not like bronze weapons, and the other thinks they do not mind. Three boys from the flint weapon village, Bimo, Amer and Grune, were friends, until Bimo is given a beautiful bronze axe, which is stolen by Grune. From the start the author makes it quite clear that ~~Grunes~~ Grune is a singularly bad person. The fathers from the two villages have gone to erect the holy stones at Stonehenge, and when they come back, he is teased so much, that he runs away and is made into a galley slave. Later in the story Amer is made into a priest, a miracle occurs, the village is allowed to use bronze weapons, and last of all, making a very suitable end to the book, Crune is forgiven.

I liked the book very much because the characters were very real and lifelike. The author wrote very humanly, and I felt my reactions would be the same as the characters. Though his discriptions were not particularly long or complicated, they conveyed easily and quickly what the author meant, as in this piece.

"The little village consisted of about a dozen low, round huts lying on a smooth mountain. It was surrounded by a wall built of rough pieces of stone to about the height of a man. A spring gurgled outside the wall, feeding a little stream that ran downhill."

Mr. Schmeltzer's scenes were not fast, but they were still either exciting or interesting. They compare favourably against another book with fast scenes. This passage, I think, is the fastest in the book.

"Birno stepped closer to him. "Have you taken my bronze axe?" he hissed into his ear. "If so I want it back."
Grune sneered at him. "What lies in the ashes doesn't belong to anyone And therefore I have every right to keep whatever I happen to find there.""

The book portrays well that then a village was much more of a community than it is now, Also that the people were completely dominated by religeon.

I enjoy the book very much, and greatly recommend it. The author definitely knows what he is talking about, and I imagine he liked writing it.

As a matter of interest Kurt Schmeltzer now lives in Cambridge.

(14)

A Lament

Orpheus lamenting for Eurydice.

O! Dearest Eurydice, twice lost to me,
Only in Hades, the Kingdom of the Dead
Shall I ever see you again.
I have been where no man has been
before, to rescue you:
And a sudden passion made me turn
And lose you for ever in this world.
An hundred paces more and you would
have been mine for ever.
All is lost to me; never more shall I be
happy in this world;
The birds of the air, the animals of
the field,
The fields themselves; they all flock to
hear me play my lyre.
The trees bow down in sorrow at my
music
No-one could cheer me now except you,
Eurydice.

I would exchange my magic lyre for
    a day of your company,
Yea, for only an hour;
But it is impossible.
What shall I do now you are dead?
Shall I wander till the end of my days
    playing my lyre?
                never
I shall marry again, though women always
    follow me;
Eurydice is the only woman I love
And will do for ever more.

(15)

Free Composition.

A Moment of Tranquillity

I sat down. A golden fungus with buff spots was implanted in the tree trunk I was sitting on. The radiant orb of the sun, shining through the elm trees, beneath which I was sitting, made the muddy water of the river sparkle as a trout stream. How peaceful and serene it was. A robin alighted on the ground, unfrightened in the quietness, and began to pull grubs from this bountiful earth. At the confluence of the two rivers lay swans' droppings ready to fertalize the soil, in a never ending cycle. A grass snake slid slyly and malevolently onto a pile of dead rushes, to bask in the blazing sun. This was the creature that God made creep on its belly for tempting Eve in the Garden of Eden. A small insect was carried down by the the relentless current of the river, it seemed so small and pathetic. Rather like a human being, swept ~~dear~~ along by the continual, gigantic turbulence of life, sometimes gaining, sometimes losing. To what end was all this? Some day the tranquill scene will be destroyed; by man. The meadows will be built over to supply housing for the ~~already~~ ~~over-crowd~~ ever increasing population. Or will the Atomic bomb wipe out everyone except for a second Noah?

(14)

A Letter.

The Manor House,
Little Eyewink,
Oxfordshire.

27 April.

Dear Sir and Lady Hutchinson-Hall,

Thank you very much indeed for the invitation to your ball, on Friday, 13th May at 8.30 p.m. I am very grieved to have to decline this invitation, but I must be in London that day for an important debate at the House of Lords. However my son would be greatly pleased, if he could be present in my place,

I am sure you will have an extremely successful evening, and I only wish I could be there.

Yours Sincerely,
Archie.
(Lord Archibald Montague Crickleshank)

(10)

A Micro-Description.

A Piece of Furniture.

The slender curved legs of the piano-stool make it look very perky. I can imagine it scuttling away any moment, or dancing a jig round the room. The legs reflect the light from the blazing coal fire at points on its surface. The reflected golden light, strangely subdued pulsates irregulary on the shiney polished wood. The concave seat is covered with a strong material, unusually patterned in an abstract way. Some of it looks like a skyscraper block of flats, some of it a large dog tooth pattern, squares, triangles, leafy trees, and all manner of things. The corners are worn to a lighter colour, showing long, constant use. However, the stool is not only used for by people to sit on, for the ginger cat usually sleeps on it, leaving a few hairs, and an oval-shaped depression.

(14)

Encounter with a Creature

A Mouse.

I sat on the gnarled branch of the old
  pear-tree one July afternoon.
The poplars swayed gently, in the light, dry,
  breeze;
Just a shadow of a breeze.
  looked languidly around; dazedly at the
  rhubarb patch
Is there something there?
Yes, there!
There under the shady-green of the rhubarb
  leaves,
A little ball of fur.
A Mouse,
A little mouse.

It fascinated me.
How beautiful it was, but that didn't
  mean it couldn't cut oper flesh, with
  its yellow razor teeth

189

How clean its tiny [paws ~~are~~ were, and devoid
   of hair.
Its long tail looked like a tapered worm,
   complete with rings.

The mouse sat up on its hind legs;
And licked its wax-pale paws, and cleaned
   its quivering wire wiskers.

Suddenly it glanced at me.
Its body became rigid-steel, taut, frozen; and
   then relaxed, slackened.
Its liquid-berry eyes reflected pinpoints of
   light as it looked quizzically at me.
"How tall do I look to you?
As tall as a skyscraper?
Taller?"

The mouse vanished.
There was our cat, bounding across the
   lawn after it.

Why do people use mouse-traps?
Cats enjoy catching mice, and are better at it.

I rested my head against the tree-
& trunk, and continued my daydream.   ⑮

Book Review III.

Lord of the Flies.

'William Golding

This is the story of an aeroplane load
of well-brought up schoolboys who are
marooned on an island when the plane crashes.
All the children are 12 years or under and
there are no grown-up survivors. These pleasant
boys turn into bloodthirsty savages; some
with a desire to return home, others with
a desire to hunt and kill the wild pigs
that roam the island. The climax of the
story is ~~after two~~ of the boys have been
killed, it is right at the end and is the
man-hunt of Ralph. At the very end the
boys are rescued.

Though this is a good book, it is not,
in my opinion, meant to be enjoyed. I think
it is a satire on educated man. The author
puts accross very well, the fact that the

192

boys were unable to be organised as they did not accept the leader-ship of their equals. Also that they weren't used to thinking or making decisions for themselves.

"Grown-ups know things," said Piggy. "They ain't afraid of the dark. They'd meet and discuss and have tea. Then things ud be all right—."

The imaginative descriptions are very vivid and also very detailed. This means, if you want to appreciate them you cannot read them quickly. The characters seem real, because, as well as telling what they do physically, the author describes what they feel or think inside. This is most effective when Simon is 'listening' to the Lord of the Flies. Another reason why the characters are so ~~lifelt~~ lifelike is because the dialogue is more like boys speaking than in any other book I know of. Although, if you read the climax by itself, you could not imagine it happening, the pre-climax events, smooth this out. I think this is an excellent piece at the end:

The officer grinned cheerfully at Ralph.
'We saw your smoke. What have you
been doing? Having a war or something?'
Ralph nodded.*
Nobody killed, I hope? Any dead bodies?
  "Only two, And they're gone.'
The officer leaned down and looked
closely at Ralph.
  "Two? Killed?"
Ralph nodded again. Behind him the whole
island was shuddering with flame. The officer
knew as a rule when people were telling
the truth. He whistled softly.

    This is rather a strange book, but
well worth reading. It deserves its title of a
modern classic.

* A small piece omitted
                                          ⑯

194

Notes for Chineese Verse.

1. The language for these poems p makes pictures; that hint at feelinge & situations, or unfold a story in a kind of picture - shorthand.

2. A Chineese poem may be of any length. It may be very short and abrupt, or longer and meditative.

3. There are no rules about line length or x rhythm but usually the lines are roughly the same length throughout the poem.

4. Each line ought to have a distinct rythm of its own. Most of the time the lines do not "run on."

5. The choise of words is all-important for there should be no waste. The language should be as exact and delecate as possible. The present tense is usually the best, but avoid " —ing."

6. Subject matter is very various it may be real or imaginary or it may be a mixture of the two. It may be an every-day sight or experience. It may be a sudden memory or a moment of life that seems particularly vivid. It may be a story or a situation. ⑥

Chineese Verse.

Peace

The sun shined dimly through a bank
    of peaceful cloud;
Snow lies soft upon the ground.
Jagged features smoothed; crevices are filled.
Trees lie heavy with its weight.
The pond is blanketed by a soft smooth
    sheet.
Where will the birds find water

The Wind

In the winter, people curse me;
In the summer, people bless me.
For in the winter I blow the snow and sleet.
I chap peoples' legs and faces;
Their lips crack,
Their eyes and noses run.
They curse me.

In the summer I blow refreshing breezes on
  them,
I cool and refresh them,
I caress their faces.
They laugh and bless me.

The Venus Fly-Trap.

Silently waiting, it sits.
A fly passes.
It smells a sweet aroma?
It alights in the rose-red jaw.
The mouth snaps shut.
The fly struggles helplessly; and is lost.
Then its captor settles down to a juicey
  meal.
It is truly amazing what some plants can
  do.

---

(14)

Clytemnestra's speech of welcome to Agamemnon.

O, brave and noble warrior,
You have at last returned to us.
To Mycenae, and to your faithful wife.
Many long, hard years have I waited;
Fearing every minute to hear of your death.
My eyes did not dry from my weeping
All the time that you have been away.
Each day has been an endless eternity;
At night I never slept, save by potions.
You are like the sparkling stream to a
    weary traveller.
A Rousing spring after a cruel winter;
Joy after misery.
Joy as a shipwrecked sailor sees a boat
    sailing towards his island;
Joy as an explorer finds his goal.
The joy of the whole country, cannot be
    more than mine;
There will be weeks of feasting.
Now you must bath, and then the feast
    and prayer.

Thy royal conquering foot must not touch this common ground;
Priests, bring out the carpet of the Gods! (14)

In the first year the Exploration is a form of composition which is intended, through its recurrence, to develop a humble but vital tool of children's creative imagination – their attention to sensory experience. At the outset I usually spend a lesson explaining the idea to the class. My aim is to make as clear as possible just what kind of alerted consciousness Exploring, in this sense, *is*. Most eleven-year-olds have a natural disposition for it, and can be encouraged to realise it. The *Notes* (p. 139) arise out of the discussion. They are meant to fasten down the main points as we go along.

Before I offer any advice on matters of expression in this lesson, we usually spend a little time doing a small communal Exploration of a simple subject like Coming Into The Mummery or Opening A Textbook. At each stage of this any boy may put into words a sense-impression of his own, or suggest how someone else's could be better put, and a scribe writes up the expression which is generally agreed to be the most effective. In this way a concern with accuracy arises directly as a function of sensibility in action – and what is *meant* by such a note as 'Make your words as exact as possible' is made clear. We consider, too, the difference between Story-telling and Exploring; and what it means to write 'speakingly'. (The second sentence of Nigel Cooper's sixth Exploration, *Visiting the Dentist* (p. 161) illustrates both weakness and strength in a speaking style, in a conveniently small span – 'Butterflies were playing cricket inside me; the air around smelt clean, but dead.' The first half is feeble, its chatty cleverness a substitute for close attention; the second half is direct and telling, a response to the sensation's subtlety.)

At the end of this lesson – invariably a Business Period – I set the boys their first Exploration for homework. For this, as for all following Explorations, I offer a choice of two or three alternative titles. The titles thus accumulate during the year, and at each assignment I allow free choice over the whole increasing range. Implicitly, a wide variety of styles of perception is invited, as may be seen in the fact that Nigel Cooper could have chosen as his *final* subject (instead of *Having a Swim*) *Waking Up, Having a Bath, Making a Piece of Toast, Having a Haircut, Washing the Dog, Visiting the Dentist: The Waiting Room, Washing Up, Making a Bed, Mending a Puncture, Watching a Bird* or *Mowing the Lawn.*

Occasionally, later in the year, it may be useful to do a full-length Exploration in class as a communal refresher exercise. Nigel Cooper's class did this just before the third Exploration was set. Even so, a few boys never grasp very surely what Exploring amounts to. They continue to write little narratives, time after time. There is nothing wrong or objectionable in narratives as such, of course: but they obstruct the more important enterprise in this context. Most boys, however, improve at Exploring, perceptibly if not drastically, during the first year. They make the sort of overall progress that Nigel Cooper makes.

His first attempt (*Falling Asleep*, p. 141) starts uncertainly. What Exploring there is in it really begins at the opening of the *second* paragraph; and when it comes it is dir cted chiefly at the creatures of the night, not at the process of falling asleep. There is certainly some pleasant writing in the piece – I enjoyed reading of the screech owls with 'their silent flight aided by downy wing feathers', for instance, and of the grunting hedgehogs 'leaving tracks in the dewy grass' – but the way it evades the prime issue can be seen when it is compared with this passage, the last part of an Exploration of the same subject by Baker, also written during the first term:

Suddenly a wave of weariness swept over me. My mind felt like flowing whirlpools, and I felt warm and cosy. My ears registered only my breathing, and the soft crumple of my bed-clothes as I moved. When I tried to move my eyes, they were heavy and clumsey. The smell of crisp clean linen of my bed helped my body to slumber in bliss. My body relaxed and I felt as though I was floating on air with warm water flowing all over me. An endless silence fell, not a harsh silence, but a soft kind silence. Then my mind went blank, and I felt myself falling...falling...falling... The harsh rattle of the alarm bell woke me with a jerk. It was 7.30 a.m., time to get up.

As he writes, Baker does not only recall what happens, he re-creates it. The rhythms of the prose catch the very lull of the experience. And Cooper comes a little nearer to this degree of engagement in his second piece (*Frying a Sausage*, p. 142) with its several moments of good Exploring – such as the assured, straightforward opening, 'The liquid fat ouses out from the solid lump and spreads across the pan'; the moments of exact observing and reporting, 'this causes wierd contortions to project from their otherwise smooth skin'; and the touches of adventure with words, 'A delicious odour wafts up from the succulant sausages'. In his third attempt (*Climbing a Tree*, p.147) narrative takes over when he meets the owl. As narrative it is quite effectively realised, the language making its sudden spurt as recognition springs from the solid fact of the bird's presence – 'I see a pair of large solemn unblinking eyes gazing stolidly at me. It is an owl!' It is an encounter that is genuinely, though briefly, Explored there at the end of the first paragraph, I think; but elsewhere the Exploration of the *climbing* is very thin.

A real breakthrough seems to me to come in Exploration IV, *Setting Off a Firework* (p. 154). Here Cooper is consistently concerned with what matters most in the experience, and the prose speaks robustly. I like the way his first crossing-out reveals a care to be as accurate as possible – 'I struck the match it—b the stick snapped . . .' – where the taut, precise language conveys the tension of the occasion. There is hardly a word wasted here; yet Cooper's next effort, *Feeding a Pet* (p. 158), relapses almost completely into story-telling, pleasant enough in its way but with little Exploring outside the second and seventh sentences. Then, with *Visiting the Dentist* (p. 161), the skill returns in force. In this I admire the understatement of feelings (surely deliberately done?) and the striking effect (perhaps unintentional?) in the sudden shift of viewpoint as the dentist begins to drill – 'The dentist held my mouth open and contacted my tooth with the bur. Eights skulled past on the river, unaware of my position.'

Having a Swim (p. 172), which was done as the first written homework in the second year, is not an outstanding success – the sense-perception being notably less sharp in the latter half – but I was pleased with its unaffected zest and its range of impressions. When compared with Cooper's first efforts, it shows some real development. I think it is worth making Exploring a *habitual* writing activity throughout the first year because there is, in the repeated commitment, an 'opportunity for the child to develop, over a period of time, his understanding of what is involved' – and thereby to *grow* – in a 'climate of heightened awareness'. Not many of the boys grow steadily from strength to strength. It is usually a matter of sudden triumphs and equally sudden lapses. But it is rare for a boy to go through a whole year without any triumphs at all.

I try to vary the boys' diet by giving them at least one different form of composition after every two Explorations (though these alternatives may be designed to sharpen particular aspects of the Exploring art). A thoroughly successful *Description of a Fireplace* (p. 156), for instance, would depend on especially attentive *looking* (as I explained when setting the homework). In this respect Nigel Cooper's explanations of why the coke bangs and how the firebrick comes to be pink and black are not 'to the point'; but it would have been perverse to grumble. In fact, these moments of clear 'scientific' writing are sheer bonus.

Sights and Sounds at Evening (p. 169) was written from notes made during a quarter-of-an-hour spell of watching and listening in the garden at the end of the day. Some of its effectiveness may be due to the Exploring habit. At any rate I should like to think that Cooper's Explorations had had *some* influence on this piece of writing: perhaps they helped to sharpen his eye for direct and telling detail – 'As it towered above me the wooden sleepers quaked and sank in the ballast as it went on its journey' – especially in his observation of what interested him most of all, the sticklebacks – 'Young ones that have already hatched hang like black needles in the clear water'; perhaps Exploring strengthened his effort to be adequate in description – 'In the tall elm trees the wind made an irregular pulsating sound, like that of a waterfall far off'; or helped towards his sharp, clear-cut phrasing – 'Its brown fur was plastered to its sides by the damp grass.' Perhaps, too, the Exploring habit contributed something to his *second* piece of *Free Writing* (p. 168), the wholly engaged evocation of a glider's flight.

In every term I try to make some time available for Free Writing, which the boys do not always do in their Written Work Books. It is usually well worth the time spent on it, for, in response to a direct stimulus and freed from any need to worry over the finer points of spelling and punctuation, some boys write far more sensitively than they ever do in a piece of formal homework. The first piece of Free Writing in Nigel Cooper's book, however, is nothing more than a chaotic catalogue; and this was my fault. It was, in fact, the first piece I ever asked a class to write, and at that time I had not discovered Dora Pym's excellent booklet on the subject and how to tackle it. I put the opening movement of Bruckner's 'Romantic' Symphony on the gramophone and told the boys they could write 'anything they liked' *so long as they didn't stop until the music was over.* (This was an utterly foolish injunction, for of course it drove all the 'freedom' out of the occasion.) I suppose I was expecting some kind of instant mass-fertilisation of the imagination to take place. The movement was a good piece of 'programme music', and I had a vague idea that this would cause it to 'form' the boys' narrative or description as they went along. But really I did not know what I was up to. Nor did the boys. They looked very blank and bewildered during my hazy introduction to this little scheme. Some of their efforts were less wildly garbled and random than Nigel Cooper's, but there was little in any of them to be glad of – because of my own stupidity.

Next time I went about it a bit more carefully. As a starting-point I gave the boys a couple of lines of verse (saying nothing about their being poetry) and simply asked them to continue writing about whatever the words had called into their minds. A few boys went on in a free verse form, but most chose prose. And the subjects varied widely. There were kites, and beings from other worlds, and feathers in the wind, and many different kinds of bird: and as I read the pieces through there was something in almost every one that was as satisfying as Cooper's description of the glider's climbing flight – 'rather as if a noiseless space craft from another world had been spying out the green land' – with its manner of 'sedately turning like a ship in no hurry at all'.

Free Writing makes a change for the class in many ways; not least because it is not formally marked but just read, carefully commented on, and returned to the writers. It has to be done in the classroom, not as homework; and to be really free it has to be, so to speak, sprung on the

7·2

children. I remember a day when the class finished a Verse Session with about fifteen minutes of the period left over. The performing Guild had finished with a chilling rendering of this poem by Walter de la Mare, done in a near-whisper under sepulchral light.

> I spied John Mouldy in his cellar
> Deep down twenty steps of stone.
> In the dusk he sat a-smiling,
>   Smiling there alone.
>
> He read no book, he snuffed no candle,
> The rats ran in, the rats ran out
> And far and near, the drip of water
>   Went whispering about.
>
> The dusk was still, with dew a-falling,
> I saw the dog-star, bleak and grim,
> I saw a slim brown rat of Norway
>   Creep over him.
>
> I spied John Mouldy in his cellar
> Deep down twenty steps of stone.
> In the dusk he sat a-smiling,
>   Smiling there alone.

It had been done with a single figure propped against a rostrum at one side of the stage, with his back towards us, in a small pool of murky green light (I discovered afterwards that one of the boys had doubled the gelatine in the filter-frame on one of the spotlights). There was no other light in the room. From somewhere high up at the other side of the stage came the voice of a lone actor reciting the poem. He had learned the lines for the occasion. At the end of the third stanza, as if to endorse what one of the boys had christened 'the shudder moment', the spotlight went out, and we had the last lines in total darkness. When the house lights came on, it was clear that the whole class had 'enjoyed' this shock effect and so, on the spur of the moment, I distributed sheets of paper and asked each boy to write for the rest of the lesson about the most memorable shudder moment in his own life.

This was the piece that I was most pleased to read afterwards.

I meet a cat and some pigeons
I was just about to go into a houses garden called forrie. It is up red cross lane.
I looked up and some crows were sawing above me. I took no heed and went in. I rou rounded a corner and there, there was a dead, ginger, cat.
It was lying there, there was (or still is) a roller to rolle the grass.
The first thought that came to my mind was that it had been run over by it As it was crushed there was nothing else to prove what happened to it but I know one thing for shore sure   it was dead.

wood
I walked on and there just in front of me lay a heap of   /   pigeons, there must of been at least fifty of them

I turned on my heels ~~and~~ and fled least I should be the next victim of the dreaded house forrie

It was a hot day and ~~ever~~ every thing smelled awfully. (Forrie Red Cross lane left hand side) Every thing still to be found.

˙ The End

The writer of this was a boy called Roberts; one of the least able members of the class. He was also rather lazy and consistently turned in casual, half-baked homework, very messily set out. It was hard to find things to admire in it and he never seemed to *try* to do it well. If approached about his writing he quickly became surly and obstinate, though in other kinds of work – like Mime or Speeches – he could do well with a good grace. This brief piece, sprung on him as it was, was the first in which I found any substantial personal *concern* emerging. It was this that pleased me so much. The economy, the instinctive selection of only the facts that mattered, the immediacy – 'I looked up and some crows were sawing above me. I took no heed and went in. I rounded a corner and there, there was a dead, ginger, cat.' – all of these things spoke for a dropping of defences, a momentary stirring of sensibility such as more formal assignments had not achieved. I made sure that Roberts (who was known to his friends as 'Ginger') noticed that I was really impressed with this piece. And from then on I tried to include some Free Writing in the work of every term.

Free Composition (p. 185) is not the same thing: it is a *homework* assignment that I include occasionally in the second-year programme. I offer three or four titles and invite the boys to choose one of them and compose a piece in any form, verse or prose, that they have previously undertaken: or, if they wish, they can combine two forms together (description, for example, with dramatic soliloquy). Nigel Cooper chose *A Moment of Tranquillity* in preference to *Nightmare* or *Lost*, and I imagine he would have called his composition an Exploration, though soliloquy and, I think, the impact of the mime of *Orpheus and Eurydice* (where the pastoral serenity of the opening scene is shattered by the snake that bites Eurydice) have probably had some influence on it. Being a contemplative soul, Cooper uses the offered freedom of this composition simply to let his thoughts carry him along, and, as a twelve-year-old's musing, the piece strikes me as pleasant enough (rhetorical flourishes and all), though I do not think he drove himself unduly hard to produce it. Phrases like 'the radiant orb of the sun' and 'this bountiful earth' may have been stock bits of description for him; but they *may* equally have been part of an effort to make his language match the grandness he felt around him. In cases like this – and they arise quite frequently – it has always seemed safer to me to give the boy the benefit of the doubt; especially when there are other elements in his composition that one can like unreservedly, such as the frank way that the musing issues straight from his exploration of the natural scene.

The first diversion from Exploring in the first year was the Elegy, composed while the Guilds were working on the Mime of King Arthur. The first five lines of the piece (p. 144) were an optional beginning which I arranged from a snippet of Malory's prose; the rest is Cooper's own. The reader can probably detect behind the lines one of the models that I gave the class when proposing the composition – David's lament for Saul and Jonathan from the second book of Samuel. Though I also read other biblical elegiac verse (from Jeremiah) and an example of Homeric lament (Andromache for Hector), by far the greatest impact was made by 'The beauty of Israel is slain upon thy high places.' I talked a little about the cadence of grief in the phrasing of an elegy, and a little about an appropriate form of diction. The boys themselves were quick to bring up the question of lay-out. 'How long do the lines have to be, sir?' ('Not too long, on the whole. You start a fresh line when it feels right to do so – and a longer one from time to time can make a good effect.') Then someone asked about imagery. 'Can we compare things, sir, when we try. Like "swifter than eagles"?' ('Yes, certainly. But use your own ideas. Don't *just* copy what you have heard.')

The later elegy – *Orpheus lamenting for Eurydice* – was also done in conjunction with a mime performance, but I did not spend enough time recapitulating the leading qualities of the elegy style with the class: so, many of the boys wrote a sort of re-telling of the story which did not make Orpheus' grief very apparent. Cooper's piece (p. 183) was one of the most successful on this occasion. Perhaps the absence of sentimentality in it, the *direct* sense of loss and regret, is due in *some* measure to his involvement in the mime-experience, although he was not one of his group's Master Players.

Clytemnestra's Speech of Welcome to Agamemnon (p. 198) arose directly out of work in mime too, but it was probably not as valuable an enterprise as either of the two laments. In working on the key-episode of Agamemnon's arrival at the palace, I had read a translation of Clytemnestra's speech in Aeschylus' play. In the discussion that followed, the boys were quick to fasten on the Queen's brazen assurance and the underlying menace of her words. We spent nearly a period exploring the leading ideas from what she said in mime-expression; and the

dramatic life of the speech began then to be an experience. The homework assignment came later, when the performance of the whole story
was in its final stages, and for most of the boys it amounted to little
more than an exercise in paraphrase, I think. I was short of ideas at the
time and set the homework thoughtlessly and in a hurry. The exercise
probably did nobody any actual harm. But there was probably less
positive 'culture of the feelings' in it for most of the class than in the
dramatic soliloquy which had been set at the beginning of the year.

I think Nigel Cooper's *Soliloquy* (p. 174) catches some notes of fear and
desperation quite well. The darkness has real presence – 'My fingers
grope out. The dry, bare floorboards have protruding nails' – which
leads the speaker to a yearning for the outside world – 'How I long for
a blue sky, trees swaying in a gentle breeze, and birds singing beautifully
in the green bushes.' (Cliché-feeling?) Although the background to his
predicament is not made clear, his panic is – in the jumpy, disconnected
questions. But Cooper has forgotten (or found too difficult to achieve)
one other element that I stressed as important to this piece of homework – the adoption of a 'character' different from his own. So the
language remains, essentially, schoolboy-talk – 'Why is this happening
to me? There are millions of people to choose from. Why me?' Some
of the boys who chose one of the two alternative titles for this piece (*A
Gladiator Before His Last Fight* and *Frightened Animal*) got away from
the schoolboy idiom a little more successfully.

Apart from the Elegy, diversions from Exploring during Nigel Cooper's
first year came in the form of Balladry and Book Reviewing. The *Notes
for Ballad-makers* (p. 149) were dictated after more than a fortnight's
work on traditional ballads in Guild Verse Sessions and, like the *Notes
for Explorers*, they sum up a lot that was treated at length in class. I
had frequently asked the class to chant the ballad-pattern with me –
'Te-tum, te-tum, te-tum, te-tum...' We repeated it almost *ad nauseam*.
My *hope* was that all the boys would thus have an instinctive sense of
the way the words should go along the lines when they came to compose
their own individual ballads. (I generally tried to end the Christmas
term with ballads, and set the do-it-yourself task as a holiday assignment. Some of the boys needed a lot of time for it.) *Most* boys, flush
with the work of Verse Sessions, can manage the rhythm-pattern easily
when we make a composite ballad in class; but some of the less gifted
ones have a very unsteady hold on the rhythm outside the classroom.
It is chiefly for *their* sake that I am so specific in Note 1.

In spite of this, I'm afraid the holiday task becomes something of a
nightmare for a few boys. They just cannot hear the pattern their words
are making when they try to compose a ballad by themselves; so the

result has a very hit-or-miss air. Here, for instance, are the last three
stanzas of Salter's ballad called *The Highwayman*.

                                        like
        The highwaymans horse 'twas   /   a flash of light
        His dagger like the Ivory moon,
        His cloak like a great black bat,
        His hair like a stragling typhoon.

        The Highwayman shouted I'll fill you with lead.''
        the excise men said ''We'll split you in two
        ''I tell you I'll shoot I'll shoot I'll shoot''
        ''Remember before you do, there's twelve of us and one of you''

                                    excise
        He shot the first of the   /   men
        ~~But after~~ then he fell and broke his ~~varmit~~ neck,''
        Here ends this bloody tale,
        Along by the rushing beck.

Nigel Cooper found rhyme and rhythm to be more manageable in *The
Sinking of the Nancy Lee* (p. 152). Its confident, unforced swing and the
pointed use of the repetition (as, for instance, in the frame made by the
first and last stanzas) are the best things about it. It has much of the
spirit of a 'real' ballad, but the story never comes to a climax and Note
4 has slipped from the boy's mind in the stress of composing. *The Train
Robbery* (p. 175), done a year later, droops sadly in the feeble con-
trivance of several of the rhyming lines and in the casual mixture of
diction – now free-and-easy, now poetic.

For comparison's sake, here is a ballad on the same theme made on
the same occasion by Cooper's class-mate Liddell. It is one of the dozen
best ballads that emerged from that particular assignment, though not
the best:

                            Ballad 2

                    The Great Train Robbery

        The Robber Chief sat in his den,
        A'racking of his brain.
        The problem he had set himself,
        Was how to rob a train.

        A plan he made, a crafty raid.
        His gang he called together.
        If any man disclosed his plan,
        He'd reach the end of his tether.

        His scheming mind he used to find,
        A farm close to the rail.
        He planned to set a hold-up there,
        And reap a crop of mail.

"These are my orders for tonight,
And see that they are done.
Our objective is the bags of mail,
In carriage number one."

It was the Robber Chief who spoke,
As they crept towards the line.
And as the men concealed themselves,
They joked to pass the time.

The Royal Mail was on its way.
At sixty it was steady.
But far away in the dying day,
Everything was ready.

The brakes are on, the steam's cut off.
The train grinds to a halt.
Out of the night the gang erupt,
And launch a sharp assault.

The guards are coshed, the mail-bags grabbed,
And into lorries stowed.
Minutes later the job's complete,
And the gang is on the road.

Back to the farm the lorries rush,
With their multi-million harvest.
The loot is shared, but some are scared
And leave the hide-out fastest.

But one of the gang has left a clue,
And the Yard picks up the trail.
The leader slips away through the net,
While the rest are sent to jail.

The Robber Chief sits in the sun,
On the sunny coast of Spain.
He raises his glass and drinks a toast,
To the Royal Mail Train.

Though very little of the story here is 'told by using the voices of the characters in it', this ballad seems to me to be full of felicities – as, for example, in the skilful way the narrative progresses in flashes of detail and in the sheer energy of the language (the bracing internal rhymes are a device that Liddell picked up from his own ballad-reading). Cooper's two ballads are more typical of the *average* offerings.

I introduce Book Reviewing towards the end of the first year, as an extension of the technique for Reading Reports, spending a period discussing the ways and the means with the class, and building up *Notes for Book Reviewers* (p. 163) through dictation, point by point. I have found that it pays to dwell on the nature of 'evidence' at this stage, since some boys find it difficult to grasp just what is meant by 'supporting an opinion with quotation or reference'. The first Book Review fills two homework periods after this lesson – one period being meant for each section of the review. Thereafter I aim to set one review per term. When handing back the first attempts, I read aloud extracts from some of them where evidence has been used successfully, in the hope of bringing a little enlightenment to those boys who still have not got the hang of Section Two.

Nigel Cooper got the hang of reviewing from the start, and his first effort (p. 165) might well have been quoted in class to show the careful and effective use of quotation (even though his final judgement – that Percy Westerman's 'ingenious idias were highly successful' – is supported with no evidence at all). The majority of boys seem to grow better at reviewing as time goes on: and Cooper certainly does. In his second review (p. 180) his evidence at one point clarifies his opinion in a striking way. He speaks of Mr Schmeltzer's 'fastest' scene, and the extract that he then quotes does not illustrate any rapid sequence of events. He is, I think, dealing with the notion of a dramatic *tension* without knowing a term for it. He does something of a similar kind in his last review (p. 192) when he wrongly describes as 'satire' his sense of the fable element in *Lord of the Flies*. And although he is puzzled by this novel's mode – '. . .a good book. . .not, in my opinion, meant to be enjoyed. . .rather a strange book, but well worth reading' – he does appreciate its chief qualities with finesse. The review seems really 'in touch' with the book as a whole.

Like each of his classmates, Nigel Cooper transferred each of the pieces mentioned so far – except for the two passages of Free Writing and the dictated Notes – to his Fair Copy Book (a title to be explained shortly) together with his *Micro-description, Encounter with a Creature* and *Chinese Verse*. Like Clytemnestra's speech, the *Micro-description* (p. 188) was a homework that I set too hurriedly. I remember thinking that a renewal of Exploring might be useful at this point in the second year if the boys did not immediately consider it to be old hat. 'Micro-description' as a title was a thin attempt to disguise what I was really aiming at – and the boys saw through it almost at once. I was holding forth about the prefix 'micro' and the fact that it should lead them to give especially close and detailed attention to their subject when Paterson piped up with 'You mean we do it like for an Exploration, sir?' 'Er – yes, Paterson.' 'Oh, I thought we'd finished with them.'

The *Letter* (p. 187) was not copied into the Fair Copy Book because neatness was crucial to the assignment in the first place. I asked the boys to write a letter declining an invitation and to set it out as though their exercise-book's page were a sheet of notepaper. This gave me the chance to teach a little useful information about some formalities of correspondence, matters of presentation and punctuation, points of courtesy. There was some need for this as not all the boys were sure how to do the address and date, or how to start and finish, although most of them had written real life thank-you letters. To add a touch of human interest to the exercise, I invited them to adopt an invented identity. I neither invited nor forbade humour. Nigel Cooper's tongue-in-cheek entry into the ranks of the aristocracy – where he hits the manner off very graciously – was probably his way of enlivening an exercise he found basically dull.

The remaining exercises in his book served various purposes. Those on pp. 143, 159, and 171 were presented as handwriting exercises, but all three had a further point to them. For instance, the task of learning three stanzas from *The Wife of Usher's Well* early in the first term – before they had made an official start on balladry – brought the boys a foretaste of metre and ballad-style. I hoped that their appetites would be whetted rather than blunted, for the stanzas were not very difficult to remember. I tested this passage, like the other two, by having the boys write it out from memory during a Business Period. The passage about Hector and Achilles is taken from E. V. Rieu's translation of *The Iliad*, from which I had read some extracts when launching a Mime. The piece focused the boys' attention on some details of action and character that were directly relevant to their performance; and perhaps the boy-appeal of its description of the death-blow lightened the chore of learning it for homework. 'We have heard of the fate of wicked men justly punished' is a key chorus from *Philoctetes*, and I think everybody in the class grew more involved with the hero's predicament for having learned the piece by heart. In other years I have tested passages of memorised verse in an oral way by distributing the boys in pairs all round the room and having them recite to each other: but for some reason I seem to have been obsessed with neat handwriting in this class.

Words from 'Philoctetes' (p. 160) was a way of ensuring that each boy read the play at least once before starting to act it. When I gave out copies of the text at the end of the second term, I asked the boys to make lists of all the words that were new to them, writing their meanings opposite. This gave practice in using the dictionary to those who most needed it; and I hope it implied that the play's language was rich and accessible rather than difficult and daunting.

The collation of references to Time in *Julius Caesar* (p. 178) was done when performances had reached the end of Act III. It involved the boys in some close attention to the text, and it directed their concern towards one element in Shakespeare's dramatic craft – the way he quietly screws up the audience's excitement in the first half of the play with repeated reminders that time is passing and the murder, therefore, drawing nearer. After pointing this out, and instancing such a line as 'The clock hath stricken three', I asked each boy in the class to select and copy out for homework a dozen striking examples of such 'reminders' coming before the assassination. (This was not one of Nigel Cooper's brighter efforts. He copies carelessly from the text, and goes on past the murder.) Sometimes, when the class has been doing *A Midsummer Night's Dream*, I have asked for a similar collation of lines that contain the word or idea of dreams and dreaming.

There is never enough time in a school year to include all the kinds of writing one would like the class to try. I must leave out of this chapter the various forms of composition – such as newspaper-reporting, dramatic dialogue, alliterative poems, blank verse – that were included in other years in place of some parts of the programme that Nigel Cooper's class followed.

In developing a programme of written work for his children a teacher has to make a selection from all the kinds of prose and verse that he believes to be valuable and relevant to them. He has to try to keep a balance between English-as-an-instrument-of-communication and English-in-the-service-of-imagination (not that either can be wholly separated from the other in any piece of writing). I hope that this balance was a reasonable one for Nigel Cooper's class.

Each boy in the class keeps a Fair Copy Book in which he enters each piece of his *creative* writing once I have read and marked it in his Written Work Book. This arrangement gives practical point to correcting, and it encourages the boys to take some sustained pride in their work. Also, it quietly asserts a significance in creative writing that is different from that in exercises.

The Fair Copy Book is larger, shinier, different in colour, stiffer-covered and altogether more splendid than the standard issue. In it a boy may illustrate or decorate his work as he wishes, but nobody is penalised for not wishing to. Everyone designs his own frontispiece, supplies the book with a Contents page, and embellishes the cover to his taste. I try to encourage real achievements of personal book-making, and lay much stress on the importance of *space* and clear handwriting in making a piece attractive to the reader's eye. Since some boys will put plenty of care into making the adornments and give little to the fair copying itself, there is usually need to repeat advice against making decoration too obtrusive. I try to make it clear, through comment and discussion, that *accuracy* is the first criterion in this work, and design the second; but there are always one or two boys whose fair copies, though truly beautiful to behold, contain quite as many mistakes as their originals, though not always in the same places. All the same, fair-copy-making is a worthwhile thing, even for the boys whose work, like Nigel Cooper's, is relatively free from serious flaws in the first place. While some boys are lazy over lay-out when first writing a composition, because they know it will have to be fair-copied in any case, others draw confidence at the time of writing from knowing that they will have the chance to put right what they get wrong in the trying matters of spelling, grammar and punctuation. Most children do not *want* to make mistakes in what they are asked to do. In Fair Copy Books they have a means of expressing pride in their work for its own sake. I think it important that an English teacher should deliberately sustain his children's capacity for this kind of pride whenever he can (it is quite a different thing from self-satisfaction, of course) simply because the capacity is *bound* to be bruised by accident from time to time in an educational relationship.

When I first started the work of marking compositions I corrected each boy's writing to a standard of total accuracy. I fondly imagined that I could do this with each homework assignment and still remain clear-eyed and sensitive to the substance and expressiveness of the writing. It proved not so. Marking took me a very long time (four to five hours to tackle thirty Explorations) and I often felt so grumpy after bespatter-ing a boy's composition with a rash of red ink that I wrote some carping comment at the end of it about his lack of care. I was irritated by the sight of my own correction-marks and by the sheer length of time I had spent imposing them. If and when any appreciation for the creative quality in the work of the more backward boys entered my written comment, it tended to be grudging or incidental.

My wish for precision in every detail of spelling and punctuation amounted to an onslaught of nagging through correction-symbols: and nagging is a goad to itself. My comment at the end of the piece of work was all too often a mere declaration of the dissatisfaction that my cor-rections had already made quite plain.

All this was a far cry indeed from some of the wisest of all the wise advice that Douglas Brown left me:

Comments matter more than marks or the corrections. Try hard, however tired, to put some intelligible phrase or sentence of comment that shows you have read and con-sidered the piece. *Never* 'good', 'poor', 'satisfactory' or even 'fair'. I think 'excellent' is in another category: it means, in effect, 'words fail me' and can be so understood. Try to make your notes, then, a real comment. And – until you are sure of your boy – rely on praise, indulgence and optimism.

There were, I suppose, two or three boys in each class every year, whom I became 'sure of' speedily and so I knew that their sloth really needed a spur. In an exceptional class their number might rise to half a dozen. But in my early days I set about giving the spur to at least half of the class; and in doing so I made myself increasingly dissatisfied and irritable.

I think, now, that the less gifted boys were seriously hindered and depressed by having their work corrected to a standard of absolute accuracy. The sheer multitude of errors made fair-copying a labour from which carefulness departed, along with all trace of pleasure, long before the end. Slowly it dawned on me that I was merely bruising both the boys and myself; and so at last I began to correct selectively, going for the more important errors and letting the rest pass.

This, for instance, was what I did to Salter's three ballad stanzas.

                                       like
' The highwaymans horse 'twas   / a flash of light
   His dagger like the Ivory moon,
   His cloak like a great black bat,
S His hair like a stragling typhoon.

," The Highwayman shouted I'll fill you with lead."
." the excise men said "We'll split you in two __
    "I tell you I'll shoot I'll shoot I'll shoot"
    "Remember before you do, there's twelve of us and one of you"

                              excise
   He shot the first of the   / men
   But after then he fell and broke his varmit neck,"
   Here ends this bloody tale,
   Along by the rushing beck.

I felt that this was enough of an intrusion. If he took good note of these corrections he might have found others for himself. When I returned his book to him I made it clear that I had left a fair smattering of mistakes for him to detect for himself. I hoped, too, that he would look carefully at his own piece when I discussed in Business Period some of the more common flaws in the work of the class as a whole (on this occasion, matters of capitalisation and the punctuation of direct speech). Salter's fair copy emerged far from perfect: but it was better than his first presentation. While he was making it, I hope he felt more like a detective than a criminal.

Most teachers have a favourite method of indicating corrections. I use a system of signs intended to avoid too blatant an interference with the boy's writing. Most of the time I put an underlining on the page (double line for a mistake in punctuation, single line for spelling) with a sign in the margin. Signs are simple to devise – S for spelling– a stop with a circle round it for a full stop; a query likewise for a question-mark; T for tense; and so on – and I spend half a Business Period early in the first year making sure that the class grasps the various symbols. Using the margin like this preserves courtesy and keeps the display of one's interference to a minimum. It implies, I think, that one wants to be more of a helper than a fault-finder, more co-operative than hostile – an implication worth struggling to carry into every aspect of one's work, even into matters as minor as spelling.

When Nigel Cooper writes about the 'headgehoge gunting', his mistake is a slip of the mind and the pen. When he writes about 'succulant sausages' or the 'gigantic turbalence of life' his mistake is part of his adventure with an expanding vocabulary. Neither error is of a kind to merit *censure*. If one's children explore life and the resources of language enthusiastically, one must surely *expect* mis-spelling as a consequence of the excitement of writing. Good writing issues from a kind of daring, in an effort to express a strongly felt experience, and if one treats spelling mistakes as if they were reprehensible, one probably suppresses one's weaker pupils' willingness to show much of that daring. In refraining from too much censure, one is quite likely to find, among the straight mis-spellings of known words, the occasional invented word, which is sometimes a real creative achievement. When Nigel Cooper described the dead sticklebacks as lying 'mortive' on the muddy bottom of the river, I felt that the word registered splendidly both his recognition that the fish really were dead and his wish that they weren't. Hovering somewhere out at the edge of his verbal resources there were, no doubt, the words 'mortal' and 'mortifying'. 'Mortive' seems better than either, here. I put no correcting mark near it. It seemed as important to leave that word alone as it was to correct 'stragling' in Salter's ballad, his tendency being to miss double letters repeatedly.

At about the time I began to teach Nigel Cooper's class, I remember resolving to make all my comments on written work include some considered remark, conveying admiration for *something* in the composition. But I did not always fulfil the intention. At the end of a long day, a pile of exercise books can dull one's edge long before one reaches the bottom of it. I think, now, that it was churlish to write after Cooper's first Exploration – 'Fair, but too untidy. And are the night-creatures the only things you see and hear and think about? They are almost all you have explored!' – and again, after his second Ballad – 'Not very exciting because the rhythm and choice of language are often too weak. You hardly seem interested in the story.' But I was probably weary – and only halfway down the pile – at the time.

Both comments were potentially destructive. They offered Cooper nothing to relish, nothing to help him feel that his fair copy was worth

doing. Such bald disapproval is useless – probably worse than no comment at all – whereas expressed approval is always *potentially* constructive, no matter how brief it is. It does not have to be very acute, but it
must be sincere, and offered without gushing. None of the following
comments on Cooper's work is very bright; but I do not *regret* any of
them as I regret the other two.

> Your comments on the book are thoughtful and interesting.   *(Book Review II)*

> An effective lament expressing a restrained grief well.
> *(Orpheus Lamenting for Eurydice)*
> Fascinating; all through.   *(A Micro-description)*
> Very acutely 'explored': a very good effort indeed.   *(Encounter with a Creature)*

In *Sights and Sounds at Evening* Nigel Cooper writes:

> In the river was a dead rudd lying on its side its silvery scales upwards and its tail bent
> downwards into the depths. In the shallows stickelbacks, tiny in comparison, guard
> their nests to the death as can be seen from the several bodies lying mortive on the
> muddy bottom.

Here (as in so much good writing by children about the world around
them) much more is registered than the mere facts of the matter. The
exploration of nature is infused with awe and liking which the boy
expresses with instinctive art: as Polixenes says, the art itself is nature.
Surely a teacher's energies in a marking session are better employed in
making a note that will directly convey to the boy an admiration for
the way he has written about the fish, than in making a note that points
out that he has changed tense from past to present at 'In the shallows...'
and ought to be consistent in his fair copy. The 'mistake', in this instance, is like a goldsmith's hall-mark; it puts the stamp of genuineness
on the work. Cooper has taken the impression so strongly that it becomes,
quite naturally, present in his creative imagination.

Tact in correction is difficult to define and impossible to prescribe:
but I am convinced that a part of it lies in a teacher's care *not* to give
spelling and punctuation top priority; and a greater part of it lies in the
concern to put *appreciation* before censure.

The reader may care to decide – as a way of summing this chapter
up – how he would 'correct' this Exploration, which was written by
Campkin towards the end of his first term in 1 A.

Making a Parcel

> I spread out the colourful christmas paper on the dinningroom table. It crickled and
> crackled as I did so. For a moment I gazed at the cheerful puctures of father christmas
> being chased by a heard of rane deer. In the next picture father Christmas was up a tree
> with the rane deer around its base. I slightly smiled at the picture and then picked up
> the present I was about to wrap. It was a small clockwork train that had a whiste that
> scared the life out of our cat. I did not want to lose the key so I had put it into the train

cabin and clamped the break leaver down over it. The key rattled faintly as I lay it on top of the paper. I monouvered it round to see which way it would be easyer to rap it in. I soon fond that it was best to lay it sidways along the outer part of the paper. I began to role it up The paper rustling all the time. Some of the ~~spard~~ sparcling frosting that is stuck on the paper came off on my hands I licked it a tast of glue hung in my mouth. I heard the clock in the hall strike 6.30 p.m. "Supper soon" I thought. I had better hurry up. I grabbed the special christmas selotape that was decorated with holly and worked with my nains to get a grip. There was a long drawn out F A U U U T as I pulled. I picked up the sciccors and cut it after thre attempts. I stuck down one end, then the other, stapping the tape down hard. Then I wrote out ~~the~~ on the little card.

> TO Heather
>> with Love
>>> From David.

It did not look neat because the card did not absorb the ink well and it looked ~~blul~~ blurred. I stuck the tab to the pacel and went off to supper. I would clear up after wards.

12. And arithmetic?

A full report on each boy's work and progress is given each term.

School Prospectus

This chapter will be very short. It is about the awkward business of marking.

Part of the awkwardness belongs to the very idea – for the essence of a subject like English has nothing to do with testability. The bread-and-butter skills of literacy are important, of course, and some kinds of test (with the marks pertaining) may encourage expertise with them: but they are not the essence of the subject. *That* lies in whatever capacity for sensitive living may be helped to grow by the kinds of relationship in teaching and learning that are encouraged in the classroom. The essence lies in experience of certain quality, in and among people: and you can't catch that with marks, any more than you can measure commitment with a thermometer.

But, more awkwardly, boys *expect* to be given marks for their work. However much one argues to the contrary, they persist in believing that, in English, and in the rest of the curriculum, marks must *prove* something. So they demand them.

Even more awkwardly, the powers-that-be in the school demand them. A 'full report' on a boy's work means, in practice, that each main subject teacher must give him a termly position-in-class, together with two A – E grades (one for Attainment, one for Diligence). After these figures and letters (e.g. '15th out of 31. B: B – ') there is room on the report-form for a remark (or for two remarks if the teacher writes a miniature script or adopts an ultra-telegrammatic style). It seems to be an unwritten rule that position-in-class must be arrived at by totalling up marks for the term. And in my experience unwritten rules are as difficult to affect by argument as boys' expectations are.

In this situation I resorted to quiet compromise. There seemed to be more future in it than in open defiance.

So, I produce a form-order at the end of every term; and I tell the boys what it is when they clamour for it. But I always make it clear at the same time that it's a form-order that relates only to the markable – i.e. their written work – that I produce it only because report-forms oblige me to, and that I don't consider it to give an adequate indication of anyone's overall worth or achievement because what is individually markable is not *more* important than their classwork in Guilds and Companies (where an attempt to be classifying individuals with numerical assessments would simply defeat the whole Mummery purpose).

At the end of a term my register will probably contain, for each boy in the class, a couple of marks for his Reading Diary, a mark for his Speech, a couple of marks for his Fair Copy Book, a few marks for notes and exercises: and four or five marks for his imaginative and creative writing. Most 'essence' is reflected in that last batch. So I try to make it *count* for most in each boy's sum total, by doubling these four or five marks, or (if necessary) tripling them. In this way each boy's position-in-class is a little more than half determined by marks reflecting his personal sensitivity, and a little less than half by marks reflecting the bread-and-butter skills of accuracy, neatness, correctness with grammar, spelling, punctuation and so on. (For, as one has periodically to insist in the course of staff-room discussions, these latter skills really are no *more* the concern of the teacher of English than of anybody else. All teachers whose subjects involve a child in written language share direct responsibility for his grasp of them.)

For Fair Copy Book purposes I correct spelling, punctuation and the like, in the way I have described; but I don't take these things much into account when deciding a mark for composition. I'm interested, rather, in substance, expressiveness, tenacity, a care for language, a way with words, and so on. With all creative writing – except for 'free writing' which by definition goes uncorrected and unmarked – I bear in mind a mark-scale which has 20 as a rough sort of maximum, but is really more geared to the notion of 15 representing a good piece of work. When giving back the boys' work in Business Periods and discussing it with them, I offer them *this notion of a standard*, not the idea that it has been marked 'out of' a set figure. (This may seem a trifling point, but it does have some tempering effect on the spirit of competition based on individual marks.) Marks over 15 move increasingly to excellence: marks of 10 and below mean that the work, alas, is poor (about one case in every seven or eight, in the early days). In practice I don't think I have gone above 19, but given a piece that was that much better I wouldn't hesitate to go on up by several marks. 20 has no special prerogative for being a king figure, any more than 7 – which is as far down as I've ever had to go – can call itself rock bottom.

Other written work – notes for this and that, handwriting and memory tests, quotation collections, letter-writing, and Fair Copy Books – I mark out of a fixed maximum of 10 (which anyone can attain with care) with 7 representing 'satisfactory' and 5 'not careful enough'.

So marks for creative, personal writing span a wider scale (7/8–17/18) than marks for formal skills (5–10). Every so often in Business Periods I remind the class why this is so. Nigel Cooper's Written Work Book, where the mark for each piece of work is encircled at the end of it, shows the scheme in action.

When considering Reading Diaries I also have to mark over a wide scale, the boys' reading habits being so various. Again I take 15 to represent a good standard (something like four or five careful entries), and I don't mark to a maximum. It is not very unusual for the prolific and attentive readers to score over 20 (the record to date is, I think, 25), whereas the neglectful may rate as low as 5 or 6. I think it is valid to count in the Reading Diary marks unadulterated for the term's total, the reading habit being such an essential aspect of 'English': and I preach from time to time on the theme that laziness here can undo all one's good work in other fields.

Speeches seem to me the one *Guild* activity where marks for individuals can legitimately be taken into account for form-order calculations. When each term's Speeches Sessions are over I take in the timekeeper's notebook and, for each boy, divide by three the marks awarded by the class, add them to my own mark (to the nearest whole number) and enter a total out of 20 in the register.

Any scheme that aims to measure human powers of sensitivity and imagination with numbers is bound to be biased and idiosyncratic; as every human consciousness is. In marking various kinds of children's writing on the lines described, I hope to be acknowledging certain definite biases; and to be asserting their importance responsibly.

One further kind of marking remains to be mentioned – the marking of Guild and Company performances in the Mummery lessons. This I do with less residual uneasiness than I feel when marking compositions. From the outset of Mummery life I make it clear that it is the whole group effort (not star acting performances by individuals) that earns the mark. For routine performances I mark out of 10, with a bonus mark (that may be fractionalised, or withheld altogether) for preparation and 'putting away' procedures. Most of the time these performance-marks range between 5 and 9. For specially grand undertakings – like final, full-dress mime-performances – I mark out of 20. I keep a careful note of the marks for each class, and publish a detailed score-card at the end of each term, announcing overall winner and best single Guild achievements. Each new term brings a fresh start, of course – that's an important tactic.

The reason why I approve of marking and competitiveness and fighting to be top *here* and not in written work is that the mark brings to focus a communal endeavour, not individual assertiveness.

13. 'Conclusions'

As a practising teacher, and a would-be practical one, I try to bring things-as-they-should-be a little nearer to things-as-they-are. The latter is something we are all supposed to know, and modern teaching goes through all sorts of antics to ensure that it starts just where 'The Child' does: never ahead, never above. Our 'democratic' considerations lay a similar stress on the importance of 'The Average'. This is reasonable: if you make no contact, you plainly cannot teach. It only becomes dangerous when too low an estimate is put on these abstractions (*Child* and *Average*); when you credit people with so few, and such feeble, interests that you fail to stimulate interests which are actually present, or fail to stir those half-vacant places in their minds where interests could grow.

> From the Advertisement to *Our Living Language*
> by A P. Rossiter

Dear X,

Thank you very much for reading the draft of the book and for sending those comments and questions. Let me attempt an answer to the points you raise.

You say you wonder whether the Mummery approach to English would work with children who are 'less able' than grammar school boys. Instinctively I'm sure the answer is 'Yes, certainly it would'; but I'm really not sure in what terms ability is to be measured. Intelligence may be assessed by I.Q. tests, but a high I.Q. does not *necessarily* make one 'more able' as a person; indeed it can obstruct emotional and imaginative sensibility. I suppose that the boys I taught must have been 'more able' in *some* ways (in the skills of literacy, for instance) since they had all passed a competitive examination to get into the school. But I wouldn't have wanted to teach them on different lines if they had all been more or less illiterate, for the principle of collaborative dramatic activity seems to me a proper basis for teaching and learning English at almost every 'ability-level'. The details of its practical application will always need to be tailored to the local circumstances.

The things I believe to be *fundamentally* valuable in the Mummery approach are these:

(i) It treats drama – by which I mean enactment that brings to life the word – as the proper medium for *English*; the right way of tackling the subject.

This is better than calling Drama a separate subject, making it distinct from English work in the pupils' eyes and equipping it with a specialist Drama teacher – though that in turn is better than having no dramatic activity anywhere in the curriculum. Since our prime aim as teachers of *English* is 'the very culture of the feelings' our teaching procedures ought surely to reflect the fact that this culture is a dramatic experience.

(ii) Literature is at the heart of the approach.

This, with a sense that 'Literature' means more than merely 'what has been written in our time', is perhaps the most important point of all. You suggest that the Mummery programme doesn't give enough attention to contemporary writing. Visitors often urge me to be more 'modern' – recently, for instance, I was pressed to give the Guilds *The Royal Hunt of the Sun* to work on 'instead of all that out-of-date Shakespeare' (I found the attitude behind this remark confusing) – and some teachers, I know, feel that almost all pre-twentieth-century literature is irrelevant and useless to their pupils, especially to their 'less able' pupils. But I really do not see what many of the most ardent advocates for contemporary literature claim – that it has an inherent virtue simply by *being* contemporary and is therefore, somehow, good for children today. The stamp of 'now' may enable some sort of immediate identification to take place; but recognising images of facets of the contemporary scene is a different thing from imaginative experience; growing absorbed in dressed-up documentary reportage is not the same as responding with an inner movement of sensibility. To give children a more or less undiluted diet of the up-to-date, 'realistic' literature that fills so many current courses and textbooks seems to me to aim for sociological awareness rather than extension of imaginative experience. I do not deny that sociological awareness is an important part of Education; but it is not the prime aim of English. One of the major functions of the imagination is surely to free the mind and feelings from the tyranny of the immediate present. Teaching children English by making the literature of their more or less immediate environment into their staple fare strikes me as not only starting where 'The Child' is, but obstinately staying there.

I'd want to credit children with greater interests, greater potential resources in the 'half-vacant places in their minds', than such an approach allows for. Edwin Muir is right, absolutely right, when he says 'we are bound, even when we do not know it, to the past generations by the same bond that unites us with our neighbours, and if only for the sake of preserving the identity of mankind we must cherish that connection'.

Cherishing that connection is, in a nutshell, what the Mummery approach tries to do.

(iii) In working together to make 'English' happen, the children take on real responsibility, and a creative 'discipline' is built into the co-operative structure of the class.

I can best illustrate this with a memory. One day I was delayed unavoidably in the staff-room for the first quarter of an hour of the period following the mid-morning break. A Second Form was supposed to be acting *Julius Caesar* in that lesson. I could not get a message to them, so they were left entirely to their own devices. When eventually I reached the Mummery, I found one Company acting its allotted scene to the other. (No colleague or passer-by had given them the tip to start: I checked on that possibility afterwards.) The auditorium was in darkness and there was complete attention to the performance on the stage, which had obviously been going on for some minutes – Brutus was just leaving the Forum, having introduced Antony to the Roman citizenry. Someone had moved my desk to the back of the room, in case I managed to join the class, but clearly my absence was of no immediate concern. The 'English' was what mattered, and they were getting on with it. I slipped quietly into my place to watch, and the play continued with scarcely a pause. It was an extraordinary incident, and very humbling in the way it made 'Sir's' dispensability blatantly obvious: but at heart I was more pleased than staggered. It was a striking demonstration of the very bond that Edwin Muir speaks of.

The Mummery 'method' takes up roughly one-seventh of the weekly curriculum-time of a class in the first and second years. This ration reflects plainly the central rôle of 'English' in 'Education', and offers it some real chance of working to some effect. I think that the chance is encouraged by an arrangement whereby one teacher looks after all the English a class does for a two-year period. The habits of trust that sustain a creative relationship are only acquired gradually. The children have to grow to trust each other, to trust the material you offer them, to trust the standards you hold to: you have to learn to trust their latent and developing abilities, their capacity for personal and social responsibility towards experience. All of this has the best chance of happening where there is a long-sustained acquaintanceship. (For this reason too the teacher's freedom to arrange lessons in sequences of one kind of activity at a time is valuable; it makes possible an increasing depth of day-to-day involvement in the work.)

As Rossiter says, if you make no contact, you plainly cannot teach. I think the best 'contact' occurs when the children's roused interest in your subject is what is leading them on (as was happening with those second-form boys). If a teacher can establish with his class a working relationship, a working structure, and a working programme, which together aim to keep this 'contact' – in which the subject-matter itself will be doing the better part of the real teaching – the rest of his work is a kind of watchful maintenance-engineering.

You are quite right when you describe the Guild idea as 'a sort of game'. It's played perfectly seriously, though; without (I hope) becoming a solemn or overweening affair. I suspect that you find the Guild-terminology uncongenial, with its 'Masters of the Revels', 'Masters of the Tiring House' and so on. In which case, as I said in chapter 4, do away with these names and use others; but don't abandon the group-'game' principle. Groups like Guilds are a way of making a partnership in which children and teacher can 'play' together, though not in the same style. The adult is not expected to stop behaving as an adult in first explaining and then enjoying the game (for that would be to lose the essential stance for the everyday maintenance work). The child is not expected to be any more 'grown up' than he really is in adopting a rôle in the Guild. Their relationship should be of that distanced kind which David Holbrook describes in chapter 11 of *The Exploring Word*; a relationship in which the teacher 'may be found by the children to be an adult, when tested, and show himself an adult who can allow children to be children. Only in such a distanced relationship – in which the adult knows he is an adult, and the children know where they are – can love and sympathy be given, and creative "giving" and "receiving" take place.'

One way in which children may 'test' a relationship with you is, of course, through deliberately 'naughty' behaviour. I didn't mean to give the impression that in this respect boys in the Mummery are as good as gold. There are always those who, individually or in a concerted effort, will throw a spanner in the works from time to time. They don't often do this with a vicious intent; but they do it with cool deliberation. The results, as you can imagine, are often spectacular – the stage-lights switched on, or off, at just the wrong moment, piled-up rostra 'accidentally' knocked over in a black-out, a sudden entry on the scene in quite outlandish garb, and so on. Usually the disruption gets a general laugh, is hastily patched up and the performance goes on. I may or may not get drawn in, but at the end of the lesson, in talking to the class, I usually refer to the incident, not wrathfully or sarcastically but in a way that simply shows I'm not deluded about its nature. The *attention* for their spanner is, of course, what most pranksters are after, and having got their laughter and recognition they will usually call it a day. More persistent 'wreckers' usually cause their Guild's performance-marks to drop sharply. I point to the reasons for this in class (one doesn't need to name names to make oneself clear) but it's the felt pressure of mounting exasperation from the rest of the Guild that usually brings about a change of attitude. Discipline of this kind, as well as 'a creative discipline', is maintained more by a sense of sociability than by fear of punishment from a single authority-figure.

But to return to your concern for the feasibility of a Mummery-style approach to English with other people than first- and second-year grammar school boys – 'What about less literate children, mixed and mixed-ability classes, older children?' I believe that the fundamental aspects of the approach – the basis in collaborative dramatic activity, the essential rôle of Literature, the sharing of real responsibility – are proper ones at *all* levels of secondary English. I haven't found convincing evidence that they're *not* (though, admittedly, my experience of teaching in the kinds of class you mention has not been extensive – so you may say I haven't looked hard enough).

'Every human being', writes Edwin Muir, 'has to begin at the beginning, as his forebears did, with the same difficulties and pleasures, the same temptations, the same problem of good and evil, the same inward conflict, the same need to learn how to live, the same inclination to ask what life means.' That statement is no *less* true of less literate children than of anybody else; and it implies, very powerfully, Literature's crucial importance – that it speaks to us of the identity of mankind. I don't believe that children who cannot read and write fluently are deaf to its voice. They will not express their feelings very easily in the acts of reading and writing: but they are not therefore feeling-less, not handicapped in other modes of expression, not cut off from the experience that lies in much of the finest Literature, not disabled from *receiving* the word. Read to them Malory's story of the death of King Arthur, or Lawrence's 'Snake', or 'Hath not a Jew eyes?', or (almost) anything else that your heart is in, and you will see that.

I imagine that if you were teaching a class of less literate children, with the equivalent facilities, contact-time and group-structure of the Mummery approach, you would not find them less responsible or less capable of collaboration than more literate children, if you had taken enough care in giving them the means of order at the outset. After doing that, you might well find that you wanted to draw up your English programme with its ingredients in different *proportions* from mine, but I hope we'd want the same ingredients, and want them in each term – drama, mime, poetry, speech, reading and writing. You'd want, I should imagine, a larger proportion of class-time for reading, aloud and privately, and for writing, both 'free' and more formal, since the best way of improving these skills lies in practising them: and you might want to begin to 'tailor' other things a little like this:

Little or no book-in-hand acting (at first?) but much improvisation from your own readings (and/or recordings) of literature and the ensuing discussion.

Shakespeare (in due course) not in such quantity, but perhaps with the termly aim of a key-sequence from a play set into its context, attended to in the word, and then interpreted in a 'dance-drama' style.

A place for mime and movement as basic tools of expression, supporting (and overlapping with) improvisational drama and poetry; not always as a separate art-form.

Less expectation of quantity in the personal composition of poetry at first; more emphasis on group-poems. Possibly an ideal of 'a-poem-at-a-time' for performance purposes, rather than 'a programme of verse'.

A call for a shorter, more informal style of 'talk', rather than a 'speech', from each child once a term. Perhaps a less weighty etiquette, but some sort of ceremony upheld.

As you see, I shy away from making detailed prescription for other teachers. I don't feel that any of the material I have written about in the previous chapters is 'beyond the grasp' of less literate children (nor, of course, that it is the *only* Literature that it is appropriate to take with young secondary schoolchildren): but the particular attitudes and tactics that lead their imaginations into *possession* of it are not reducible to rules of thumb. What I would contend is that it is dangerous to put too low an estimate on those abstractions 'Child' and 'Average' *because the consequences of doing so will degrade real people*; and that as teachers of English we have a moral obligation to start *ahead* of 'The Child', if we are genuinely to educate children and ourselves.

As for mixed-ability classes – which is what all classes are really – I would only point out that a Mummery style of organisation, by whatever name, is *designed* to turn a mixture of abilities to positive account. In a comprehensive school the *range* of abilities will, of course, be wider than in the classes I have taught most, but the Guild principle should become all the more relevant for that. It does not categorise anyone for good and all as a one-skill person. It does not treat some skills as first-class and others as inferior, but draws on all with a communal and creative purpose. It helps to establish a truly educational atmosphere, in which people who are timid may acquire confidence, the over-confident may learn modesty and tact, and those people with special talents may both exploit them and learn to appreciate the value of different ones: an atmosphere in which people come to depend on each other: an encouraging atmosphere for weak abilities of most kinds – and for strong ones – to grow stronger in.

The viability of the Mummery approach does not depend on all-boy classes. Girls will take to it as readily as boys at the age of eleven and twelve, though in some mixed classes there may be a tendency for all the girls to choose to be actresses and all the boys to choose to be technical experts. I think it's wise to forestall this possibility by the way you 'explain the game' at the outset. If it's well 'rooted' when the children are aged eleven and twelve, in single-sex or mixed classes, the approach can go from strength to strength in succeeding years and even become a positive 'stabiliser' for mid-adolescents. Its fundamental principles do not change as the children grow older, but the tactical interpretation should grow and develop with them. A very practical and stimulating account of one such interpretation is given in Keith Crook's article on 'The Senior Mummery' which now exists at the Perse School and is chiefly used by third- and fourth-year classes (*The Use of English*, Volume 19, Number 2 (Winter 1967), p. 130).

As you point out, it is not vital for a room in which drama may take place conveniently to have a built-in stage or bench-desks such as I inherited. (In fact, the Senior Mummery has neither.) The essential features are adequate space, black-out and some storage facilities, fairly simple lighting resources, the means of playing and making recordings, and an adaptable set of rostra – features that can be combined quite other than Mummery-wise, of course.

You go on to say 'Surely it's best to think of a Drama Room as being more of a general "workshop" than the Perse Mummery – a room which may be used by classes throughout the school, when drama is relevant to their work, in a more "impromptu" way.' That view seems to rest on the assumption that drama is a sort of audio-visual aid that can be made available, sporadically, to assist in many subjects. It can indeed be that; but it has its greater significance in being the essential medium of 'English'. Something like a Mummery seems to me to be basically relevant to the pursuit of studies in the subject (which has altogether as much claim to a room of its own as Music or Geography or Art). A class that *habitually* works together in such a room is likely to build up for itself a sense of human community which extends well beyond the four walls. This sense of human community, one of the distinctive qualities through which English should validate a central place for itself in the school curriculum, is much *harder* to build up when conventional classroom conditions are the rule and sorties to the drama room the exception.

Finally, you asked me to estimate the effect of 'tradition' on my work at the Perse: and an answer can only be implied.

In her book *An Experiment in Education*, Sybil Marshall describes tradition as 'the condition of the future being in the past', and she goes on – 'This is what we inherit, not the benefits or ills of the past, which are but unimportant details, but the power of time gone before to nourish and sustain us in our own time.' I have a sense of that power when I remember the teaching of Douglas Brown. From it, in my boyhood in the earlier Mummery and in later years, I learned more about English, and what matters in it, and what matters in teaching it, than I can ever properly declare. This book is both a gesture of gratitude and an attempt to declare what I can. A great deal of what I have done as a teacher has been modelled on Douglas Brown's work; and I hope there has been living, developing spirit in it, not just inert copying, since I felt far more stimulated than constrained by the tradition of English-through-Drama at the Perse.

All tradition involves you in repeating something: if you repeat a *meaning*, and can enhance it to even the smallest degree, then you make 'tradition' into a living state; if you merely repeat a form, without imagination, you make it into a relic. This is also true of our contributions to a literature.

To end at my beginning, with one further quotation from the essay that gives this book its epigraph –

Imagination tells us that we become human by repetition, that our life is a rehearsal of lives that have been lived over and over, and that this act, with all that is good and evil in it, is a theme for delighted and awed contemplation.